Archangel

Also by Keith Korman
Swan Dive

Keith Korman

THE VIKING PRESS
NEW YORK

Copyright © 1983 by Keith Korman
All rights reserved
First published in 1983 by The Viking Press
40 West 23rd Street, New York, N. Y. 10010
Published simultaneously in Canada by
Penguin Books Canada Limited

LIBRARY OF CONGRESS CATALOGING IN PUBLICATION DATA
Korman, Keith.
Archangel.
I. Title
PS3561.O66A89   1983   813'.54   82-10858
ISBN 0-670-13063-X

Research assisted by Howard Schott

Printed in the United States of America
Set in Videocomp Garamond

For my Mom
And
For Chris

> Lovers and madmen have such seething brains,
> Such shaping fantasies, that apprehend
> More than cool reason ever comprehends.
> —*A Midsummer Night's Dream*

Blue Vista Flats
Summer 1933

First to Wake

I'VE SEEN YOU WHERE YOU NEVER WERE,
AND WHERE YOU NE'ER WILL BE,
AND YET YOU IN THAT VERY SAME PLACE,
MAY STILL BE SEEN BY ME.

The railroad tracks were quiet and dark. Dawn like a fine pale grindstone honed the sky's featheredge, the knife drawn from its dark scabbard, whetted and ready; off in the distance the woods reached for heaven like bandits of the night, and trees murmured, whispering among their branches. Overhead a wisp of cirrus clouds stretched like a dark eyelid across the horizon.

The haggard drifter squatted between the rails on a wooden railroad tie. He squinted at the faint rosewisp clouds in the east, making out the dark brown hulks of two houses built by the rails. No sound came from the houses; they were peaceful and asleep. The hard straight rails were still. On either side the fields lay bound in the summer's dawn. No grassblade stirred. The ground was neither cold nor warm: eternal topsoil, tilled, gouged, plowed, pummeled.

Even as he squatted on the railroad ties, wide out in the open silence, the drifter never saw them coming. They sneaked up on him slowly, the way-station workmen, slithering close to the ground. They slouched close, cramping their footfalls to smother them in the dark. Then they struck, two men shooting out of the blackness. The Bull with the big bald head carried a policeman's nightstick, and he swung the billy as the drifter turned to look. The drifter's simple fragile eyes opened wide as the billy struck. Nailed on the knee, the squatting man fell sideways, cracking his skull on the rails.

The fight was finished then, but the other Bull came in for licks, kicking in the groin, the spine, the jaw. The drifter rolled on his shoulders, and the Bull with the big bald head used the nightstick on his ribs. The twisted man shuddered when he breathed; the Bulls stopped and watched him. The drifter gasped breaths of thin air, the gulps catching in his throat. Shallow draughts . . . thinner . . . gone . . .

The drifter did not gasp again; he coughed up drops of blood and mucus between his teeth. The Bulls were watching, and they stood loose, hands on their hips like soldiers at rest. The Bull with the big bald head held the nightstick in one hand; he looped the leather strap around his wrist and let the billy hang. The other Bull prodded the body with his boot toe. He spat on the ground—for himself, for the pleasure in it.

"He gawn."

Not much else to say. The Bull with the big bald head took the dead man by the hair and knotted his thick fingers for a good grip. The smaller man took a wrist and the two pulled together, the dead man's boot heels dragging along the ground. They hauled the heavy flesh away from the sleeping houses; they hauled him quite a distance, a quarter mile at least. Past the railroad way-station's own workhouses, past the coal tender, under the water tower, the two men struggled with the body till they reached the trestle spanning the river. They rolled the body down the bank, and chased after it, their knees pumping in the high riverbank grass, the iron trestle rising above their heads.

Baldy had the big ideas. "Git some rocks . . . rocks sink 'um."

"No, stupe!" The second Bull jammed his pink face close, jaw working; his red hair seemed to stand on end. "You want him sunk right under the trestle? Let him float! Let him float!"

With two fingers the Bull with the big bald head pulled at the flesh under his chin. The other man sidled alongside the big man's ear. "He be outta the county inna hour. Less mebbe."

No more discussions. They rolled the body to the water, taking it to the middle of the current where the river ran strong. The water flowed around their waists and higher to their chests, each parting the water in a V south as the river curved. They let the body go, sending it off with a helpful shove; the corpse was a log face down, arms spreading from its sides. The current drew the body on.

Splashing up the bank, the two Bulls turned and watched the body drift. The flesh wrinkled in tender rolls at the back of the bald Bull's neck. He kneaded the creases with his fingers and wagged his head from side to side, as if to shake loose the sight of the dead man from around his eyes. "Didja hafta kick him so hard? You din't haf to."

The other Bull was hard like knotted wood; he pressed his flushed face, glowing like a bright copper cooking pan, close to the big man's snout. He pointed at the billy dangling from the bald Bull's wrist. "You din't have to use that stick."

The rolls of flesh at the back of the big Bull's neck furrowed like a worried brow. Baldy backed off. No time to hang the blame. No point in making trouble now. Enough was enough; that drifter was gonna stay dead, like it or not. No changing that now. He faced up the bank away from the river, the polished nightstick swinging as he moved.

The wiry Bull rubbed a hand through his red hair, and it shifted across his scalp in a wave like a good shoebrush. "Ah, the hell with it." Disgusted, he followed the big Bull up the dirt bank of the river.

The bank sloped to a lip where the trees and scrub rose like a low fence, spotty in places, with gaps to crawl through. Back of the bank, in the bramble thick and heavy with leaves, the brushwood trembled. The bald Bull marched by first, careless in his bluster; scrambling from the river, he kept going like a huge dog straining at the leash. Never far enough. Never fast enough. He bustled blindly through the underbrush.

"Hold it!" The red-haired man stopped. A sodcutter blade moved in his hand. The big bald Bull doubled back to the bramble; the other parted the bushes. "Well lookee here . . ."

They saw a youth crouching in the dirt on his elbows and

knees; he twisted his head to the side, eyeing the open space above him.

He dug his elbows in the dirt and tried to scuttle back into the bramble, but the scrub was too thick. Cornered, he twisted his neck again, and his hair fell back from his forehead. The bushes were parted, and with the sky opened up he could see one man's legs, and under his pants the man's hard knees stuck out like balled fists. No place to crawl, no space to back off, no hole to scurry in headfirst. He stood up slowly, spine stiff, bones cold and brittle. The Bull's pants were still soaked from wading in the river; the man's thin red mouth was set and drawn, still hard from the water's chill and the empty soul that floated in the river. The Bull's thin neck was slick with sweat from dragging the body down below the train trestle, where the rails were laid from bank to bank, silent iron like a huge serpent stretched across the water.

As if in a trance the young man clutched a tin can. The brambles caught him around the arms and chest, saplings snagged his arms and wrists, reaching to tie him down. The tin can fell from his hand and hit the ground, spilling fat rust-red worms, which twisted over themselves in a living knot and slowly scattered in the dirt. The worms stretched out like India rubber bands and crawled in all directions.

The Bulls stared, cornstarch dry and quiet. Then the Bull with the big bald head cracked a grin. "It's the Walker boy. That's Drake Walker's boy. His name's Buck. Hey, boy . . . your name Buck?"

The kid opened and closed his hands as they hung at his sides. His fingers spread to five and then clenched to a fist, like hanging weights from a scale. He was lanky, rank-haired and strong. Each finger's tendon ran up his forearm to the elbow, and the tiny muscle tightened like water's flow down a slight grade. He knew the Bull with the big bald head was the foreman at the railroad way-station. His name was Simple.

The one with the blade was called Meriwether. The red-haired man was ripping and frayed, like a tear in a bedsheet that keeps on going; his fingers clung to the sodcutter handle. He was so sure of the blade in his hand that his eyes never moved to it, never left Buck's face. The freckles on Meriwether's pale pink skin seemed painted on.

"Looking for fishbait, fella?" Meriwether rolled his eyes up in his head and winked at Simple. The big bald Bull smiled back and then ran a rough palm over the skin of his pate. He edged toward Buck.

"I know you're Drake Walker's boy 'cause you got your pappy's pretty face. Don't he have a pretty face?"

Meriwether coughed as though catching pollen in his throat; he brought the butt handle of the knife to his mouth. "Yeah. Yeah, he have one." Then his eyes were back on Buck, the knife down and steady in his hand. "How about it? Fishbait?"

A red fireball sun cleared the tops of the trees, laying hot rods of molten light down the steel rails bolted to the trestle. Meriwether's red hair took the sun deep in its bristle. Buck Walker licked his lips, finding a sandy grit of dirt, a hard grain against his gums. Past the trees and scrub and down the riverbank he could see Yellow River flowing, in some places over the rocks breaking stride, in others deep and slow. Beyond Meriwether's shoulder Buck saw the dead man, shirt soaked and back to the open air. No sign of blood, no rose shadow swirling in the water. No marks on the trail where the Bulls had dragged him to the water's edge. And no hint of care in Meriwether's pale blue eyes. The dead man floated aimless. Meriwether cut a leaf with his sodcutter, the blade slicing easily through the green veins splaying from the stem. Best answer the man.

"Yeah . . . fishbait."

Meriwether, hepped and tense, smiled as if he had known it all along. He laid his hand upon Buck's shoulder and drew him from the bramble. Below Buck's belly his gut folded, and a fistful of bubbling water sank below his spine. Meriwether's fingers were thin metal bolts. They clenched and sank into Buck's shoulder muscle like winter cold. "Everybody knows there's lousy fishbait by the river."

The bushes behind Buck's back poked their sapling points at his shoulder blades; on one side Simple smiled, and on the other Meriwether held the knife. "I didn't find too many good ones."

Meriwether wanted to play a little more, jab the tender flesh and see it jump. "Think you'll fish today?" He stooped and picked up the last nightcrawler inching by his foot. The Bull held the worm head to tail in one hand, and slid the knife blade in the loop. "No fish gonna eat this."

The knife moved and the worm was sliced in half, like good meat under a butcher's hand. Nightcrawler blood welled from the severed body and ran along the bright blade's edge, glistening over the metal. "Pick up the worm can."

Buck reached down and the bubbling pressed in his gut. He squeezed his stomach; his belly was loose, and below his spine he tried to shut the bubbling with his thighs. The can was in his hand and he held it out. The sun was up and the other worms were back in their holes. No squirming on the hook today. The severed worm dangled from Meriwether's fingers, and two drops of blood fell to the ground. Buck held the can tight; the bloody pieces dripped over the can's open mouth.

The tin can trembled; Buck's hand felt steady, but his arm was cold and the can kept shivering. The sun's light was cool and distant, its heat falling away as the living blood flowed from the worm's cut body.

A black hatchet flashed across the glare, a shadow racing on the ground, wings outspread. Buck flinched and a rusty brown screech owl soared above the train trestle. The bird ignored the men and swooped to wheel over the river, circling the body floating like a log, face down. The owl's amber eyes flashed as it turned, sunlight catching the liquid center. Buck's palms were stiff with no blood in the flesh. The two Bulls edged a little closer. Meriwether dropped the writhing worm in Buck's can and it kept twisting, head to severed stump. Again, Meriwether reached for Buck's shoulder and his stiff fingers held like meathooks. He brought the sodcutter blade easily up between Buck's legs. Buck saw the nightcrawler's blood spread across the metal. Then the blade's edge vanished in the joint of his crotch. He felt the sharp edge on his pants' inside seam.

Meriwether pursed his thin red lips. "Don't go fishing for a while. People drown in the river. They go down for a little dip and never come back."

Meriwether withdrew the sodcutter blade, wiping the worm blood on Buck's inseam. He held the blade up to the sun and the blood was gone. The Bull's voice was soda sweet. "You run along now, young Walker. Don't let me catch you digging fishbait up here again."

Buck rubbed the free hand on his leg. There was a wet spot high up on his thigh, near the tailbone. His bait can was moist where his fingers curled around the metal. Inside the worm seethed, kissing its own bloody stomach, looking to mend its clean-sliced stump.

Simple and Meriwether moved back, giving Buck room. The owl wheeled again and Buck took a step between the two Bulls. They did not stop him. He took another step and neither man grabbed for his wrists. He looked over his shoulder. Simple was grinning and Meriwether had crossed his arms over his chest. At the fourth step Buck ran and the Bulls let him go. Their laughter rose in the morning air, chasing his heels.

Buck dashed like a crazy man, clawing through the vines and scrub, he ran hell-bent and driven, not caring. Past the way-station, knees chopping down the wooden railroad ties, past the hulks of two houses, he ran curving with the rail line south. His throat burned with a hot sucking wind that gave no air, each gasp hollow. And then familiar ground, where the steel rails crossed the U.S. Route. He slowed when he saw the black and white striped ding-dong lights hanging motionless and silent, as though tarred and feathered and run out of town. He stopped short and slumped to the ground against a railside tree, chest pounding. The sucking wind lulled in his throat, and tiny salt drops stung his eyes.

He shook his head and the air flowed cooler down his gullet. A body in the river and an owl in the sky. He clenched his fists and the finger tendons slid up his elbow to the forearm. He unclenched his fists and the pink returned to his knuckles.

Fishbait.

Floating in the river . . . fishbait. He touched his fingers to his pants crotch and his gut bubbled. His fingers came up stained with worm blood. The hollow breath in his throat seemed loaded with bitter wood smoke. He grabbed out for a handful of brush leaves, wiping the blood on his fingers away, clawing at the leaves and tearing off a thin cluster. He wiped the leaves between his legs, getting the last worm blood left from Meriwether's blade. A bird sang three notes and then stopped. He threw the branches to the ground.

Buck rubbed the back of his hand across his eyes, and the salt came up from his skin. Before him a wall of trees rose up beside the railbed, the sun lancing through the trunks and vines. Within the trees the sun fell in a lightshaft clearing. Sun glinted off metal on the clearing's far side. Drawn to it, Buck left the gravel railbed and passed through the wall of trees. The trees parted like a curtain of smoke as he entered the open space. The metal glistened on the clearing's edge: a car, black and rusted, had been driven off the U.S.

Route and down the railroad tracks, driven off the tracks and left to rot.

Chrome splayed into Buck's eyes. He brushed a tear-drop crumb from his cheek and saw how the broken-down car was sagging on its axle, tires flat, spokes bent and bumper dented. He squatted down, leaning his back against the car's door. Above his head the open driver's window gaped like a mouth, the window glass gone without a trace. Long ago he had played here with his sister, Tina, and the car was rotted even then.

At his feet the dead leaves crackled, and he tried to hush the noise, stilling his feet, the wind snagging in his throat again. The leaves on the clearing floor rustled underfoot.

Not his feet though, and the sound shot through him like thin bones snapping in a fire. Then quiet . . . *Shshsh!* The clearing was empty and nothing stirred. A few drops of sweat gathered at Buck's back, the back that turned on the Bulls' hard laughter. The back that turned on a body floating in the water, back to the heavy footfalls and an owl in the sky. It did not matter that Buck had seen them throw the body in—he dangled like a severed worm, Meriwether holding him between thumb and forefinger, the sod-cutter blade drawn across his groin. Still warm and bloody. Fishbait.

The dead leaves crackled on the clearing floor again. This time the rustle was louder, the leaves catching like a child's ragged breath. The hard metal of the car door was at Buck's shoulder, and he looked from side to side. Up at the front of the clearing the steel rails shone through the trees, and on either side the woods grew dark and tangled, shadowed like tall men crowded close together in a nighttime room. The crackling leaves brushed nearby, their sound withered and dry.

Buck looked under the car, half expecting to see Meriwether's hard boots and dirty ankles on the car's far side.

Nothing.

Buck could still feel Meriwether's hand reaching for his shoulder, fingers stiff and cold, pulling him from the riverside bramble. Fingers pulling on Drake Walker's boy, with his pappy's pretty face. Buck's gut bubbled—tell your pappy that a dead man floated and the worms crawled in all directions. Tell him what?

No chance he'd go looking for a body dragged miles by the current. No chance he'd make the Bulls pay for their own hard laughter, with no bruise to show for it and not a scratch from

Meriwether's blade. The leaves crackled and then went still. Buck looked fast under the car.

No boots. No ankles. No man standing ready to lay a hand on him again.

The car's metal was warm against his shoulders. Something light as a gnat-wing grazed his ear. He brushed it away and touched a soft lump; out of the corner of his eye, something dangled from the car window.

Buck came out of his squat, feet pushing him away from the car's dead metal, the gushing air pounding in his throat. A white hand dangled limp and lifeless from the car's open window. A finger stirred and it moved. Then the hand gripped the window ledge hard, and two eyes peeked above the metal rim.

"Scared you, Bucky?" Tina's head bobbed like a jack-in-the-box over the ledge; her dark hair was tousled and blown in a mess around her ears. Her bright eyes gleamed as she watched her brother sprawled on the ground. She had been hiding in the clearing all along. "Bucky, you're not mad—are you, Bucky?"

Buck was on his feet, his balled fist came down hard on the car's metal roof; the metal thundered, sent birds squawking in the trees. Tina's hands were at her ears.

Buck's balled fist hit the car roof again. *"What the hell?"*

Tina twisted in the open car window. "Now, Bucky . . . hold on here."

"You think you're funny?" His gut was bubbling and loose.

Tina's head vanished from the window frame, and she ducked back across the car seat. More leaves crackled, and she appeared slinking around the car's rusted rear fender. She was small, her little girl's snub nose leading the way. Her clear fresh skin was drawn tight across her cheeks, and her eyes darted, her limbs quick, ready to break and run.

Buck lunged for her as though pricked by the Bull's sharp blade—the anger rising in him, sour spittle in his mouth.

No use reasoning, Tina jumped—her skinny legs a blur, she dashed for the wall of trees and the rails beyond.

Buck whirled, and his fingers snagged her dress's shoulder strap. The strap slipped from his fingers and she was gone. The gravel skittered on the railbed and Tina glanced back when she reached the top of the hump to see if Buck had chased her.

She was pouting and baffled, but she let the questions pass.

Tina looked down at her knees, scarred and scabby from playing in the dirt. Then her eyes were back on Buck, standing like a strong dark shadow behind the trees' dusky shape. "The hell with you, Bucky."

Buck said nothing. So she stuck her tongue out and then turned on her heels, running home free. Buck let his sister go. At just sixteen years, Buck had a good five years on Tina. Five good reasons why he ought to smack her head for spooking him with a girly prank. The pounding in his throat faded into his blood's steady pulse; he watched his sister run, running like he ran.

But not chased by the river's flowing current and Meriwether's hard jackal laughter. Meriwether said people drown in that river. The Bull knew for sure. Up on the railbed a dust devil whipped to life from the wooden ties. The dust devil twirled, a spinning gyro top, big as a man, skipping down the railbed, following on Tina's heels. The ochre funnel danced like a dervish and then collapsed, vanishing as the exhausted breeze perished and the devil with it.

The Bulls were not afraid of him. Not when a body floated miles on its own. They laughed at him and the knife's edge flat against his inseam, at the worm blood wiped between his legs, at the worm cut and dripping. They laughed as he shivered in the sight of a murdered man. They laughed, knowing he would never tell a soul.

The drifter's body floated. It drifted past snags and sunken logs, rough rocks, and stayed in the deeps of the riverbed, feet dragging in the running water. The body floated, shirt bulging with an air bubble, downriver where the U.S. Route jumped the river over a one-lane bridge. Girders and planks, concrete pilings poured over the rock on the riverbank, and steel spans set. The dead man swirled in the backwater; the owl dipped in the air as the body passed under the bridge. Under the water the drifter's boot snagged on a metal hook sunk deep and rusted in the concrete piling. The current buoyed the body up and pushed it close to the steel supports, the shore in the bridge's hollow. The dead man bobbed in waist-deep water, resting and hidden, silent under the metal spans.

Day Fever

HARK! HARK! THE DOGS DO BARK!
THE BEGGARS ARE COMING TO TOWN,
SOME IN RAGS, AND SOME IN TAGS,
AND SOME IN VELVET GOWNS.

The church was wood. Painted white. Up the stubby steeple, squat like a house on a house, the clock chimed once on the half hour. Roman numerals, copper, on the clock's single face were dusty green in the early morning sun. The Blue Vista Flats town square was empty and the great oak planted at its center was oddly free of blackbirds, those nuisance creatures so often perched on the telephone lines. The sound of the flies droned stupidly in the cool house eaves. Hidden from the light. No flies visible. No evidence that the damn things breathed.

Tacked to the clapboard by the side of the church doors a printed poster hung by a single nail. The public notice pinned there two weeks ago never stirred, motionless in the still midsummer heat. Two weeks was plenty of notice, public or otherwise, so everyone knew the score.

AUCTION   Aug. 4th

Five Head Horses
Farm Machinery incl:
McCormick-Deering Tractor,
Grain drill, binder, mower,
hay rack, and articles too
numerous to mention . . .

MOSS GREENE ******** OWNER

PARKER WATTS ******** CLERK
(President Blue Vista Bank)

SHERIFF TATE **** AUCTIONEER

    Preacher Simon opened the double wooden doors of the church and with rough wedges propped them against the clapboard, one door covering the poster. Standing taut like a sapling on the worn plank steps of his church, Preacher Simon breathed the stale dry morning air and stared through the leafy branches of the giant oak across the square. Opposite the church was Lepke's Diner, built from shiny sheet metal, now dull and tarnished. The diner was constructed in the style of a railroad parlor car, with rounded corners and curves where the roof met the walls. In summer, only a ratty screen door kept the flies out, and the long glass windows on either side of the door were grimy from kitchen grease. At the booths and counter the vague forms of early risers moved slowly, reaching for coffee, for doughnuts, for whatever Lepke served.
    Beyond the diner several houses lay quiet; their dry weathered rooftop shingles curled and pried at the rusted nails that held them fast. Lepke's Diner and the houses were on the south side of the square, with the eastern corners of the buildings lit up bright in the sun. No different from any daybreak. Except that it was August 4th, and for Moss Greene, "Owner," this was the day of financial atonement.
    Preacher sensed the dawn's promise. Preacher was not going to preach about the promise, and he was not going to holler. He was not about to say what God already knew. No point to lay blame for Moss Greene's failure. Because when a man went broke, even

a good man, that man could only look to himself for the answers and the simple truth of it. Moss Greene was busted, getting bought out, kit 'n' kaboodle.

Preacher dug in his black trousers pocket and felt two nickels warm against his fingertips. He held them in his pocket till they were moist from his hand. Now unable to make out Lepke's patrons behind the window glass in the diner, Preacher glanced east, shading his eyes against the rising sun. The square barely covered an acre; the only proper building on it was red brick and two stories high. The west facade facing him was dark. On the south end of the square nearest the diner was the First (and only) Blue Vista Flats Bank; the corner wall was sharply defined in an angle of sunlight. The bank's windows were barred and the shades pulled down.

The building's middle door was the sheriff's office and jail. Also barred. Bart Lowell's Barber Shop was closest to the church. Bart kept his windows bright and clean. The peppermint barber pole outside the door had long since stopped turning, but Lowell polished the brass ball on top nevertheless. Nobody wants a dirty barber, not if he is shaving your chin, plucking the hairs from your nostrils, or wrapping your face in a hot towel. Bart Lowell rented the Rooms-To-Let on the second story, when occasion demanded. Preacher never heard any complaints. Bart obviously kept the rooms clean, too.

Preacher looked for movement in the brick building; nothing stirred—not a window shade, not a curtain. At Preacher's right hand, Hanson's Garage & Gas was empty. The two red pumps were padlocked, and up the oil-stained concrete ramp the garage door was shut. Hanson had built the wooden garage in 1919, painted it once that same year, and let it peel ever since. The garage was Hanson's last compromise with the horseless carriage. The first was pawning his old horse off to a neighbor with oats. Hanson also owned Hanson's Goods Store, Feeds & Sundries. His store took up the last corner of the square, a deep wooden house that ruminated on its stone foundation; same side as the garage but farther down, near the diner. Hanson's porch sagged. A cardboard sign was taped to a window pane: ABSOLUTELY NO CREDIT, scrawled, faded, now nearly illegible. Safe to say that if you needed credit, you would never get it. Who would bother asking?

Preacher Simon took off his broad-brimmed black hat and wiped his forehead on his jacket sleeve. He held the two nickels in his pocket; the coins were very wet now, the pocket lining of his trousers almost soaked through. From out of the darkness of the Goods Store porch a fly darted into the light; it made a small quick circle in the air and shot back to the cool of the shade. The little buggers were alive. Heat or no heat, when the flies went broke they kept the failure to themselves. Didn't take much to keep a fly happy; most often they didn't even need credit.

In Lepke's Diner, Lepke, the stout walrus of a chef and sole proprietor, switched on the tall standing fan by the screen door and ran his open hands over his belly to hike up his pants. When the fan moved from side to side the blades made a clean sweep of the booths, the counter, and the grill. Lepke stared at the man sitting at the counter, not quite sure what to make of his familiar but silent customer.

Yohanna Johns bent over his coffee cup, his gristly-bone back to Lepke, hunched with a determination seldom seen so early in the morning. The old farmer's spine ridged up his overalls, protruding caustic and severe. Come to bid on some of Moss Greene's property, Yohanna Johns had shown up on Lepke's doorstep just as Lepke opened the diner. Ready and waiting, his early presence foreshadowed his purpose. He waited for the auction and was ready to bid. Ready and waiting, as if an early rising could forestall all comers who risked their money and bid against him. So he arrived like a thundercloud ahead of the storm, to scare off the feeble-brained, the weak-hearted, and anyone else who dared to claim an article of Moss Greene's property that obviously deserved better hands. Granite determination was all that kept Yohanna Johns from springing to his feet, shouting, "Ten dollars! Twelve dollars! I'll pay whatever it takes!" thrashing his finger in the air.

Lepke knew all about determination: in addition to the diner, Lepke also owned the county grain elevator by the railroad waystation. He had seen the farmers come in their trucks loaded to the breech. He had seen some arrive joyous, others pensive; some had come despondent and some walking, but dead. Two steps from the grave, or worse, two steps from the road, which stretched east and west and vanished in a point. Lepke was glad of it all when he let their trouble pass him by, sending them away from his grain elevator, back to their crops or onto the road that yawned before their ruined hopes. Lepke would have none of it. The great fear was getting on that road: cropless, farmless, homeless. Drifting. Avoid it at all costs—kill if you have to, but don't get on that road, because you'll never come back. Broke, sober, and somber, that road was one long gray grave. Everybody said only the dead could Rest-In-Peace, but out on that road the drifters took over. And nobody ever accused a drifter of resting. Though Lepke had not seen Moss Greene in over a month, he was sure the bankrupt "Owner" had tombstones in his eyes already. Couldn't be any other way. You did not have to be a prophet to know the vultures were circling over the carcass, sniffing at the twitching body, like Yohanna Johns and the others who holed up in the diner waiting for the morning to pass.

The standing fan hummed in Lepke's ear, blowing his thin hair onto his forehead and into his eyes. He brushed the strands away.

"Wanna bet Preacher'll bid on something? Yohanna? Now I'll bet you Preacher's got his eye on some little piece . . . bet you twenty cents. Twenty cents says Preacher's gonna make a bid."

Somewhere in a back booth a customer began to snore. Yohanna Johns kept on sitting hunched over the counter, silent as an old knot of discarded soup meat; he shrugged his shoulders and said nothing. Lepke had no intention of bidding himself, not even for something useful as a table lamp or a set of tin spoons, but he could see old Yohanna was after something big . . . a thresher, maybe a mower. Maybe even a tractor. The wiry farmer would spill his own story quick enough. Lepke tried again.

"Who wants to bet?"

Another long snore, choppy but deep and croaking, from the back booth. Yohanna Johns swiveled around in his stool. He stroked the thin ligaments on his knee and frowned. His eyes, deep in sockets carved out with ladles, jittered and then suddenly went steady. "Preacher let the bank turn his church into a roadside billboard, didn't he?"

Lepke said nothing. Yohanna stroked his knee a little harder. "Didn't he? Well, didn't he?"

Lepke noticed Yohanna Johns' neck muscles were corded like a butchered turkey's. The old man never seemed to suffer. Dry or wet, good harvest or bad, Johns always kept pace. He had the acreage, he had the three dumb sons to help him, and an old whore's toothless smile—if you ever caught him smiling. A rare occasion. Now a widower, when his wife dried up and died like a withered stick, Yohanna Johns was left with just enough energy to fight the Good Fight, as Preacher would say.

"Wanna bet?" Lepke swept the thin strands of hair back over his scalp and he saw the old farmer's Adam's apple bob in the buzzard's gullet.

"Wanna bet?"

Johns swiveled back to his coffee. "Bet yourself."

The snoring stopped abruptly. At the back of the diner J. J. Baskum clawed himself out of the booth in a waking frenzy. Caught unaware: "Tell my wife I'm not here!"

Baskum straddled the arm of the booth seat, one leg hanging into the aisle. In his hurry to rise, his thigh jammed. He was wedged in tight—stuck. His eyes were red, and his jacket bunched under his armpits. J. J. Baskum. Farmer. Husband. Dastard. Fool. If any clod in Blue Vista Flats or Bone County worked as little and yet reaped as much they'd thank their lucky stars, praise the Lord and sin with the Devil. Not J. J. Baskum.

He hated his wife, plain and simple. He'd snagged himself some tenant farmers and he stayed afloat. The machinery on his farm never seemed to rust. His chickens laid eggs, his cows gave milk, his house never leaked and his fields produced. Yet for all that he was a sorry case. His wife took him to task. And often. Yet they stuck together day in and day out, and nobody thought that was strange. Baskum just did not have the guts to throw the fat squaw out the door. But this was the truth: J. J. Baskum was a coward. Baskum knew it, and his wife knew it. If nothing else, his yellow belly and his wife's nagging gave them something in common. His two front teeth were gold—knocked out by the lady, most people suspected, knocked out sometime after the honeymoon was over. So now Baskum, too, came as a bidder on Moss Greene's property.

Yohanna Johns stared down at his cup. "Cool off, J. J."

Baskum jerked his armpits and pulled at the sleeve of his jacket.

"Your wife ain't called." Johns dabbed his spoon in a coffee puddle. "Lepke's making a bet."

Baskum eased his stocky trunk back into the booth, slapping

his hands to his face. He rubbed his eyes and sighed. "God bless her. Absolutely. What time is it?"

Lepke shrugged. He never pried for details, like some bartenders and countermen who claim they knew a man better than his spouse. The facts were obvious to Lepke: neither the wife nor the mistress can truly judge their customer—and bartenders least of all. No one trusts a drunk's slurred speech. The mistress only knows his fits of passion and his wife only the lulls between.

But when unaroused and sober, most men seek a refuge from work, from women, from weighty thought and forced laughter. Lepke breathed his diner's stale air; he inhaled the traces of men's thoughtless moments, of idle company and the pointless trickle of conversation that filled the space of empty minutes.

Lepke went around to the back of the counter, put on a grease-stained apron and poured himself a cup of coffee from the dingy hot plate next to the grill. In the booth Baskum dropped his hands from his face and adjusted a threadbare white necktie that pinched his neck like a noose. He tugged at the tie knot, loosening the choker. As his fingers dug at the knot, Baskum managed to bend a collar point under the tie loop, and this gave him the appearance of a fat little schoolboy who had tied his neckband for the very first time.

From the side of the counter Bart Lowell, the barber, came out of the bathroom buttoning up his fly. Lowell was a small man with moist eyes and beautifully groomed hair. When he finished buttoning his trousers, he held his hands away from his body like a surgeon and walked down the back of the counter to the sink. Lowell was a dainty man, pink-eyed as a hamster. He turned the hot water tap and let the water spill over his hands for a moment before getting the soap. He lathered, rinsed, lathered, and rinsed again. He did not pick up a dish towel from the sink; he shook his hands in the air to dry them.

The pay phone on the wall near the toilet began to ring. Bart Lowell snapped up the earpiece with two damp fingers and answered it. J. J. Baskum began frantically pointing at himself and shaking his head. He wanted nothing to do with the phone, whoever was calling.

"Yes," Lowell said into the phone. After a moment, "Sure." And then, "My pleasure."

Lowell turned to the booths by the window, the earpiece of the phone in his hand. Baskum's tie had now slipped from the collar completely and was pressing the flesh around his neck.

"J. J." Lowell held out the phone. "It's your wife."

Moss Greene.
"Owner."
Moss Greene was going broke. Gone broke, in fact. Nothing was simpler. Easy to do. Lean like a sapling, he stood in the open door of his barn, holding on the wooden door jamb. The Greene farm was fifty acres rolling away without a stump in the ground. But his place was on the auction block nonetheless. Moss Greene was one payment late on the joint C&C Railroad–Blue Vista Bank equipment loan and mortgage. The damn bastards would not even let the harvest come. One damn payment late and the debt was called in. No piece of the cash crop was good enough—they wanted cash and title. Parker Watts, the banker and co-lender on the loan, filled in as County Collector. No cash crop, he explained; the C&C Railroad wants cash.

Cash. You can't eat the stuff. You can't smoke it. You can't grow it. It does not smell nice, and it is no good for tinder. The greenbacks are no good for the holes in your shoe soles; unlike rags, you can't plug the cracks in the clapboard with cash. But that never stopped the railroad from wanting it, and it certainly was not going to stop Parker Watts from collecting it, and Moss Greene suffered the hopeless feeling that even when each credit-purchased piece of machinery was sold, the sum tallied up and the land title transferred in bold blue ink with signatures and counter-signatures nothing would remain, no scrap left over that the family once called their own.

Moss had watched as Parker Watts strode around the farm, a clipboard in his tight fist. He tallied up the livestock. He tallied up the grain stores. He tallied up the machinery, right down to the pitchforks, the shovels, the axes, the awls, the half-barrel of nails, and he counted the horseshoes hung on the barn walls. And after Parker Watts counted every little thing and estimated its value, he took a deep breath, and the cocky skinflint even eyed the barn itself, as if to measure how well it would burn and whether anyone would pay for the privilege of tearing it down and carting it away as firewood.

Then lickety-split like a rabbit, Parker Watts had the whole she-bang typed up and called it an "inventory." Moss Greene considered this just another word for robbery, but kept silent. The good banker had a hundred copies of the inventory mimeoed and set the stack on Sheriff Tate's desk. Within a week the stack was gone, snapped up like a free morning newspaper. And one by one, in ones and twos, the cars came up the road. Some folks brought gifts, as if they were making a house call, but mostly they came just to look around. Some did not bring gifts at all, but strode right into the barn like they owned the place already, kicking the wheels on the thresher, pulling back the horses' lips and peering at their teeth, fingering the point of a pitchfork, wondering, scrutinizing, considering.

But some neighbors came with bad looks in their eyes. They shook their heads and muttered things. They talked about their children, and they talked about the future. They talked about the new President's foreclosure freezing, some New Deal, and the Agricultural Adjustment Administration, the Triple A. The Farm Union sent a man who stroked his chin. And then Parker Watts appeared again, saying something about the Reds. He liked the New Deal, Watts claimed. And Moss Greene remembered when Parker Watts closed the bank in March, only to reopen, proud and smiling, proclaiming the health of the Republic, glory to God, and pass the pie, sister.

But the Farm Union man went away, and so did Parker Watts. The AAA was not everywhere at once and never knew where to look, so before Moss Greene could count the days, he woke. August 4th had dawned. The awesome foreclosure day arrived bright and cheerful like August generally was in Blue Vista, the only difference being that the day was slow-fated and Moss Greene had gone broke. The day arrived, the same as any other, the sun coming up in the east, the birds on the telephone wires chirping about nothing at all, and Moss Greene stood at the door of his barn peering inside for what the world knew would be the last time. Last, because all his machinery, his cattle, his horses, his chickens, his hogs, his grain piled up in the silo, his spade with the worn handle, everything that made the difference between living and starving, between working and rotting, was up for auction. House and foundation, anything and everything, sold to the highest bidder, for better or worse, for richer or poorer, when the gavel do us part. Three days' grace for packing the personals. Then by golly: *get out!*

The pity was, he could not stab a finger in the air and say, 'Yes, I remember, I remember the day I went broke.' No such luck. No one to blame. He could not meet a payment, he knew he couldn't, he told Parker Watts that simple fact, and Watts smiled. Not to worry . . . not to worry . . . I'll take care of everything. He sure did. Not a damn thing Moss Greene could do about it.

Across the yard he heard the door of his farmhouse open and the scrape of feet standing in the door frame. Liza was up, letting the children sleep, for no work would be done today. No point in shaking the children out of their dreams, calling on them to feed the chickens. The cows could be milked whenever the kids got around to the job. No hurry—the 4th was auction day, and Liza woke and stood on the farmhouse porch from habit alone.

She stared at her husband standing at the door of the barn, vaguely noticing the blackbirds perched on the barn roof, waiting as they always did for the chickens to be fed so they could freeload on the scraps after the rooster stopped strutting and his little women had been stuffed to the gizzard. But what struck her was the way the early morning sun glanced off her husband's back. His shirt clung to his shoulder blades and his spine, stiff under the shirt cloth, seemed strained today, strained as never before, even when he used to pull a plow himself, before they bought the horses, the water wagon, the tractor, the reaper. Strained under a lack of weight, free for once, failed forever—close to breaking. That was the way things ended.

Without turning to face her, Moss pushed the sliding barn door on its rails till it was full open. The barn inside was cool and dark; cobwebs full with dew caught the morning light as they hung from the beams and trembled as he passed. Moss Greene's two great dappled mares were quiet in their box stalls. Like two grand old ladies biding their time the two horses knew Moss was near them, and they breathed deep, the air jetting from their large soft nostrils. Two sets of ears twisted, perking as Moss' footsteps fell close by, and the two horses turned together, each in its big stall, to see if Moss had brought them oats or an apple.

Moss took the bits and halters off a nail by the box stalls and laid the tack over the first dappled mare's great head; then he led her gently from the barn. The mare followed him, always willing, always trusting, her large chestnut eyes blinking in the bright morning light. Moss hitched her to his clapboard wagon, and the horse bowed her head, letting the ringed harness slide onto her neck. She waited patiently in the traces as Moss went to fetch the second great lady, to team her up beside her sister. With both horses hitched, Moss filled two nosebags with four or five handfuls of oats each to keep the mares from nibbling on people's hats or shirts at the auction if they stood too near and did not pay attention. Moss ran his hands across the graying wood of the wagon's slats and heard the porch boards sigh under his wife's feet.

"Children up?"

Polite and foolish: he'd have heard them if they were. Liza looked at his shoulders, his spine under the shirt cloth, and the small hairs at the nape of his neck.

"I thought I'd let them—"

"Right." Moss turned around.

Liza smoothed out her dress and touched the braided hair that fell over one shoulder. At her feet on the porch their black hound thumped his tail and perked his ears. The dog lifted his head, eyes bright in the morning, happy and unconcerned. Liza looked at Moss. "You'll want breakfast . . ."

The dog thumped his tail again. Moss shrugged as he stepped away from the wagon. His boots kicked up the gravel in the yard; the stones skittered as he walked to the house. The dog leapt off the porch after a rolling stone, bounced it off his paw, and went chasing. Moss stopped at the door. Liza stood and faced him. Taking the braid from her shoulder, she tossed it onto her back. Moss did not try to squeeze past her into the house. He stayed quite close for a moment and saw where her braid met in three, weaving in waves from her scalp. "No rush for breakfast."

In her bed in one of Bart Lowell's Rooms-To-Let, Eve opened her eyes and blinked dully at the soft light touching the window frames. The body next to her in the bed was warm and heavy. She did not recognize her companion. The big lummox had the sheets drawn over his head. Yes, definitely a man. But which man? The lump began to snore in short little sucking bursts.

Sheriff Tate.

Again? That made it twice in a week. His wife, June, was gonna throw a fit. Maybe twice a month the Sheriff could claim drunkenness, offer the poor alibi of waking in a ditch, but not twice in the same week. Not a chance—June would not believe it. She would raise hell this time, for sure. Eve felt for her nightgown which had rumpled up around her waist. Her mouth tasted sticky and sour. A dresser with a mirror leaned against one wall; on the dresser was a bottle of Seagram's, three quarters empty, and next to the bottle some loose cash. Tate should have left in the middle of the night. She should have dumped the sucker in the gutter. But as she eased out of bed, her head felt filled with water sloshing against her ear. No. No chance of throwing him out last night. She would have forgotten the money, tossed him a party favor, and that would have been no good at all.

Her head reeled slightly as she stood up, and she grasped the dresser for support when she crossed the room. Sheriff Tate's loose cash amounted to four one-dollar bills and a fiver. Eve took the five and two of the singles, folded them and tucked the money in the top dresser drawer. She closed the drawer without a sound. She let go of the dresser and turned; more water sloshed in her ear. The bed was far away, but she managed to crawl back under the covers and stretch out flat. The snoring stopped abruptly and Sheriff Tate shifted under the sheets. Eve poked the lummox somewhere in the shoulder.

"Time," she whispered.

Tate grunted. "Lemme be, June."

Eve poked Tate hard this time and whispered loudly in his ear. "This ain't June, Tate."

Sheriff Tate sat up quickly in bed, the sheet falling off his head. The water was sloshing around in his skull too. He blinked his eyes and clapped his hands to his ears. "Oh . . . Jesus."

Eve lay on her back and stared at the ceiling. "If He's even listening He won't approve. Leave now and you'll be home before six. On the way you can think of an excuse. But don't ask Jesus."

"Oh Christ . . . damn." Tate was putting the pieces together.

Eve stretched and wriggled her bottom down into the mattress. "Yes, well like I said, if you get home soon you can soak your head, plead with your wife and show up at the auction looking like a Sheriff."

Tate rolled out of bed and crawled over the floor on his hands and knees. "Pants . . . shirt—"

"On the chair, darling."

Tate stood up. He found his pants, shirt, and most of his clothes and leaned against the wall as he pulled them on. The Sheriff was certainly a sight; didn't look much better than if he *had* slept in a ditch. Eve reached down and scratched the warm hair between her legs.

So last night it was Tate. Before?

The day before—alone.

The day before that—skinny little Watts. The banker was a hit-and-run driver; Parker Watts shot from the hip and barely said thank you. And the day before that . . . Bart Lowell. Her dear dear brother-in-law. If her sister only knew. Bart was a funny one all right. He always came up in his barber's smock with nothing but his underwear on. But then it figured, because her sister Claire possessed an evil streak. The evil ran right through the woman: not mean, just a quiet wildness. Not a bad sister. A cuckold, but not a man. Had a doxy for kin.

J. J. Baskum was pretty ordinary. Always said 'thank you,' and Eve could never help asking, "How's your wife?" Baskum hardly flustered; he always nodded his head sadly. "Oh the same, the same."

Yohanna Johns was the weird one. Never did a thing. The old farmer liked to look, touch her breast gently, and smile to himself, off in a trance. But Johns never paid for the pleasure. The poor man, seemed not to miss his wife now that she was gone. Eve would tally up and settle that account some day. No bills unpaid. No debts outstanding. No free rides.

Sheriff Tate buttoned his pants and swayed toward the dresser. He grabbed the few bills Eve left without looking at them. He waved them in the air. "Didn't pay you last night."

Eve smiled. "Oh, this one's on me, Sheriff. Just settle things with June. You can come back again and pay me double."

Tate's belly hung over his belt. Cramming the cash in his pants pocket, he turned to go. "Keep the bottle."

The door closed and Eve stared at the ceiling. That sloshing water slowly drained from her ear. The pressure passed and her head cleared. A breeze pressed in through the window and the door to her room was sucked open as if by a ghost's passage. Across the hall Parker Watts began his waking ritual. Eve slipped out from under the covers, shut her door and waited, her ear close to the door and every sound in the hall.

Parker Watts lay awake in his bed across the hall. When he heard the heavy footsteps fading down the hall, he got out of bed gingerly. His feet barely touched the floor as he went to the washbasin. His bladder was full and pressed, but he ignored the urge to urinate. He took a damp cloth and washed the crusty sleep from his eyes. He found clean underwear in the dresser and discarded the pair he had slept in. The dresser yielded clean socks, and sitting on the bed, he drew the socks up his calves, snapping on garters to keep them taut. The garters fit snugly around his calves, just under the knee. They were striped red and silver. The red and silver garters were a present from his mother, given upon his graduation from a Philadelphia accounting school. He wore the garters every day.

Watts then stood before the mirror hung over the washstand and dipped the cloth back into the water. He wrung the washcloth out over his head, getting his hair damp. Very carefully, he combed back his hair, parting it on the side. From the closet he took a light wool gray suit, a starched shirt, a burgundy tie, and a fresh collar that hung on a peg. He laid the suit on the bed, buttoned the collar to the back of the shirt, and put the shirt on. Standing before the mirror, he threaded the tie through the collar and pulled the knot tight.

The shirt was starched and clean; the cotton was pressed so two sharp creases plunged to the tails. The shirttails covered his flaccid thighs but stopped short of his knees, dimpled and pale. The urge to pee returned but Watts would not give in.

He found his shoes, polished the night before, and put them on. He used a stiff Fuller shoe brush to buff up the shine. The shoes were wing tips, probably the only pair in Blue Vista Flats. Last of all he looped an Elgin wristwatch around his wrist. Another present from his mother.

Opening his door a crack, Watts peered down the impeccably clean hall that ran the second-story length of the rooming house. Bart Lowell's Rooms-To-Let had four available rooms: Bart and

Claire occupied their own, Parker Watts' room was obviously taken, and Eve's room was generally double occupancy. That left one room to spare. As the "salesmen's" room, so far, it had been empty for quite some time; paying roomers were in short supply. At the far end of the hall were the stairs that led to Lowell's barbershop, and a back exit that the roomers used. The stairs were narrow, and the landing at the building's end had been boarded into a small room, no bigger than a walk-in closet: the toilet and tub. Baths were 5¢ extra. Watts took two baths a week, but he used the toilet every day. And that, of course, cost nothing.

Gartered, shoed, socked, in shirt and tie but pantless, Watts threw open the door and walked quickly down the corridor, keeping on his toes so his wing tips made little noise. The first door he passed was on the back side, away from the square. This was the empty room. The next door he passed overlooked the square, and this was Eve's room. Eve was part of Bart Lowell's family, so to speak. Bart was married to Claire Lowell, and Eve was Claire's sister. This made Eve Bart's sister-in-law.

And that made Bart Eve's brother-in-law.

Didn't it?

It surely did.

Eve paid no rent; she ran the town's telephone switchboard out of Sheriff Tate's jail, and kept out of trouble. Eve was unmarried —that had its problems. Eve liked to drink, and that had its problems. But then Eve worked on the assumption of see all, do all, say nothing.

And from time to time, Parker Watts had indulged the fancies and passions of the woman. After all, Parker Watts was a man.

Wasn't he?

And Eve was a woman.

She surely was.

So when Parker Watts did indulge the woman in her baser instincts, he did so purely for medicinal purposes. The discreet use of passion kept a man fit. So his mother always said. But he could not stop Eve from gratifying herself, more often than prudence allowed. And so he had to trust her only to see all, do all, and say nothing. But seeing him walking down the hall in his almost new cotton shorts, his shoes, socks, garters, his shirttails and tie was not part of the bargain. The young president of the First (and only) Blue Vista Bank had a certain dignity and prestige to uphold. The financial weight of the community rested on his shoulders. The loans he approved with the different lenders (from the railroad to the insurance companies) kept Blue Vista Flats and Bone County a flourishing and solvent economic unit. For the most part.

No gentleman put his shoes on last, and no gentleman tiptoed down the hall barefoot, and most certainly no gentleman was caught by the landlord's sister-in-law strutting to the toilet in his underwear.

Watts passed Eve's door and then passed the Lowells' room, slipping into the toilet at the head of the stairs without incident. He brushed his teeth with his tie thrown over the shoulder so he would not spot it. He urinated carefully with a sigh of great satisfaction, shaking himself with a flick of the wrist and dancing a little jig just for good measure. He flushed the toilet and peeked out the door. The hall was empty.

Stepping brightly down the corridor he moved smoothly past the Lowells' room, past Eve's room, past the empty room—

"Hold it right there, sucker."

Eve.

With as much dignity as possible, Parker Watts let go of his doorknob and turned smartly on his heels. Eve leaned on the door frame. She wore a bathrobe. Her hair was pinned. The bathrobe belt was tied, and Watts could just make out her cleavage. She was graying in wisps, and she was fighting to keep her figure. Husbands can afford to be tolerant where customers will not.

"Yes?" Watts was polite.

Eve measured him for a moment. One of his garters was slipping and needed to be tightened. Other than that, and the lack of his pants, he was perfectly dressed.

"You left the toilet seat up."

Parker Watts looked down the hall. The bathroom door was closed.

"How can you tell?" Watts did not want to argue, but the evidence denied this claim.

"You always leave it up."

"I see." Watts turned toward his room. "Well, next time..."

"Now."

"Perhaps," Watts tried, "I could put on my—"

"Now."

Parker Watts let go of the doorknob, turned swiftly back to

Eve, brushed past her and walked down the hall to the toilet. He was not going to make this encounter any ruder than it was already. Watts knew better. Do what she asked and let her have her way. A man and a gentleman—but a gentleman nevertheless. He reached the toilet door and opened it. The toilet seat was down.

Eve's voice danced down the empty hall. "Have a jolly time at the auction, Mr. Bank President."

Parker Watts heard a door slam. Then another door slammed. His door. Locked out, keyless and barred from entry! The woman had locked him out of his very own room. What possible motive made her do a thing like that? What nonsense. She was a child. He would have to get the key from Bart Lowell.

"Bart's over at the diner." The hair on Watts' knees went prickly and cold. Claire Lowell stood in her doorway. She was a smaller woman than her sister, Eve, and was not graying yet. She held her first morning cigarette between two fingers; the other hand rested on her hip. The cigarette smoke drifted out into the corridor. Claire was not pretty, not by magazine standards; not by the magazines Watts peeked through. A brown mole clung to her upper lip. The mole was not especially big, nor especially ugly. The small brown blemish sat at the edge of her lip, long forgotten. Claire was a woman who would not notice the fault. She was a trifle hard. Like her sister, she almost never backed down.

"And I don't have the key."

Watts waved the cigarette smoke from his face with a fluttering hand. Claire took another long drag, exhaling more blue fumes in a cloud.

"Where'd you lose your pants?"

Drake Walker sat in the metal seat of his tractor and looked down along the long red engine hood, shaped like a great locust's armored back. He rode up above the wheat field's flower tops, the crop spreading below him like a sea and the tractor became a vessel, plowing through the swell. Drake Walker, duly honest and solid, saw that Moss Greene's failure was not entirely straightforward, that not everything met the eye. Nothing illegal. But if a man could work his whole life long, sweat the hours through, if he put his trust in a banker's arms, only to go bust when the C&C Railroad called in the loan, then the world had changed. And Drake wondered if Moss Greene's fate might be his own if he stretched his resources too far, too fast.

Drake's peace with the world began at his scalp and rose rank-haired; he brushed off any threats and men's jealousies like the sheared clippings in a barber's chair. He kept peace with the world in the bidden circle of his family, and he kept his peace with the future in Buck's strong arms. No son's failure was born out of his father's honor. In Drake's own arms he had the boy's supple strength. Strength enough and his conscience too.

When two of Drake's neighbors failed in '32, they joined their land to his and he took them on. Any one of them would have done the same for him. You got along. Stand by your neighbor—he'll stand by you. On this principle Drake Walker kept his family and his son in a circle of peace. So far he had succeeded.

The Walker farm was called the Eastern Range; it lay east of Blue Vista Flats. Long ago, Drake's grandpa left the knoll at the farm's center wild and untouched. The knoll was left as the family had found it, deep in the wild grass with one lone cedar pointing up to the sun and the sky, throwing a long shadow in the morning across the field and then toward the town.

Now Moss Greene was busted and only three farmers in Blue Vista Flats were solvent. J. J. Baskum was the first. Yohanna Johns was the second. And stretched as he might be, Drake was the last. Last in the county most likely, and last to take on his neighbors as tenants. Baskum took on his share and made his tenants' lives the worse for it. Yohanna Johns took on no extra responsibilities, no extra load; he would not trade off produce for another man's mortgage payment. But Drake felt the earth under his feet when his two neighbors came to him bareheaded and ready to fold. There was no letting them hit the U.S. Route and blow away in the wind. They stayed on and they worked. When the Farm Price Index dropped, Baskum's tenants threw away another year of their lives, their hope tattered and in shreds, but Drake's tenants kept their silent watch and Drake his promise, handling their debt alone and nothing else.

Drake Walker, sitting in the tractor seat, turned off the

motor and hopped down to the ground. He strode up the tiny knoll and dirt scraped off his boots onto the long wild grass. He stopped at the top of the knoll and stood in the cedar tree's shadow stretching west from the rising sun. Drake could see the better part of Bone County and Blue Vista Flats. Two roads formed a cross at the town square. The U.S. Route which passed smack in front of Drake's farmhouse ran east and west. County Road 6 ran north-south. The C&C Railroad line came up from the south, curving around the eastern edge of the Eastern Range. The tracks ran parallel to the U.S. Route, but the rails were laid a mile and a half away and Drake's farm spread in between. Last, Yellow River crossed all routes and rails; the river followed County Road 6 twenty yards from the road's eastern shoulder, until the water reached the town. Then the river ducked under the U.S. Route and washed another half mile south before bending west and flowing out of sight.

Drake Walter, J. J. Baskum and Yohanna Johns all took water from Yellow River. In dry weather each man coveted that stream like the sole hussy in a miners' town, but no one more so than Baskum. The river cut right through the middle of his property, but even so he coveted it like an only child. "Give him an inch," people said of Baskum. And he took it. Yellow River was all Bone County had when the rain failed. Then the water was hauled up the drying banks with buckets and water wagons, with home-made pumps—anything just to keep the soil moist. The river was ten feet deep and in some places more; forty feet wide, but in some places seventy. In drought, parts of the riverbed broke the waterline like dry dead bones dusting in the sun. No one liked to see that.

When Drake looked north he could see the railroad tracks and his tenants' houses, old and rotting. The houses stretched along the black tracks—houses built while Drake's father was still alive and when people thought the town would grow toward the railroad and not along the U.S. Route. But popular opinion proved incorrect and the farmers took over the houses. They had worked the land beyond the tracks, until they failed.

Failed with the bank's loans outstanding and Parker Watts sniffing at their heels. When they came to Drake, they came without a hope, because when the bank took something away, Drake knew you never got it back. Sure, he took on their mortgage payments. Sure, he took a cut of their cash crop. What else to do? What else?

Let them sell out to Parker Watts? Let them auction the equipment? Let them drive out to the U.S. Route?

But now Drake was full up on debt.

Moss Greene knew it too, and did not even bother asking. Half the country out of work, a pocketful of auction money, a couple of gallons of gasoline, nights in the Hooverville, and the road again, looking for work—that's all Drake saw for Moss Greene now. You leave your children and your wife in the cardboard city and down the long strip of macadam you whisper to yourself that you'll see them again and you might even believe it.

So Drake's tenants stuck on and kept working. He wanted them to keep living in their houses. The alternative was poverty, no work, and of course, the U.S. Route led forever down an endless grave. So Walker and his tenants planted and that was what counted. In three large strips they sowed: closest to the railroad tracks was wheat. In the middle, circling the knoll, corn. Nearest Walker's farmhouse, barn, and vegetable garden, they planted cotton and a strip of alfalfa. The droughts of '31 and '32 pushed yet more farmers out onto the road. Yellow River fell to only a foot and a half—Drake and his tenants irrigated, loaded up their water wagons, and sprayed their fields. When the first dust storms blew, the land was wetted down, and only a sixth of the crop was lost. Others lost much more. In Oklahoma the dust piled up three and four feet deep against the sides of houses. Preacher said it was God's will. And some folks believed him.

Looking north up County Road 6 and Yellow River, Drake could just make out Lepke's grain elevator, monstrous and silver, rising over the railroad tracks. Dwarfed by the elevator, the C&C Railroad's water tower and coal tender squatted over the steel strips and wooden ties, black with steamed-on dirt and oil. Hidden was the railroad's workhouse where the Bulls marked time, worked the track, the ties and steel, were masters of their company's land and all else that came across their tracks. More than once the Bulls trespassed on other people's land. And this led to trouble.

Preacher called the Bulls' civic thrashings "God's judgment on the sinful." But then Preacher was a mule that brayed when it oughtn't.

With his hand Drake felt the stiff cotton weave of his overalls, the stitching tight down his thighs. The fabric was faded from soapy water and washboard scrubbing. When Eddy, the tenant, made soap out of pig fat, all the people on the Eastern Range, Drake's family included, washed with Eddy's soap and hung their sheets and clothes out in the wind and bleaching sun. The fresh-blowing air killed the smell, but you could not get rid of all the odor. The smell from the soap was pig fat, and that was a whole lot different from the lily-white fragrance that clung to Parker Watts when he sat behind his teller's cage in the bank and counted out your money or scratched out a deposit receipt. When the Eastern Range families sat in Preacher's church they were given plenty of room, for the soap's piggy odor clung on relentless. There would be a pew empty front and back. Drake figured that God could smell them just as clearly out in the range, so the next Sunday the Eastern Range families stayed away from Preacher's church. Preacher asked for Drake and his tenants, but some of the congregation just shrugged, and others giggled. The pig-fat odor never reached Preacher in his pulpit, so he was aware of who was missing, but unaware of what he missed.

Down the knoll Drake saw where the tractor's engine was exposed to the air, the block dirty with black grease, the wires snaking from the spark plugs and the oil filter on one side dry where the dust blew up from the wheels, and on the other sticky from the slick engine sweat. When he looked back out across the fields, Drake could not see Moss Greene's farm, but northwest up County Road 6 the farm lay, nonetheless, waiting to be plucked clean for the love of money, or some such nonsense. Moss Greene needed his farm and Bone County needed Moss Greene. The situation was as simple as that. Because the C&C Railroad was short on cash they called in their equipment loan, and the land's title, mortgaged, fell over like a domino. Because Parker Watts, that little snippet, co-lender with the Railroad, put up half the money, he collected, proud and brave—upright, a conscientious, pea-brained squirt, counting someone else's money with the hands God gave him.

It wasn't fair.

It wasn't right.

Drake did not have to think about it. Moss Greene was down and beat. Squeezed. Ripped to shreds and scattered in the dirt. And not much was going to be left when the gavel struck: Sold!

Sold! Without a thought, without a hope, without a prayer in the world. And the U.S. Route beckoned, straight and flat, work or bust, hit the macadam or starve. Denver. Reno. Des Moines. Los

Angeles. Hooverville—the tin-and-cardboard shacks, the squalid sewage ruts, the campfires that gave no heat in the night. No doctors, no sheets or pillowcases, no clothes, no baths, no chair to sit in, no table to eat at, no windows to look out of, no nothing.

Drake turned and looked up at the cedar tree, a green spike climbing into the sky. He moved close to it, where he could reach out and take a branch in his hand. The tight green conifer barbs pricked the tips of his fingers. He pressed them hard against the skin to see if any blood would come.

J. J. Baskum slammed the screen door of Lepke's Diner behind him as he stepped out into the square. He looked over to Hanson's Goods Store, but Hanson was nowhere in sight. Preacher had disappeared into his church, leaving the front doors open and the auction poster hidden. The diner's screen door squealed again and Bart Lowell stepped up beside Baskum. Lowell took a long thin comb from his breast pocket and ran it through the sleek dark hair on either side of his scalp, slicked razor-smooth and flashing a sheen.

Suddenly Baskum was looking at the bank. He nudged Lowell and pointed. On the second story the rooming house hall window was open. Two eyes, darting, peeked over the windowsill.

"What the . . . ?" Lowell put the comb away. The eyes at the second-floor window disappeared. A figure rose from behind the ledge and Lowell recognized Blue Vista Flats' esteemed bank president.

"Parker?" Lowell called. Watts waved, his hands fluttering like nervous pigeons. "Parker," Lowell called again. "What the hell are you doing in my hallway with nothing but your panties?"

From the open window Parker Watts' paper voice drifted across the square. "The key." His hands trembled again at the windowsill. "I'm locked out."

Bart Lowell walked toward the bank, looking up at the window. "Mr. Watts"—Lowell wasn't smiling—"if you can't get dressed by yourself you better leave my place. You may own the first floor of this building, but I definitely own the second. That clear?"

From the second story Watts pleaded. "Just gimme the key."

"You may not realize how serious I am."

Baskum chimed in. "He's serious, Parker. The man's serious."

"Please. The key."

Lowell stood under the window and pulled a massive key ring from his jacket pocket. Methodically he picked the first key on the ring, contemplated its purpose, discounted it and went on to the next.

"Please." Parker Watts was ready to go down on his knees. "Can't you bring them up? We'll look through the ring together."

Lowell glanced at the window; the key ring slid around his knuckles. Losing count, he sighed and stepped quickly around the side of the building and disappeared. Parker Watts withdrew from the window.

Alone in the square, J. J. Baskum shoved his hands in his pockets and looked over again at Hanson's Goods Store. He tapped the ground with his toe, letting his patience dribble away.

"Hanson!" Baskum hollered. "Hanson! Get your butt out here."

In the shade of the sagging store porch Baskum saw the screen door open and Hanson shuffle out. Hanson was smoking a cigarette which he plucked from his lips, flicking the ash into the air. The flies in the shade of the porch jumped, spinning over his head as Hanson waved the cigarette.

"Quit yapping." Hanson's teeth were brown from nicotine. "Why don't you get that shit-heap of yours backed up? I got the goods stacked inside."

Baskum's battered green pickup was parked at an angle in front of the diner. He got in, pressed the starter, and backed the truck toward Hanson's porch.

The pickup nearly rammed into the porch boards. "Whoa!" Hanson skipped back. Baskum cut the engine; it coughed once, misfiring, gurgled, and backfired, belching blue smoke into Hanson's face.

"Damn you." Hanson waved the smoke away, dragging on the cigarette stuck in the corner of his mouth. Baskum hopped out of the cab and stepped up on the porch. Hanson went through the screen door without bothering to hold it open. The door slammed before Baskum reached it, so he grabbed the handle; the hinges squeaked, and he nearly tore it down.

Hanson's store was stacked high with goods. Against the walls stood barrels filled with flour and barley. Baskum smelled the forty-gallon pickle drum in the corner even though it had the lid on. A long wooden table served for a counter, stacked with bolts of material.

A couple of glass jars were filled with candy and licorice. Cured hams in cheesecloth hung from the reddened wood ceiling.

Hanson had piled Baskum's order by the door. A sack of flour. Ten pounds of salted fat-back wrapped in newsprint. A sack of dried pinto beans. Baskum grabbed the corner of the flour sack and backed out through the door. Hanson took the fat-back and followed him. Baskum, sweating, hoisted the flour sack over the gate of the truck and dumped it on the bed. Hanson threw the ten-pound chunk of meat in after the sack. The wrapped meat bounced off the sack and rolled on the bed of the truck. Baskum went back for the sack of beans. He dragged the bean sack out and threw it in with the rest.

Baskum stood up straight, his filthy white tie askew. "Got your book?"

"Yeah." Hanson dropped the cigarette from his lips and crushed the butt. "Let's go."

They circled the tree in the square once before getting on the U.S. Route west. Two miles out of Blue Vista Flats they turned down a dirt road and headed south toward the river; they passed Baskum's house and barn. The road split into deep ruts and the two men jostled shoulders in the cab. Baskum heard the sacks flop against the metal walls of the pickup like the dull thud of dead bodies.

The fields gave way to a sparse wooded copse; the car was just able to squeeze between two solid trees. Past the trees a clearing opened up at the bank of Yellow River and stretched fifty yards in both directions.

Two small shacks and a chicken coop were set back from the river's edge. One shack was made of wood, the other from scrap sheet metal. Windows no bigger than hand Bibles, cut with tin shears in the walls of the metal shacks, were dark and vacant. Clotheslines were strung between the huts and wisps of smoke drifted up into the air from holes in the roofs. Trash was strewn in the clearing: some of it valuable for patching, tin sheet and such; some discarded like motor parts and bald tires.

A small dog scurried around to the side of Baskum's pickup

and began to scratch at the gate on its hind legs. Baskum cut the engine and heard the sound of Yellow River flow over the stones. A chicken clucked somewhere in a pen. Baskum blew his horn twice and stepped out of the cab. Hanson got out too and hiked up his pants. The Goods Store man had his small black book in hand. At the back of the truck the dog was still pawing at the gate; still standing on its hind legs, it scratched the metal trailer. It whined once as Baskum came around the back of the truck.

Baskum gave the dog a sharp kick on the thigh and it fell on its back with a yelp. He moved toward the dog again and the mutt headed for the river at a slow trot, teeth bared, but still retreating.

Hanson saw the pale drawn face of a woman in the doorway of the tin shack; she held a curtain back from the door, but when she noticed Hanson looking, she dropped the curtain and withdrew into the darkness. From the woods on the far side of the river, men's voices rose like thin smoke; then splashing in the river up from the bank, two men passed their shacks and stepped into the clearing.

Henry was lean and dark; a shotgun, breech open, slung over one arm. A broken gray felt fedora with the brim snapped down cut across his eyes. He walked smooth and silent. Henry's brother was a crushed little man, thin in the hips and bowlegged. A wormy straw boater slanted across his head like the tilted rings of Saturn. His eyes were watery and flitting. The brother held three dead rabbits from a piece of string knotted around each rabbit's neck; he looped the string over a sharp corner of a shack as he passed, letting the rabbits swing slowly. Blood was splattered on the rabbits' fur. As the two neared the truck their voices fell to murmurs and the murmurs died to silence. The crushed little man wore a shirt without a collar. Henry's boots had no laces.

"Gentlemen." Baskum flourished a hand over his truck. "I've come with provisions."

Henry stared down at his laceless boots. The crushed little man looked off into the woods as if bored. "What's the matter, Henry?" Baskum's gold teeth flashed. "Ain't you low on provisions?"

Henry looked up from the ground and his eyes narrowed slightly; he shut the gun breech and squeezed the trigger on the empty chamber. The dry click of the firing pin cut through the water rushing over the rocks in the Yellow River shallows that washed behind the tenants' shacks.

"Hey!" Henry shouted in the direction of his shack. Hanson saw the curtain in the doorway pull back again and two tin cans were tossed into the air. They landed a few feet from the men and rolled, stopping near Henry. He bent over picking up the cans, the muzzle of his gun scratching the dirt as he stooped low.

Henry's brother fetched cans from his own shack and came back with a scoop. He handed the scoop to Baskum, who got up on the flatbed and cut open each sack with a penknife. Henry wanted five cups of flour and four dollops of pinto beans.

Hanson opened up his book, found the page with Henry's account and entered seven cups of flour and six scoops of pinto beans. Henry's brother wanted eight ladles of flour and nine scoops of pinto beans. Hanson licked the point of his pencil and entered ten ladles of flour and thirteen dollops of pinto beans. So it always went.

When each man's cans were filled, they walked back to their shacks, placing their dole in the shadow. Then they were back at the truck again while Baskum unwrapped the fat-back. "Even-Steven?"

Henry grunted in approval; he produced a long-honed hunting knife from somewhere on his body. "Just in half is fine."

Baskum cut the chunk in half. In his little book Hanson divided against a twenty-pound chunk instead of a ten-pounder and each man's account reflected a double dole. Each brother took his chunk and went back to his shack. Baskum tied up the two half-empty sacks with a bit of cord and jumped down off the truck. Hanson snapped his ledger book shut and wiggled his toes to keep from grinning.

Henry had pulled the curtain away in the door of his shack and stood looking at the truck. Baskum put the gate up on the flatbed and moved toward the cab. "I want to see everybody in the south pasture tomorrow." Baskum went around to the front of the truck. "We're gonna do some irrigating."

Hanson got in the cab and put his ledger on the dash. Baskum started the truck and eased it through the row of trees onto the dirt track.

Henry, standing in the door of his shack, let the curtain slip and listened to his wife moving in the darkness.

"Get yourself proper." Henry's wife sighed as she rubbed the metal cans together. The cans were full now, but soon they would empty—charged against the cash crop and charged against the rent. She was a big-boned woman, her hair lank and falling across her shoulders in a tired cascade. Henry spoke again in the darkness. "Forget the cans."

She looked at him, her eyes always adjusted to the darkness; the skin around his face was dry and tight.

"I'm taking you to an auction."

She could not see his mouth when he spoke. It was a kind mouth. It had always been kind to her.

"Forget the cans."

Out on the U.S. Route in Baskum's truck, Hanson lit up another cigarette. He looked at Baskum driving, right fist planted solidly on the wheel, left elbow resting on the window ledge, the hand propping up his head. Hanson did not care if Baskum worked his tenants till they were ragged in the dust, nor if Baskum kept the purse strings tied around their throats. Baskum's tenants' luck was down. And Hanson was gonna make sure his own luck stayed right where it was, if not just a nudge better.

"One fine day those tenants of yours are gonna skin you, J. J."

Baskum shrugged, and the truck jolted in a rut. "Maybe." He looked at Hanson. "But if they do, that bank ain't gonna feed them."

"Food." Hanson shook his head in disgust. "I wouldn't call that stuff—"

"Sure." Baskum was smiling; as if bored he drummed a tattoo on the steering wheel. "But they eat it."

Buck Walker heard his father's tractor rumble in the Eastern Range fields. Buck ducked around the side of the farmhouse and sat on the front porch in a spot of shade. The early morning shadows had begun to shrink along the ground.

The U.S. Route was empty; in fact, no automobile drifters or trudging sundowners thumbing for a ride had passed by the farmhouse for over a week now. The steady flow of ratty vagrants was held up somewhere, maybe at the county's borders beyond the last hill east. And yet, out of the east the road came anyway; half a mile away the blacktop clawed through a wall of trees and then dipped into a gully. The U.S. Route ran up out of the gully and coasted by the front porch of the Walker farmhouse.

The U.S. Route jumped Yellow River and blew into town, circled the great oak in the square and kept going west, the drifters along with it. Of course, the railroad Bulls kept the vagrants vagrant and Sheriff Tate would, more often than not, back the rail workers. "No sense in tempting fate," the Sheriff was known to say, as if this excuse explained anything at all. Buck had seen enough unknown strangers limping sadly out of town to know the Bulls were never gentle. "Accidents" and "mishaps" were commonplace; sprained necks and broken fingers were the most common of all.

Now he found himself a guilty witness, fouled by a chance encounter and the grown men's threats; when Meriwether dangled a severed worm, its body bleeding on the tin can, fate seemed far away. Far away when all that stood between him and the Bull was his pretty face and an owl wheeling in the sky. To say something, point or shout? Neither pappy nor his sweet face could hold off the Bulls' hard laughter—no use to chase a body vanished in the river.

The sun rose inch by inch, and inch by inch the long lean morning shadows from the farmhouse and the telephone poles shrunk into themselves, their phantom traces dissolving in the light. Where the blacktop broke the woods the trees burned green, unnaturally so. Buck could see them very clearly, as though the veil of heat-soaked air had ceased to shimmer. No dust blurred the road; the air was clear with only sunshine. The wood's leaves in the distance stood out sharper than a knife's burnished blade: green fire, the day's own.

The sound of an automobile droned up into the air. The engine hummed softly and Buck looked west toward Blue Vista Flats. Nothing coming from town. Buck shielded his eyes eastward against the low-slung sun and the flaming green trees; the car's rumble grew louder. The clear lens of heated air wavered, shimmering like a curtain; from out of the gully a four-seater Model A came up over the nearest hill. A screech owl cut through the air close to the car's bumper, disappearing into the sun's molten gleam. The car kept on and a few feet from where Buck sat on the porch, a man-size dust devil whirled to life. It dipped and spun, then shot down the road, straight for the gaining car.

The Model A glistened as it moved, pushing a tissue of simmering air. The sun splayed off the headlights' chrome and lanced straight to the back of Buck's skull, dazzling and keen. As the car bumped down the highway the chrome flashed, jangling his eyes. The Model A coasted toward the farmhouse. The dust devil whirled down the road, smack down the middle of the blacktop, a wind eddy spinning head-on for the car.

Buck held his breath as the Model A kept rolling. The tires spun over themselves; the bumper rattled and cut the duster in half, blasting it to smithereens. Again, the air simmered like a boiling sheet of glass as the car roared down on the farmhouse. Buck found himself grinning—grinning as the glare from the chrome headlamps glanced and flared. He noticed that the wall of trees half a mile distant was not burning green in the sunlight anymore. The trees' color was duller now. He flicked his eyes to the sky: no clouds.

Then his throat was tight and Buck felt the blood throb wild and windy in the tips of his fingers. The car had just blown up out of the gully, haze and all. He had never seen it clear the trees, half a mile distant. The Model A, the shimmer of heat, the dust devil blown to nothing.

Buck's fingers grew cold and he rubbed them on his legs. Well, maybe the car was stalled at the bottom of the gully.

Or maybe a thousand things. But he definitely, positively never saw the car come out of the woods in the east. The car's engine whined as the driver released the clutch; it slowed to a roll, the glare blanched off the windshield, and the road dust swirled into the air before the wheels. The driver braked; the glare flashed once from the chrome and then died as the car stopped right in front of the porch. Now Buck could see who was who and what was what.

The car was no better than a wreck. Paint was flaking everywhere, the chrome pitted. Two racks were bolted onto the body. One rack was on the roof and the other was the shape of an L which hooked onto the back of the roof and sat on the trunk. Both racks were piled high with belongings, all manner of things tied around the car: steamer trunks, chairs, a table with its legs sticking up in the air like a dog sleeping on its back, suitcases with rags poking through the holes, a storm lantern without a glass, a commode seat without the commode, wooden tent stakes, a light metal grill for cooking, some pots and pans, drained water bags, a gas can . . . the collected, gathered mess of a roving life.

The back seat was strewn with blankets and the whole back half of the coach was a rumpled mess with ragged curtains hanging every which way, a worn-out overcoat with a felt collar hung on a hanger, a small black wooden cross taped to the window partition —even a clock sat on the rear window ledge. The clock was a ship's timepiece, a sailor's clock with two recessed studs for winding. The round face of the clock had a hinge and a latch, a porthole. The glass was cracked and both hands hung improbably at the number six.

Then Buck noticed the windchimes. The windchimes dangled from a hook in the roof: Chinese windchimes, mother-of-pearl. The chime pieces were flat discs, water-thin. One small hole was drilled through each disc so a strand of thread could be knotted and the chimes hung overlapping like the scales of a fish. A bamboo bar supported four sets of chime pieces; hanging, wavering columns, the sets of chimes were side by side, so they twisted and touched.

Buck looked at the windchimes and then at the open windows at the back of the car. The rush of wind would blow over the car's hood, through the cab and out the back, flowing right across the windchimes hanging in the current. Wind and windchimes in a drafty car, and yet he never heard their precious ting-tang song as the Model A came up the road.

"We need water, son."

The voice was very low, reminding Buck of a tune he had heard somewhere before . . . maybe just one note on the church organ. The driver was a woman. Not very old, but not a young bird either. Her face was creased: road dust had a way with faces, gave the skin a second layer.

Even though the car's roof threw a shadow on the interior and even with the light blanching this way and that off every bit of pitted chrome and dirty black metal, still the woman's eyes shined as she stared at Buck. She stared soulless, the eyes in her sockets flat and vacant, threatening the daytime with nighttime madness.

Her shiny eyes made him shiver, but then she put her hand to the open window, and Buck's eyes fell to a man sitting slumped down in the passenger seat. The woman leaned out of the passenger window. The man's head just barely grazed the ledge. The tufts of hair on his scalp moved when he raised his head.

The man was not even a man: an aged boy—could've been about Buck's age at sixteen—could've been a whole lot older at twenty-five. Traces of gray shot through his patchy hair, yet no bristle or beard grew from his chin. The boy's skin was smooth and pasty, the texture of bread dough painted with egg white. His face was open like a pie pan and nearly as round. When the aged boy looked over the window ledge, Buck saw that his nose was crooked and his eyes were shallow squints with no crows' feet or wrinkles. His lips were thin and very red, and when he opened his mouth, the gash under his nose parted pink and moist. His palate was cut as if someone took an ax to him when he was still a child. Buck heard the sucking noise from the cloven face, the sound of a preserve jar popped open, and the aged boy showed lots of pink gums and only two teeth.

The woman leaned closer, leaning right over the young man, and her face was square in the window frame. The creases of dust seemed to fall away from her forehead and she smiled, showing gums like the man—but more teeth and straighter.

"Water, son."

Water. Buck's shoes were nailed to the wooden porch. Need water. The woman's brow furrowed deeper up her forehead, the lines rippling her hairline. The young man with the flat squinty eyes opened and closed his toothless mouth, and the gash made a muc-muc slurp. Need water.

"Can you hear, son?"

Buck nodded but kept staring. The aged boy closed his lips with a final muc-muc and shut one eye, but not quite; his pie face never squeezed the eyelid completely shut. It dropped down, and the muscles in his face were slack and limp. He looked at Buck with one eye.

"Can he talk?" Buck whispered.

The lines in the woman's face eased away, and she touched the side of the boy's head.

"Lomax just thinks." As if in response, Lomax's other eye popped open. Buck managed to stand up, his tailbone stiff from the porch boards.

"You need water for the radiator?"

The woman nodded. Lomax stared deadeye. A drop of sweat trickled down Buck's arm. The woman needed water.

"You wait here." Buck turned toward the farmhouse.

Sitting in the metal tractor seat, Drake Walker jostled and bumped down the dirt track that cut through his fields straight to his farmhouse. As the tractor ground down the access path he saw the barn door slide open. His wife, Sarah, stood in the clear patch near the garden between the barn and the cotton row. She looked up at him coming down the rutted track. Beyond the barn, beyond where Sarah stood, beyond the farmhouse and the storm cellar dug into the ground, a black Model A was parked on the U.S. Route. Sarah had not noticed it; from where she stood in the garden the car was mostly hidden by the house. Drake pointed, the distance still too great for shouting. His arm, stiff and straight, jounced as the tractor rumbled in the ruts.

She turned and saw the black car too. She waved, taking a step toward the house. Then the back door opened. A lanky little girl of eleven burst into the clear patch; she hopped to the ground from the back porch, lifting her knees up high to run. Sarah wanted Tina in the house; the mother tried to herd the girl back where she had come, but no chance. Tina loped away, slipping from her mother's reach, twisting and tripping over backward into the vegetable garden, snapping the string where the peapods twined. Her other hand clawed at the tomato patch cheesecloth awning, shredding it along the frame. Drake saw Sarah raise her hand. She was shouting, but the words were swept up into the early morning daylight and never reached Drake's ears. Tina danced up from the ground, a bit of cheesecloth clutched in her hand.

Sarah stopped shouting and her hands fell to her hips. She tried a new tack and cocked her head round the side of the house where the black Model A sat out on the road. Tina had not seen the car either, but now she saw it. Wary of strangers, the girl stood stock still and the cheesecloth scrap fluttered to the ground. Without a command, without a threat, Sarah turned on her heel and stepped up on the back porch. Tina, shy as a polecat, was right behind her mother, nearly sliding in around the older woman as the back door opened.

Plain old terror, righteous fury, they never worked. Tina and Buck had the rabble in their blood. From where?

You couldn't say. But threats were useless, punishment pointless, discipline hopeless, and like breeding stray dogs, the results were haphazard. Loved children never had a fear of God, or parents either. And pain never bought respect.

The back door closed and the garden was empty. The tractor's groan trembled in the air around Drake's head. He could not push the machine any faster. He had a ways to go. Lucky thing Sarah had seen the motor car.

Jesus Christ Himself with white spats and a gold-tipped cane would not be safe around Sarah, not that woman, not ever. Some gals were cut from Adam's rib, and some were not. Sarah was wired together with piano strings, but she could not be plucked, struck or played. She worked the house, the field, the barn—even though most wives said only nigger women bent down in the dirt. With sharecroppers, okay; but an upright farmwife in Bone County never touched a hayrake. Sarah didn't care for fashion, and Drake didn't care what other wives did or didn't do. When Sarah worked, so much the better. Married at sixteen, pregnant at seventeen, pregnant again at twenty-three, now thirty-five with one front tooth missing, and another going rotten. When she smiled, you could see the gap. But when she lay on her back and guided him along, she was still sixteen and flush, eager, never failing to surprise, drawing him over her thighs again.

Now, where the hell was that boy?

Buck was in the kitchen. He found a half-gallon can and set it under the hand pump that was bolted to the kitchen counter. The pump spout spilled into a tin basin. Buck could just edge the can into the basin and under the spout's lip. He started pumping the handle; the pump went *squonk-squonk,* gurgled, and flowed. Sarah slammed the back door behind her. Buck did not turn around.

"Who are they?" Sarah was not interested in any smart lip.

"Drifters."

Sarah came up close behind him at the pump. "No handouts."
Buck kept on with the *squonk-squonk*, the can filling.

"You deaf?"

Squonk. Squonk. "You want them out of here. Okay. Water for the radiator. You give them some water and the car'll keep going. You don't give them water and the car'll just sit out there."

The can was full and Buck stopped pumping. He faced his mother. Tina was edging around the kitchen table, trying not to get in the way. Buck sloshed water in the can. "I'll charge them a penny —how about that?"

For a second Buck figured his mother looked ashamed. No, if she did, her expression lasted only a moment; when it came to food or money, there just was not enough to go around. Water was cheap. Except in a drought. In a drought, parts of Yellow River's bed broke the waterline, shale slabs like tombstones in the sun. An evil sight for even the best of times.

"Don't charge them a penny."

On the road the woman had gotten out of the Model A and propped the hood up with a thin metal bar. She touched the radiator cap and jerked her finger away, the engine hissing.

"Lemme do it." Buck hopped off the porch and the woman stepped back from the car. He set the water can down by the front tire, and taking a ragged handkerchief from his back pocket, he dipped it in the water can. He wrung the excess back into the can before the wet rag could warm from his hand and unscrewed the radiator cap half a turn, unlocking it. The radiator hissed and steam shot out from around the loosened cap.

"Give it a minute."

The woman edged around to the driver's side of the car. "I hate machines." She touched the metal fender. "That Mr. Ford, he took the magic out of travel."

The mother-of-pearl windchimes hung motionless from the car's roof. Open windows, windchimes and wind—the rush of air as the car coasted down the gully lip. Buck could only dance around the issue. "Didn't see you break clean of the woods."

The woman made no remark. Lomax was now asleep; the pie-face's eyes drooped but were not closed completely. His mouth hung open slightly and his lips trembled when he breathed. The woman was looking at the engine.

"Thanks for the water." She glanced at the farmhouse. Tina had slipped quietly onto the front porch and was leaning up against the clapboard side. The woman tapped the metal fender. "Your ma thought maybe we'd steal something." Lomax was snoring and his breath whistled through the gash. "You got a name?"

"Buck."

The radiator cap had cooled somewhat by now; he took it off without redipping the rag. Getting the water can from the ground, he poured the water down the mouth of the radiator. The water hissed and bubbled away. Steam rose out of the open radiator and curled over the engine like white snakes, coiling, twisting themselves into thin air. The radiator stopped steaming and Buck replaced the cap. He lowered the thin bar which propped up the metal hood, covering the engine.

The folds of blankets in the back seat began to churn slowly; rippling in scattered waves, the material bunched together and then stretched tight. A hand came out of the folds, and then another; the hands clutched at the fabric, and a head outlined itself under the blanket. The hands pulled again and the folds fell away from the face.

A girl. Buck looked closer. Older than a girl. Maybe his age, maybe a year younger, maybe two years younger. Maybe a year older. No way to tell. From inside her skin, deep rosy grace spread like warm oil across his forehead, her youth and age mixed together. And her eyes seemed to tell him many things, but not in words that could be heard, written down or saved for later. Her eyes were calm, fertile as a grown-up lady's eyes, betrayed only by her child's coy spark and brown as those of any Indian scout crouched in the prairie.

She sat up in the back seat, the blanket wrapped around her shoulders. Her hair was tousled and her lips weighed down with sleep.

"We still in the state?" She seemed sunk in a dreamy cushion, her eyes veiled and narrow as she looked at Buck, the pale murmur of her words a faint breath in his ear.

"No, darling." The woman rested both hands on the engine hood, taking the weight off her feet. "We left the state two hours ago at least."

"Your daughter?"

The woman nodded, and she looked at Lomax snoring in the front seat. "You've already met my son."

The girl shook off the dreamy dregs of sleep. Her eyes moved over Buck closely, roving and then stopping, weighing him inside and out. "Who are you?"

Buck leaned one arm on the car roof and poked his head into the window. "Who am I?" He cocked his head to one side. "Well, who are you?"

The girl brushed her hair back with her fingers and shook her shoulders as if peeved. "If it's any of your business, my name is Drew Moon." Her dark eyebrows came together and suddenly a pleasant lump of mucus gathered in Buck's throat; his ears warmed slightly. Drew dismissed Buck with another shrug of her shoulders. "The car overheat again?"

"Radiator must have a leak." So this was Mrs. Moon. . . . "Buck here got us some water."

At the sound of his name, Drew looked at him. She softened some. "Thanks."

"It's okay. Your brother almost slept through."

"Lomax?"

As if awake and listening, Lomax's vicious harelip twitched, stretching the gash back across his gums as far as it would go. Dreaming. Through his cleft palate Lomax took a deep breath, and his jaw hung open. He made a noise, just a syllable: *ruh.*

Not a real word, but a sound, a dreaming sound, *rahh-uhh.* Mrs. Moon looked at her son sharply. The color drained from her face. She glanced at Drew, and Buck noticed that the girl's blanket had fallen from her shoulders. Drew was staring at Lomax as if he would speak. "Ruhh . . . " Lomax twitched. His mouth came together with a muc-muc and glistened with saliva. As if slapped, his head whipped from side to side. His eyes snapped open and for the first time appeared to focus on something.

"Ruhh . . . " His lips quivered. "Ruhh . . . " Lomax was trembling and his pasty skin quivered. Drew stroked the back of his neck and that seemed to calm him. She massaged his neck and he breathed a little easier. Mrs. Moon was still pale and with her fingers she tapped the car's warm hood as if a solid object reassured her.

The tractor jolted like a clumsy oaf down the rutted access path. Only fifty yards to the house and Drake wanted to hurry the doltish thing along, but the damn machine chugged on at its own pace. Drake jiggled the steering wheel and the front tires edged up a rut. Drake rode with the sway. The sun beat on his brow and he shielded his eyes against the glare. The tractor's steering wheel jiggled and bumped down the rutted track. Jolted, he was jounced from the metal seat, falling sideways, watching the large tires pass, throwing dirt from their grooves. Drake hit the ground hard, one arm under his ribs. The tractor rolled on its own for ten feet or so; the gas pedal rose, the clutch jumped and jammed. The motor stalled.

He stared at the stalled tractor, incredulous that the soulless thing could turn on him so. His ribs ached when he tried to breathe. Drake's head was very light and he wondered whether he had caught a leg under the big tire, why each breath held no air . . . what he had done to deserve this. . . .

Close to his face he saw a bird's feather resting lightly on the chipped earth. The airy feather stirred on the ground and the breath bubbled in Drake's throat and burned his ribs.

From behind the house Buck heard his mother shout, "Oh good Lord! Drake!" Buck wrenched himself away from the Model A and tore around the house. His mother stood frozen by the garden, fingers knotted in her hair. The tractor had yawed off the access path; his father lay on the rutted dirt track, one arm over his waist, the wrist limp, twisting, fingers toward the chest.

Tina caught Buck as they reached their mother and all three ran the dozen yards up the access path. They took Drake by the armpits and dragged him down the rutted track, laying him out on the clear patch of ground between the barn and the house. Drake's face was a strange shade of yellow; his eyes were clamped open and he gasped for breath.

Tina, nervous, danced around in a blur. "Get a doctor, Bucky. Get a doctor! A doctor! Bucky!"

Drake opened and closed his mouth like a fish gasping in the air. "Ribs . . . " His face turned a darker shade of yellow and his tongue, swollen, pressed in his jaw. Broken ribs could rip and jab, tear into the stomach, puncture the lungs. Buck ran to the pickup truck, threw himself in the front seat and pressed the starter.

Click-click, like the battery was dead. Oh God, oh God, start, damn, start, damn.

Click-click. Click-click. Don't die. Don't die. Oh God, click-click. Buck glanced back to the vegetable garden. Click-click. Tina was just standing there, doing nothing. Click-click.

Then he saw: Mrs. Moon had come round the side of the house and was kneeling by his father's body. A breeze wafted into the car, cooing; the air shivered and Buck heard the quivering ting-a-ling, ting-a-ling of the windchimes dancing brightly from their strings. The breeze cooled the heat behind his ears, and the windchimes' sound touched him on the cheek like a gentle hand or a wishful kiss. Buck got slowly out of the cab as the chimes' glassy twinkle evaporated in the hot morning air. Mrs. Moon was whispering in his father's ear. She touched his chest. Drake held steady under her healing fingers, not flinching.

Buck walked to where his father lay stretched on the ground. He heard Mrs. Moon say, "I've got to know." Buck saw his father nod, like he understood. Mrs. Moon tapped his rib cage. Nothing.

She tapped his belly where the rib cage stopped. Drake gasped. Mrs. Moon nodded to herself as if finally realizing; she massaged his stomach once.

"Breathe," she commanded.

Drake sucked air. "Hold it." Mrs. Moon stroked his belly again. "Let it go." Drake let the wind rush out.

"Breathe." He sucked air; she stroked his belly.

"Hold it." She pried into his gut with the tips of her fingers.

"Let it go." The wind rushed out.

"Breathe." Drake's face took on a rosier color as the yellow passed away. Mrs. Moon's hands pressed into his belly again. "Hold it."

This time the pain eased from his face and when Mrs. Moon said, "Let it go," Drake exhaled, normal and easy. She stopped commanding him and Drake breathed as he wished. But Mrs.

Moon kept kneading his belly like dough and Buck could see his dad was going to be all right.

Sarah looked at Mrs. Moon in disbelief. Tears had run down her face, racing away to the hollow of her throat, and she wiped them off.

Tina stood off at a distance, watching. "Go get your father a drink." Mrs. Moon did not expect any back talk. "Water." Tina shot off to the house as if spanked. Mrs. Moon looked Drake square in the face.

"You're damn lucky, Mister. You got steel ribs. If they'd broke, I couldn't have helped you. But they wasn't broke—one bruised maybe, but we can fix that. Your guts got jostled around, and your breathing muscle was punched too hard. You'll ache for a day or two and I'm gonna tape you up."

The back door slammed and Tina gingerly stepped off the back porch, holding the water can with both hands. She walked, deliberate and steady, careful not to spill any over the metal rim. She put the can down beside her father.

"A chair." Tina paused. Mrs. Moon had further orders. One crooked finger kept Tina from dashing off. "While you're in the house make some paste outta flour and bring an old bedsheet." Mrs. Moon looked at Sarah. "With your permission, of course." Sarah sighed deeply. No answer needed. Tina was still standing by the water can. Her child's face suddenly went liquid, the sudden panic of her daddy's sore ribs. Tina's eyes were full and wet.

Sarah clenched her teeth. "Git."

Tina bolted, her arm up around her face to wipe her girly tears away.

Sarah held Drake's head while Mrs. Moon tipped the water can to his lips. He drank some and rivulets ran from the corners of his mouth. Tina returned with the chair.

"Don't hold his arms, grab his waistband."

Buck took one side of Drake with both hands and his mother the other; they lifted him slowly and placed his behind on the chair. Drake held his breath while they moved him, and when comfortably sitting upright, he breathed deeply again. "Your name?"

"Mrs. Moon."

Sarah was eyeing her. "How did you know about—?"

"Was a nurse more than once, in gay Paree. The Great War." Mrs. Moon sighed, as if puzzled and slightly disturbed. And then to no one in particular, she said, "Oh, don't let them fool you—they'll always say the same thing. All the wars were great."

"How many wars?" Buck asked.

Mrs. Moon did not answer. Buck watched her eyes go blank as bone china, a vacant animal stare. No answer. The fragments of right and wrong . . .

Tina came out of the back door with the sheet over one arm and a bowl of flour paste. Mrs. Moon took the folded sheet and tore it into strips, said, "Thank you, child," and matter-of-factly turned back to Buck.

Buck saw the woman's eyes were clearing, the bonded candor in traces round the whites. "One war is enough for anyone. You understand."

Buck, who had seen no wars at all, hoped it wasn't awfully bad; he'd heard all about war, and hoped he'd get a chance at least to see a small one. He watched the Moon woman to see if he could understand things better, as though from her nursing the war itself would appear before his eyes.

After Mrs. Moon wrapped a broad swatch across Drake's ribs, she tied it off. She dipped her fingers in the paste and applied the paste to the tape. Drake started to squirm as the paste soaked through the strips, irritating the skin on his chest. "That'll dry and tighten a bit." Mrs. Moon kept spreading the paste. "In a few days the tape'll come away from your chest—take it off then. When you go to the privy, you may see some blood. If you bleed more than twice, you get in that pickup and get to a hospital."

Buck couldn't help looking at the pickup, cursing it and cursing the damn click-click of the dead battery. "It needs a jump."

Drake said nothing. But then he looked at Sarah for a long moment. Sarah turned and went into the house. Gingerly, Drake got off the chair. "Take it back in the house." Tina took the cue and followed her mother, dragging the chair. Drake offered his hand to Mrs. Moon, and she took it. "If there's anything . . ."

"Your boy got us some water. That's what we needed." Mrs. Moon abruptly dropped Drake's hand and walked back around the house. Drake watched her go, the corners of his mouth curling into a smile.

Buck stood in the clear patch, not sure what to do. He had seen dream readers, the faith healers and the wonder-makers, the rainmakers and the tonic merchants; the common thread that strung them together was that, like lawyers, doctors and bank clerks, they handled money, and each had a price. All Mrs. Moon wanted was some water, and she'd already got that.

Buck edged away from his father and followed Mrs. Moon to the U.S. Route. No use in pushing the feeling off—he wanted another look at Drew Moon, wrapped in blankets back of the car, her hair tousled, her eyes heavy and vague. Another look to keep that moment of her waking in his mind, that moment... as he stood beside the car, her question "Who are you?" something formal, something to bridge the gap. In fact, when her eyes measured the space in which he stood, all rhyme and reason fell away: she knew "who" he was and "why."

Foolishness. Like click-click and a dead battery. This could only be foolishness, mother and daughter with a twisted runt blowing up the road out of nowhere, headed nowhere, driving a junk heap. The girl could not know anything more about Blue Vista Flats or the townspeople than what she had seen already.

And yet... and yet. A dull heat surrounded that Drew Moon, dull like a fire's embers' final glow, just hot enough to spark and roar again. Maybe all women were like that: where stifling innocence was shed like clothes on hot, sweltering nights. It all felt hopeless, for if Drew Moon had tasted a man before, what possible use could she make of himself? Always the older men waited in bars and diners, knowing what the world could offer, knowing what they had taken, how much was left, looking at Drew Moon and knowing what her body could do... knowing she would do it for *this* reason, or for *that* reason, or for no reason at all, except that maybe she had done it before, and the time had come to do it again.

Worst of all, the car's radiator was now filled with water, ready to go and nothing held the Moons from driving through Blue Vista Flats, out of Bone County and into the state beyond.

Mrs. Moon was in the driver's seat of the Model A and Lomax sat on the passenger side as before; his eyes had lost their focus, and the muscles in his face were slack and smooth. Drew was not in the car—Buck looked up and down the road, but the U.S. Route was empty. Mrs. Moon started the car, and as the engine revved, a wall of high grass parted at the side of the road and Drew stepped onto the macadam. Her skirt was hoisted around her thighs and Buck saw the color of her skin was not lily white but tanned and ruddy. Drew caught him staring and dropped her skirt.

"You could have used the little house . . . " Buck's throat thickened. She sashayed toward him.

"Maybe next time." Then she was back in the car, pushing the blankets over to one side.

The front door of the farmhouse flew open and Sarah came out onto the porch holding a glass jar. His mother stepped down off the porch and paused when she saw Lomax. Sarah took a breath when she saw the cloven face. She pressed ahead anyway and leaned down to the car window.

"For you." Sarah held the jar and thrust her arm over Lomax so Mrs. Moon could see. "We get crab apples here in the fall. I make a preserve; this is from last year. Once you break the seal, eat it every day till you finish it; otherwise the preserve will get moldy on toward a week open. You can drop the jar off when you come back through."

Mrs. Moon took the jar with both hands and set it on the seat between herself and Lomax. "I'll return it."

Buck believed her.

Sarah was still leaning on the car window; Mrs. Moon, finger outstretched, touched the side of his mother's cheek. "Remember, everyone gets everything they want."

Sarah backed away from the car. Drew looked at Buck and he backed away too. His chest was tight, as if sewn with tiny threads. Drew's hair was not tousled anymore and wisps moved around her face when the car drove off. Buck found himself waving and grinning monkey wild; the engine groaned and the car bumped down the road. For a moment he was sure Drew waved back, but then it seemed that her hand was only a piece of ragged cloth flapping out the window and that, indeed, Drew Moon was looking forward through the windows now and not looking out behind.

He saw the windchimes clear enough, hanging from the car roof in a drafty interior. Silence. No precious chatter sprinkled over the engine's hum. Nothing. The car dwindled down the road and no ting-tang sound reached his ears.

The farmhouse looked somehow small and confining. His mother was already inside. Buck could not bring himself to follow her, to see his father taped up like a smoked ham, to hear his mother start breakfast in the kitchen, to watch Tina fooling around before she stretched the cheesecloth over the tomatoes or set the pea patch to rights. Buck went round the side of the house and found himself looking at the useless pickup. He climbed in the driver's seat and rested his forearms on the steering wheel. Through the windshield Buck could see the tall cedar on the hill. The lone cedar tree glowed, as did the woods earlier, the tree's shadow shrinking as the sun moved on.

He put his hand on the stick shift, pressed down on the clutch and jiggled the stick to neutral. The desperate click-click of the dead battery and the vision of his father lying helpless on the ground reeked in the metal cab. The memory was smeared over the windshield, over the stiff upholstery, over the dashboard and wafted like a violent odor through the truck—and with the memory—the sound of windchimes, glassy jingles, enchanting him and the reluctant truck.

He pressed the starter.

Click.

Click.

Vrooom . . . in the rearview mirror Buck saw a cloud of blue smoke rise up from the tailpipe. Parts of the cloud caught in the light and then drifted, smudging the air. He let the engine roar for a moment and then he shut it off. Tina was standing in the garden with a piece of cheesecloth in her hand.

J. J. Baskum let Hanson out of his pickup at the back of the Goods Store before parking the truck in front of Lepke's Diner. Hanson retired to his store mumbling something about "Orders delayed, shipping receipts, and Jews in the east." Baskum was not about to press Hanson for the details. Running a goods store was a jumble of knick-knack paddy-whack; fetch this, haul that, issue bills, pay bills, count your money, recount it, check it against last year, make out the orders, put 'em in the mail, wait, wait—get the dog a bone. Forget goods stores and other sundries. Go in, throw a penny for a ball of twine, and get out. Baskum wanted none of it.

Lepke's Diner was just as before. Yohanna Johns sat at the

counter, his back to the door; Johns' coffee cup was undoubtedly refilled more than once while Baskum's tenants got their dole. Bart Lowell was gone. No great loss. Lepke was washing his sink and humming *Madumwahzel from Parrmenteers, Parr-lay Voo?*

Over the grill Lepke's electric clock with the red Texaco star printed on the face hummed softly. The second hand swept slowly around and the hands pointed to eleven-thirty. An Emerson radio was plugged into an outlet; the radio was set on a ledge over the back cooking counter. A faint red glow from the heating tubes back of the radio's wooden case shone on the ledge. From out of the radio's cloth-covered speaker some joker was nattering on about the latest hog prices in Chicago.

Preacher Simon was the new arrival. A bottle of Orange Nehi perspired on the counter, with the paper straw stained from the soda hanging limp and sucked over the lip of the bottle. Lepke cut his humming short and stared out the diner's windows. Preacher and Yohanna Johns swiveled on their stools. The wheezing Model A jolted into the square.

The Model A Ford was running its last mile. Inside the crankcase, sludge piled up like dirty molasses. The oil pan leaked slow and steady, one drop every two hundred yards. The brake linings were worn to tissue paper. The clutch was so slack it engaged only at the very end and then clamped with a jolt that nearly stripped the transmission gears. The engine block was cracked and so no compression built up in two of the four cylinders; the car never drove over seventeen miles an hour. The timing was off, so the spark plugs fired in random sequence. But as the car rounded the square's great oak, these mechanical frailties ceased to matter. A charred rubber gasket in one of the two workable cylinders felt charred enough. The spark plug fired, the gas ignited, the piston rammed home, chipped the charred gasket, threw a rod and blew off the cylinder top. Mechanized coronary.

Mrs. Moon smiled, the amber melting in her eyes; she steered the car with one relaxed hand. The Model A backfired and seemed to jump a little in the air. The Ford trembled and then sagged, as all the life in its metal heart passed away. The engine died and with the last gasp of momentum the Model A rounded the oak and coasted into Hanson's Garage & Gas, slowing to a halt in front of the pumps.

The bar-framed door of the jail opened slightly and the white pull shade trembled behind the glass. The door opened all the way and Sheriff Tate stepped out onto the sidewalk. He wore a pistol on his belt; his khaki pants were clean but not pressed. Tate was the law. He felt like the law, he smelled like the law, and for all practical purposes he looked like the law. He might not have been the *only* law in Blue Vista Flats, but on this sunny morning in August Tate heard the Model A roll into town, he stood on that sidewalk, and the law came with him.

But the law also came upon him, sat on his shoulders, and slipped into his pants' cuffs. As Tate stood looking across to the gas station, he realized that the law had to deal with a Model A. Today was auction day, and that was the law too. The auction was scheduled, on the program; the Model A, unfortunately, was not. Tate saw the skinny 'cullud,' as Tate called them, come out of the dark garage. By the time Tate crossed the square and reached the concrete ramp, Ollie Cottle, Hanson's Negro mechanic, was already standing over the Model A. Cottle had taken a rag out of his pocket and was wiping the windshield. Tate could see his tattered bib-jeans and, through the tears at the knees, Cottle's brown skin winking at the daylight. The Negro was saying something to the passengers. He stopped talking when Tate drew close.

Hanson came out of his goods store and was standing on the porch, his eyes bugging for a better view. "Hey, Tate!"

Tate ignored Hanson. Cottle backed off from the car. Tate thrust his thumbs into the waistband of his trousers and rolled back on his heels so he looked easy. Like the law.

"Well. Well." Tate rocked forward on the balls of his feet and then back on his heels. "Well, what have we here?"

"Dey—dem's de Moons." The wrinkles around Cottle's brown eyes narrowed, crow's feet pinched.

"Mrs. Moon, eh?" Tate gave the old bird in the driver's seat the once-over. He walked around to the passenger seat and looked at the man with the round face. "Well, Mr. Moon . . . how long do you plan on staying with us?"

Lomax's vicious harelip parted and Tate saw the gums bright with saliva and he heard the muc-muc as the man worked his jaw.

"He talk?"

Mrs. Moon shook her head. "No, he don't talk."

Cottle stared at the back of Tate's neck; his cow's eyes glistened. "No, Sheriff, he can't talk."

Tate did not bother facing Cottle. "I heard it the first time." The Negro's eyes lost some of their color, but Tate was not looking. He was interested in the Model A.

"What's wrong with the car?"

The Moon woman shrugged. "Don't know."

"You got money to fix it?"

The old bird did not frighten easy. "I've gotta know what's wrong first, don't I?"

But Tate had been fed that stew before. "Doesn't matter what the hell's wrong with it, lady, if you can't pay for it."

"I can get the money." Mrs. Moon seemed pretty damn sure.

"Money . . ." Tate looked wistfully at the sky and wiped his forehead. "That why you're driving this shit heap?"

From the darkness of the back seat, "That's none of your business." Tate leaned down and saw a girl back there. He straightened up again.

"Maybe . . ." He dropped his hand from his waistband. "But vagrancy is my business. No money and you're up the crick. No money, and you leave the car and walk outta here." Tate looked at the Negro.

"Whaddya say, Ollie—how would you like to drive a Model A?"

Cottle thrust his hands in the pockets of his bib-jeans. "Hate drivin'."

On the Goods Store porch, Hanson clapped his hands. "That's my boy, that's my boy!" Hanson was crowing like an eager rooster on parade. "That boy'll fix 'em, but he won't drive 'em."

"Figures." Tate was not pleased. He scratched his head and looked at the Negro for a moment. Cottle turned and walked back to the garage.

"I'll look at it for you, Miz Moon, but not today . . . I'll look at it tomorrow. Today I got the Boss' DeSoto."

"That's my boy." Hanson strutted on the porch. "He's got the DeSoto."

For the second time Sheriff Tate ignored Hanson; the goods store man was a royal pain. Tate stared at the woman in the driver's seat. Mrs. Moon stared back, frowning. A trickle of sweat gathered under the Sheriff's arms; his nostril hairs twitched as if tickled with a feather. The Moon woman's eyes seemed vacant and soulless; they traveled up and down his body. Searching. Then the eyes stopped. She was staring at his ankle.

Tate heard the humming of a mosquito, but he never saw the stinger flying low to the ground. Under his sock the ankle burned and itched. The stung skin was growing hot and the ankle was welting. Tate ground his teeth; he wanted to tear his boot off and scratch like mad. He licked his upper lip and stared down at the Moon woman. "You can't stay in town."

Her hand tightened on the steering wheel. Tate glanced at his boot. The bootlace was hopelessly knotted. The ankle swelled, ballooning inside the boot leather. Tate wriggled his foot. The welt burned hotter.

Tate gulped some air. "But you can stay outside. Take the road by the church. That's County Road 6. It follows the river. You'll see a trestle and some grain elevators across the river by the tracks. And a water spigot. You camp by that spigot."

A breeze wafted across Tate's neck, cooling like peppermint, and he heard the clean tangle of windchime scales dancing close. Then he saw the windchimes hanging inside the Model A. They were motionless; he had missed sight of their striking. His ankle itched no more. The welting was gone, the venom dissolved as though splashed with water.

Mrs. Moon's face was serene and her hand loosened on the steering wheel. She wanted something more. "How do we cross the river?"

He took a slip of paper from his shirt pocket and a cracked pencil. "That railroad bridge has got a car lane on it. Use that."

With great deliberate effort Tate wrote out a message as he leaned on the car hood. He handed the slip to Mrs. Moon and the girl in the back leaned over her shoulder to have a look.

The girl read the slip out loud: "It says, 'Mister Simple—pleaze don't bother theze people tonight. Tate.'"

"Who's Simple?"

"That's the way-station foreman." Tate turned from the car and walked back across the square. His ankle's gentle throb was dull, the itch was gone, the swelling down. "You be here at daybreak tomorrow and see what Cottle finds." He walked under the oak, not looking back.

A hoarse voice croaked at him from the diner: "I never gave my permission."

Lepke. All of a sudden the diner man was getting stingy with his property. What the hell did that fry cook care if some people squatted by his grain elevators for a night? His property was safe; Lepke could live with it.

Sheriff Tate stopped at the jailhouse door. He glanced over at the diner. "No, Lepke, I did. I gave permission."

No reply came from the figure outlined behind the diner's screen door. Lepke gave up. The other figures gathered at the windows for a look-see, lost interest, and moved back into the shaded interior. Tate heard the Moons pulling things they needed for the night off the top of the Model A. He wondered for a short moment why the hell he did not just run them out of town. Then his nose hairs stirred as if tickled with a feather. He sneezed, blowing a drop of moisture on his palm and the thought from his head.

His father's face was a fortress wall, silent and dead sure. Buck saw trouble like a hot wind in that face. It was set like sun-baked bricks—the longer those bricks sit in the sun, the harder they get. And Drake was wearing his Sunday shirt: white buttons on the cuffs, the white collar new and clean, the starch stiff, making the shirt one crisp rustle when his father moved. He only wore the shirt for weddings and funerals . . . or when he had something serious to do. The auction was no reason for a shirt, but Buck saw his father's face was serious and that meant the auction was serious too: serious enough for Drake to wear his Sunday shirt and hold his face like a sun-dried brick.

Buck dropped to his haunches in the flatbed of his father's pickup truck. Through the cab's rearview window he watched Drake climb into the driver's seat. His father's taped-up ribs were tender; he held his chest erect, easing sore bones gently against the seat's backrest. He put a large palm over the stick shift and jiggled the knob.

Sarah got in the passenger side; then Tina was at the car door, scrambling over her mother's lap. Hurried and clumsy, Tina elbowed her mother's breast. Sarah scowled, her hand cupping the bruise, and her shoulders slumped. Tina barely noticed; she straddled the truck's stick shift, her knees knocking against the metal shaft. Buck gazed at his family through the rear window. Tina was looking at his father who sat steady as a hard barrel. She straightened two fingers and softly poked her father in the ribs.

In pain, Drake sucked a quart of air. He did not strike the hand away. He took Tina's two small fingers and wrapped his own around them, like pigs-in-a-blanket. Tina was smiling. She liked hands like her father's . . . big strong hands. Drake stroked the back of his daughter's head. She kissed him on the ribs.

The truck jostled as Drake's two tenants climbed in the back. Buck squeezed into a corner to give them room. With all aboard, Drake hit the pedal, let the clutch out and drove out on the U.S. Route, spitting gravel as the back wheels climbed onto the macadam. The two tenants, arm to arm, made themselves comfortable on the metal floor of the truck.

Ryder's single black eye sparkled in the morning's light and he held a cigarette cupped in his hand which he offered to Buck once and again. The smoke streamed from Ryder's hawk nose. The farmer wore a pirate's patch to cover the shriveled socket of his missing eye. Buck never knew where he had lost it. Buck glanced quickly through the cab's back window, making sure his father was looking out front, not eyes to the rearview mirror, then grabbed the cigarette and took a puff. People said tobacco would stunt your growth, but Buck had been smoking since he was thirteen and it only made his teeth yellow. Ryder once said time and more cigarettes would change all that. Ryder plucked the cigarette from between Buck's fingers before the ash had grown at all. He pulled his long hawk's nose and wagged his head from side to side.

"Boy," he hollered over the rush of wind, "you're gonna see a sight today." As if by way of explanation, Ryder balled his fingers into a fist and cracked his knuckles. The sound was lost in the wind, but not the motion. The knuckles on Ryder's hands were large as beechnuts, split long ago and healed; 'my best friends' he called them.

Buck did not know what else to do but smile; not sure, he glanced at Eddy. His father's second tenant stretched both bony legs out on the floor of the truck. His boot toes pointed like a pigeon's, ankles slightly curved. Polio.

Eddy's big round face claimed slits for eyes; some people said he was an Indian, others thought the farmer a Mex. Eddy said he was a white man, for all the good it did him. Luck had it that the men were not homestead-bound near Baskum's land, or Yohanna Johns' neither. Bad things went on that way. Eddy smoothed the hairs of his thick mustache.

"You listen to Ryder, Bucky." Eddy blinked his slit eyes. "Might be some tempers lost today—can't tell."

Tempers. Buck saw Meriwether's sodcutter catching the dawnlight, the Bull's red hair glistening in the bristle. He saw the spilled nightcrawlers inching in all directions, and Simple's bald head, smooth as an egg. They had laughed. But the two Bulls' deadeyes made him cringe, even now.

The truck whined down the road. Ryder nodded. He pointed to his eyepatch. "Eddy's talking about the auction. Tempers are bad." He winked with his one good eye.

"I can see it all now . . ." Ryder cut the air with one hand, carving to no visible effect. Buck lifted up his nose and wind rushed over his face.

There was something up Ryder's sleeve. Buck glanced back at Eddy. "So who's gonna bid on Moss Greene's stuff?"

With the question, the rushing wind seemed to stop. Ryder pulled on his hawk's nose and said nothing; his pirate's eyepatch was like a locked trap door. His good eye fell to the truckbed floor.

Eddy blinked his flat Mex eyes and kept to himself. He plucked the cigarette from between Ryder's lips and pinched the butt between his fingers.

"You're biting off a little more than you can chew. Don't swallow it whole."

Buck looked down at Eddy's legs stretched out straight, the polio toes pointed in; his thighs jiggled as the truck bumped down the road. Neither of his father's tenants would have money enough to bid on a used tin can. Forget the rest.

Not that his father robbed them—they just never had the money. Nobody said his father was a thief. But Baskum was different. People said bad things about Baskum. And Baskum would have the money to bid. That did not set right with his father; Drake wanted Moss Greene's things left be. But how could they keep it that way? Baskum's tenants hated Baskum plenty. "Think Henry and his brother'll be there?"

Eddy nodded. "No counting on him though. Henry's got the guts, but his belly's empty."

Henry was hungry all the time. Baskum kept his tenants hungry. Baskum cleaned them out. Now he could tell them how to live, what to eat. Now every harvest was bad for Henry and his brother.

Ryder rubbed his pale hair, cut so close to the scalp. "With Moss Greene gone there is only three farmers that can pay their bills and far as I'm concerned only one worth talking to." Ryder's black eye was deep as river water. He snatched his cigarette from Eddy's Mex mouth and took the last drag.

The pickup blew into Blue Vista Flats and rounded the oak tree, passing in front of Preacher's church. Drake parked his truck at Lepke's Diner. Buck was out of the truck and on the ground before the engine stopped. The two men took their time getting out, standing up, stretching, glancing at the church steps, the bank, the jail. The square was empty; the oak stood like an old sentry, eyes open and forever on duty.

Slowly, in the idle necessity of summer the sounds of horse-drawn carts and ill-tuned motor cars drifted over the square, up the County Road 6 and the U.S. Route from every direction. The clock in the steeple struck nine. And Buck saw the Model A on Hanson's garage ramp. So they had stayed. Drew Moon had not left town. Maybe they were still in the garage. Like a shot, Buck was going to dash over and see, but then he noticed his father's brick-wall face, and he remained at the side of the car. Tina was still squeezed between his mother and father. His mother was talking and Buck could see his father's stone eyes staring straight ahead. No muscles moved on Drake's face, and the only indication that his father heard a word was the slight furrow on his brow, one deep above his eyes with three smaller ones moving up his forehead like the outline of a pyramid. A smooth shiny white patch of skin clung below the hairline; Drake breathed deep and quiet and the furrow trembled.

His mother held a bobby pin in one hand, and two more were stuck in the corner of her mouth. "You're not gonna let that banker do it. You're not."

Drake blinked his eyes. Sarah went on, "You let them do it, and maybe next time. Maybe—"

Drake faced her, twisting his neck. "You're in the truck, aren't you?"

Sarah fell silent. Tina's gangly knees knocked against the stick. Drake was not through. "Didn't have to ask the boys, did I? Did I force them? I did not. They came of their own."

Sarah saw Buck watching. "Never heard us talk?"

Buck took a step back from the cab as if poked. Tina shifted her butt on the seat again.

"All right, all right." Sarah hated Tina's squirming. Buck opened the door of the cab and Tina scrambled over her mother's lap, nearly falling face down out of the truck. Buck grabbed her as she tumbled out and stood her up. Tina brushed off her dress and hiked up one shoulder strap.

Drake leaned over the wheel and faced them. "Go see what you can scrounge."

Buck took Tina by the elbow and turned to go. "Hey." His father leaned across Sarah. Buck stopped. Drake held a nickel in his fingers. He tossed it through the open door and Buck caught it in his fist. "Get that sister of yours something sweet."

"I know." Buck was all airs and soda pop. "It helps the temper."

"Don't be wise." Sarah slammed the truck door shut as they walked away.

At first Tina and Buck headed for Hanson's Goods, but once under the boughs of the large oak, Buck angled for the garage and the Model A parked on the ramp. Tina thrust her hand around Buck's dangling arm and swished her hips like a dance-hall girl. "Walk me proper," Tina cooed. "I'm a lady."

Buck wriggled and tried to pull away. Tina went off like a firecracker. "Oh no you don't!" She threw her arm round Buck's neck in a choke hold and yanked him up short.

Her lips hissed in his ear. "How much lickriss that nickel buy?"

Buck shook loose from his sister's grasp. "Enough to rot the teeth in your empty head."

Tina walked with her hands at her hips. "You don't know anything about ladies, Buck. In fact," she crept right up behind him, "you don't know anything about anything."

Buck stopped and turned around. Tina walked right into his chest. She stepped back. "Especially ladies."

"And how much do you know, Miss Smarty?"

They reached the concrete ramp. "Oh, I know." Tina with an imp's grin raised her eyebrows. "I've watched them loving."

"Who?"

"Who?" Tina teased. "Who? Who? Are you an owl? Hoo! Hoo!"

"Who?" Buck asked again. He stepped around the gas pumps and began to circle the Model A. As an answer Tina glanced back at the family truck; Drake and Sarah were still talking in the cab.

"Where have you seen it?" Buck's head loomed over the hood of the Model A.

Tina's thin shoulders shrugged up to her neck and her dress strap fell down her arm. "Wouldn't *you* like to know?"

Buck shrugged. "You can suit yourself."

He ran his hands across the metal roof of the Model A. The car was empty and the metal roof warm under his palms. Warm like Drew's tan summer thighs and the back-seat blankets wrapped around them. She could be watching him close by even now, her watchful eyes staring from some hidden place, from the church's dark open doors, from behind the Goods Store's ragged screen door, eyes shaded behind the diner's plate-glass window, blinking as she watched him, her tapered maiden hands touching, fingers laced and folded together. He shivered.

Buck looked into the shade of the garage. Hanson's DeSoto was jacked up in the back; Ollie Cottle's skinny legs stuck out behind the rear fender, heels to the ground. Buck turned from the Model A, and Drew's scent faded; the girl's faint fragrance still left on the blankets forgotten in the car's back seat. Buck walked into the garage and stood by the DeSoto. Cottle heard the footsteps.

"Who dere?"

"Buck Walker."

Cottle's legs moved and he grunted. A ratchet slipped around a bolt with a wretched metal shriek. "Damn!" Cottle rolled out from under the car. He lay on his back and looked up at Buck. The Negro wore a blue woolen watch cap; oddly, the hat was free of oil stains.

"What the hell you want?" Cottle nursed the knuckles on one hand. "Can't you see I'm working?"

"What's with the heap? Broken?"

Cottle's mouth dropped. "Dis place look like a parking lot? Of course that shit-on-wheels is broken. Now what the hell you want?"

"Where'd the Moons go?"

Cottle rolled back under the DeSoto. "If it's any of your bee's wax, they're squatting at Lepke's grain elevator, on permission of his majesty Sheriff Tate. Satisfied?"

"Yeah." Buck walked out of the garage and picked Tina up at the pumps. "C'mon kid." They headed toward Hanson's Goods. "I'll buy you a lickriss stick."

Buck jumped up on Hanson's porch and strode to the screen door. He opened it for his sister, letting her go first. "Only for a lady."

Inside the store, Hanson was nowhere to be found. The store was empty. Tina wandered up to the counter and opened the licorice jar. She took four pieces, the shoelace kind. Handing one to Buck, she folded the other two and tucked them away in her dress pocket. The last she sucked on. Buck dropped a nickel on the counter. Voices drifted into the store from out back. The back door squeaked open and slammed. Buck grabbed Tina's hand and dragged her behind a row of bales stacked three high. The voices grew louder, and footsteps shuffled on the dry floorboards. Buck recognized Hanson's voice.

"Parker Watts is counting on this sale." Hanson wheezed a rasping chuckle. "Financed that machinery three years ago—dues is dues—the time has come for Mr. Greene to pay up." The rasping chuckle again, then a deep coarse cough rumbling out of his throat. Hanson smoked too much.

Another man's voice: "That McCormick-Deering tractor. Fine motor. Moss kept that thing hummin' like a virgin in a choir. Yes, sir. That's a fine machine." The men stopped talking, and Buck heard them moving around the counter.

Hanson coughed again. "You drop a nickel?" They had found it.

"Not me," the other man said.

No use hiding anymore. Buck poked Tina in the ribs and she looked at him. He glanced upward, but she grimaced: she was hid, snug and safe. She was not about to give herself away. Buck stood up anyway, pulling Tina with him. Tina's head just barely cleared the bales. Buck was afraid his voice might crack, but he kept the tremor down.

"That nickel's mine, Mr. Hanson."

Hanson whirled around from the counter. A burning cigarette hung from his thin lips and his eyes narrowed. Yohanna Johns was with him, his hands crammed in his pockets. The old buzzard's Adam's apple bobbed in his gobbler neck.

"What you hiding for?" Hanson's smoke drifted from his lips. Yohanna Johns wasn't smiling. Thinking about a tractor maybe. Maybe wishing he hadn't been thinking out loud.

"Boy, I asked you what you hiding for?"

"I heard you, Mr. Hanson." Buck felt his voice roll out smooth like sweet dough. "Thought I saw a rat's tail when I come in."

Yohanna Johns' eyebrows rose. "Hmmph," he grunted. "A likely story."

No one spoke for a moment. A fly buzzed into the screen door with a gentle thump.

"You always got so much money?" Hanson fingered the shiny coin.

"Pa's." Tina held up a string of licorice. "Got four pieces." Hanson went around to the back of the counter and rang up the sale on the register. The register went clack, clack, Ding! and the drawer popped out. Hanson made the change. He held three pennies out on his palm.

"Come get your change, sonny."

Buck nudged around Tina and walked up to the counter. When he reached out for the change, Hanson snapped his fist shut and Yohanna Johns put a heavy hand on Buck's shoulder. "Nosy people sometimes wish they wasn't." Yohanna Johns' high breath whistled in the air. "But most often, nosy people are just plain dumb."

Tina came around the side of the bales and drew close to Johns. She poked the old farmer in the ribs with two stiff fingers. Johns sucked in his gut, taken aback. His scrawny hand dropped from Buck's shoulder. Tina poked Johns in the ribs again and he backed up against the counter.

"It's not nice talking like that in front of a lady." Tina smiled, all sugar and spice.

Buck reached out and grabbed Hanson's wrist. He squeezed and felt Hanson's knuckles rub together. Hanson's palm popped open. Buck plucked his pennies.

"Indian givers are the devil's children, Mr. Hanson."

Yohanna Johns raised his hand to slap Tina, but Buck turned from Hanson and stepped between them, his face inches from Johns' withered mush. "Lickriss is good for the temper." Buck cracked a smile in Johns' wrinkled face. "Can I buy you a piece?"

Tina hopped down from Hanson's porch and Buck followed her. The square had crowded up some. Horse-drawn wagons were pulled and braked at the edges of the jail, banked like logs around a blockhouse. More cars were parked near the diner and the church, jammed at angles. There were even cars parked near the garage and some backed up east and west on the U.S. Route. Others were parked on the shoulders of County Road 6, north behind the church and south behind Lepke's Diner.

J. J. Baskum was strutting up and down in front of the church steps. Baskum had dragged his tenants along. They gathered sullen and serious in a knot, fidgeting and useless. Henry stood with his wife and family, a broken-down fedora cut over his forehead and over his eyes. Henry looked dark and mean—"hungry" was what Ryder had said. Buck didn't know the names of Henry's kin, but he noticed a crushed little man who sat in a rig. Henry's brother had brought his son, who sat beside his father in the rig, one leg curled into his lap, twisted and shriveled.

Some farmers had come from outside Bone County. Their families stood around and Buck did not recognize their faces. Yohanna Johns' three ignorant sons stood facing the church, their backs to Hanson's Goods Store. Tina grabbed Buck's arm as he began to walk across the square.

"Not so fast. Let's have some fun."

Buck stopped and looked at the three Johns brothers: like triplets, their blond hair stood on end, slept on, never brushed, as if they all used a gap-toothed comb. They were all about Buck's age, but their late mother had left them, almost as a parting laugh, touched—maybe just a little feeble.

Buck bent so he could whisper in his sister's ear. "Let's have it."

"This." Tina laid it on the line. "I'm going to talk to Elroy. When you see me faint, toss a pebble in his ear—but be quick, the other two can't see."

"Ah-ha . . ." No trouble at all. Tina was already walking

toward the Johns brothers. Buck ducked toward the bank, dipping into the crowd.

Tina came around the three and drew up in front of the middle brother. Startled, he grinned and ran a hand over his mop. The other two eyed him, shooting glances.

"Well hello, Tina. Come to see the auction?"

The other two snickered, laughing through their fingers as they tried to cover their mouths.

"Hello, Elroy. You look fine today." Tina looked straight in his eyes; he blushed. "Yes, I'm here for the auction. Are you?"

Elroy scraped the ground like a dog searching for the sweet spot. "Oh no, we came with our dad. He's here to buy the tract—"

"Shut up, knuckleface!" The brother on the right glared. On the left, the other brother slapped his own forehead with the palm of his hand. "What a sap!"

"Oh my, oh my!" Tina looked a little weak. "What language! My ears!" She swooned, turning on her ankles, falling against Elroy, who caught her under the arms.

"Now look what you've done," Elroy complained. Tina hung limp in his arms. The other two looked on. Elroy still was not sure what to do with Tina's body when Buck's pebble fell out of the sky. The pebble richocheted off Elroy's ear and he let Tina slide to the ground. Elroy turned on his left brother.

"You oughtn't a done that."

"Done what?"

Elroy pushed him and he fell backward, sprawling in the dirt. He got up, brushed himself off and approached Elroy. "No, brother—you oughtn't a done *that.*" He slapped Elroy on the side of the head.

Elroy's eyes bulged; he charged and tackled. The two goons fell on the ground, tussling, dust flying. Tina opened one eye and peeked. The third brother now danced around the other two, planting solid kicks wherever he could. Some of the men in wagons started to shout. Tina got up and edged away under the oak tree. The fists flew fast—some hit, some missed. Yohanna Johns stormed out of Hanson's Goods, high-stepping toward the tangle.

"He's here!" As though doused with a water bucket, Elroy and his foe rolled off each other, jumped up, and brushed themselves off. Yohanna Johns halted two feet from his now standing sons and stared at them, saying nothing. The third boy moved away from the other two and hid behind his father. Elroy and his brother seemed to crowd together; each was a foot taller than Yohanna Johns, but they hung their heads while the third smiled an idiot's gash over their father's shoulder. Presently, as Johns said nothing, the two gladiators became horribly agitated. One trembled slightly and Elroy wrung his hands. The third grinned smugly over their father's shoulder. Yohanna Johns, still saying nothing, walked between the two, pushing them aside with his hands, dismissing them, and headed for the edge of the crowd for a better view of the church steps. Buck knew the Johns boys were easy prey—even without his help, Tina could hog-tie them, then hang 'em by their hocks in half a minute. Buck shook his head and dropped an extra pebble to the ground.

From under the oak tree, Tina saw her father on the far side of the church steps in front of the barbershop. Buck came up behind her.

"Not bad."

Tina shook her head. "You almost came too late."

"But I didn't hit you with the pebble, did I?"

Tina acquiesced. "You did not."

Their mother was standing near Drake. The tenants stood there as well. Ryder paced back and forth; his pants were too short and revealed ankles crusted with brown dirt. Eddy's round face was blanker than a dinner plate. Ryder hooked the thumb of one hand into his waistband; he held a new cigarette in the other.

Drake saw the children under the oak tree and waved them over. "Did you scrounge?"

"We did." Tina smoothed out her hair, tufts frazzled in the back. Buck noticed the lines under his father's eyes, like hairline fractures in dry brick.

Buck filled in. "Yohanna Johns wants Moss Greene's tractor real bad."

Drake's hairline creases tightened around his eyes. "How bad?"

This time Tina looked up at her brother; she had felt Yohanna's sharp bony chest when she had fingered the geezer. "Bad enough to call Bucky a snoop."

Ryder had been pacing behind his father, like the general's aide-de-camp; now he stopped still and pulled his long hawk's nose, the lone eye narrowed. Drake knew his man had stopped pacing —he had not even turned around to look.

"You hear that, Ryder?"

Ryder grunted. "I know what to do." His voice was low. Buck could see the liquid in the tenant's eye like heated, running animal fat. Ryder waited.

"Let Henry know that if it gets tough he can count on me."

Ryder stepped out from behind Drake. He looked across the church steps to where J. J. Baskum's tenants stood: stiff, friendly sentries called to a halt. Henry stood in front of his brother. Ryder caught his eye. Ryder pulled on his hawk's nose and Henry saw it. The shadow from his hat brim vanished from his eyes. Ryder made a fist, one finger curled to the first knuckle. Henry lowered his head and the hat brim came down like a shade.

Ryder's black eye darted to Drake's face. Henry had understood; Drake was satisfied. Buck saw his father take a deep breath and stand away. "Henry knows."

Sarah looked at Buck. "Give your father the change." Buck dug in his pocket and turned over the three pennies, dropping them in Drake's open hand. His father closed his fist without looking and slid them into his own pants pocket.

"Hey!" Eddy's round face turned, his cheeks tightening to hard lumps. His father's tenant was staring at the bank. Now the door opened and Moss Greene stepped into the sunlight. His wife, braid flying over her shoulder, broke from a cluster of people under the oak and ran toward Moss across the street. A woman shouted, "Go to him, Liza!"

Liza threw her arms around Moss Greene's neck and they stood in the sunlight as the crowd watched. Someone kept saying, "Amen, amen," over and over again like a chant.

The door of the bank opened once more: the dapper Parker Watts, president of the First Blue Vista Bank, flashed his white cuffs as he held the door ajar. Watts' wing-tip shoes were shined, his hair combed back, and he wore a tie with a stickpin. Even his vest was buttoned right up to the top. For a moment the banker seemed frozen, his heels together with the toes pointed out; one hand was at his side, holding an accounts book, and the other was outstretched, holding the door. From the darkness of the door frame, Sheriff Tate emerged.

Tate did not pause. He stepped off the sidewalk and headed for the church steps. Parker Watts danced around the lawman, following first one step behind, then one to the side, then two steps behind, then half a step closer, never quite catching up. As Tate cleared the oak, the crowd before the church steps parted.

In the crowd, Parker Watts seemed to stumble, but he caught his balance and whipped his head, feverish and furious, in every direction, looking for someone to blame. If Sheriff Tate spotted a prankster, he never let on. Parker brushed the invisible wrinkles from his suit and followed the Sheriff up the church steps to where a table had been set with chairs. The banker sat down and opened his account book, a pen in hand poised over the ledger. Sheriff Tate pulled a chair away from the table and stood with his hands behind his back. Watts drew a sheet of paper from his ledger. Tate took it and glanced at the sheet. He cleared his throat and looked around.

"I hereby commence the auction of Moss Greene's property. Parker Watts, Auction Clerk. Moss Greene, Owner. Myself, Sheriff Tate—presiding."

Parker Watts smiled. Sheriff Tate continued: "By the laws of this state, and in accordance with the banking statutes of this state, Bone County, and the town of Blue Vista Flats, public notice was posted on the calling in of farm machinery loans, a debt outstanding and long overdue." Sheriff Tate took breath. "By the rules of county auction a notice was posted for two weeks in public buildings, in private establishments and religious institutions whose cooperation was voluntary—"

Somebody shouted from the crowd, "Get on with it, Tate."

Tate looked around. "Well, I guess anyone who'll offer a bid has seen Mr. Greene's stuff." Tate paused. "I got one International Harvester thresher. Who'll make a bid?"

For a moment the crowd was silent and then Buck heard his father's simple leaden voice behind him. "Two cents."

Sheriff Tate looked down from the church steps. "What's that?"

"Two cents, Sheriff."

Tate shuffled his feet. He glanced quickly at the faces in the square, but unable to discern a mood he shook his head in disbelief. "Drake, nobody pays two cents for a thresher."

"I've seen the thresher, Sheriff." Drake was smiling, friendly. "Its teeth are dull. Two cents."

Parker Watts looked up, slapping his palm on the ledger. "The teeth are not dull! I've inspected all the machinery myself. I—"

"Two cents," Drake repeated.

Suddenly Buck realized that Ryder wasn't standing next to his father any more. Somehow all the other tenants had scattered into the crowd.

"Four dollars," Baskum called. He smirked at Drake, his gold teeth flashing, a scoffing razz—beat that, chump! Buck looked up at his father, but Drake was still smiling, palsy-walsy. Then Buck saw Baskum's tenant Henry move behind his landlord and whisper in the gleaning land rat's ear. Henry wore that fedora with the brim snapped over his eyes. Buck slipped, scurrying through the crowd. He crept close to Henry and heard Henry say, "Don't you think that's a little high, Mr. Baskum?"

Baskum shook his head. "Definitely not."

"Four dollars," Sheriff Tate called out. "Do I hear five?"

Henry's lips moved an inch from Baskum's ear. "I think four dollars is mighty high. Three cents is more like it."

Baskum shifted his bulk abruptly and looked Henry under the hatbrim. "What the hell's gotten into you?"

Henry smiled slightly, and the crow's feet at his eyes narrowed together. "I wouldn't count on irrigating tomorrow, Mr. Baskum. In fact, I'd be very surprised if you harvest at all this year. Be a shame . . ."

"Four dollars," Sheriff Tate hollered again. "Gimme five!"

Baskum checked the crowd; no one else cast a bid. "I'm not sure I like your attitude, Henry."

"Well, I'm not so keen on your fat-back neither. And I know that thresher can do the work of two men. But I'll tell you, Mr. Baskum, you ain't gonna have the hands to harvest, if you don't call three cents."

Suddenly, Henry's brother slipped up to Baskum's other side. The wormy straw boater was slanted across his brow. He tipped it up with one finger. "That wife of yours know when you go prowling around Bart Lowell's rooming house?"

Baskum's mouth dropped. He whipped his head and stared at

the crushed little man. The man's straw boater came up right under Baskum's nose. "What's her name? Bart's sister-in-law . . . what's her name?"

Baskum scowled. "Now see here."

"Going!" Tate called.

Henry's brother cooed in Baskum's ear. "Be a damn shame, Mr. Baskum . . . be a damn shame if that fine wife of yours got riled up over some little floozy."

Moisture sprinkled over Baskum's lip. The fat farmer mulled it over.

"Be a damn shame . . ."

"Going!"

"Three cents!" Baskum shouted. Sheriff Tate stopped short like a door slammed in his face. He shook his head as though water was trapped in his ear, making him hard of hearing. He looked at Parker who was breathing deep and puffing himself up with air. The crowd was watching him, eyes open, not blinking. Baskum was looking down at the ground.

"You bid already, J. J."

Baskum, fat and sheepish, thrust his hand in one pocket and turned it inside out. "Yes I know, Sheriff, but I just checked my funds, and I've forgotten the bills. Gotta change my bid. Three cents."

Parker Watts jumped up from the table. "You put in your bid! You put in your bid! You can't change it. I got it written down in the book. It's too late! Tell him, Sheriff!" Parker Watts, imploring, pleading, supplicant—his eyes popping—looked up at Tate. "Sheriff?"

"I'm afraid not, Mr. Watts." Tate knew his business. "The law says the man's gotta have the cash in hand. If he don't have the cash, he can't make the bid. That's the law."

Parker Watts was stricken. "But he *made* the bid. He made it."

Tate bent low so he could whisper in the banker's ear. "You better sit tight. I heard of this going on in Iowa. See how it goes —things could get touchy."

Tate straightened up. "I got three cents—do I hear a dollar?"

"Four cents," Drake called.

Baskum looked at Henry. "Can I bid *six* cents?"

"Too high," Henry decided. "Let Walker have it."

Baskum sighed, "That's a fine thresher . . ."

"I know." Henry relaxed. He took off the fedora and fingered the felt brim. "Works better when Moss Greene uses it."

"Four cents," Sheriff Tate called. "Do I hear a dollar?" Buck edged away from Baskum and his two tenants; he searched the crowd for other bidders. But the crowd was still, content to let events take their course. Few could afford a bid, and if any stranger was prepared to lay down cash, that stranger was holding off, or did not want a thresher. Buck scanned the sets of dead eyes, the slack jaws. No one said a word. For most of them, the banker was a rich man who never dirtied his hands, fingernails clean and palms soft as satin.

Sheriff Tate waited on the chance somebody might go for himself. Buck kept peering at the faces, peering for a face with a greedy twitch or a sly sneer. Waiting for swift fingers to pull a money sack and offer some cash.

Tate finally shrugged. "Hell, the thresher's yours, Walker."

Parker Watts flashed his clean white cuffs in the air; he gulped, the panic rising around his eyes. For a second, the banker froze. He stared at the pen in his hand and he stared at the ledger. He looked out over the crowd and then back at the ledger. "I can't do it . . ."

Sheriff Tate leaned closer to Parker Watts. "You enter the bid. No arguments. No fuss. Just enter it."

"I can't—"

"Do it. Or I'll enter it myself." Watts leaned over the ledger, hand trembling, and forced himself to enter the 4¢ bid, starting the proceeds column. Tate cleared his throat again. "Now we got here a McCormick-Deering tractor . . . ain't three years old, damn thing's got all its rubber—nice piece of equipment. We're starting at forty dollars. Who'll give me forty dollars?"

Buck turned around slowly. He scanned the crowd for his father's tenants. Eddy, his Mex face and dull flat eyes still as the ground, was keeping the three Johns boys out of trouble, back of the crowd. Eddy held a pack of playing cards in his hands, shuffling, cutting the deck. Eddy splayed his fingers and made a fan. Each boy picked a card.

Suddenly Buck noticed that his father had moved from the barbershop and now stood next to Yohanna Johns in front of the church steps. Drake stood easy next to the scrawny farmer; Buck nudged within a couple of feet, close enough to hear Johns say, "Maybe Baskum's a coward, but that don't mean I am."

"Never said that." Drake was smooth, riding Johns' ear. "But you don't need that tractor. You got one already. You need that pickup of yours much more than Moss Greene's tractor."

Johns' buzzard neck twisted and he looked over to his truck parked at Hanson's Goods. Buck looked too. Ryder's black eyepatch caught the sunlight; he was standing by the truck, leaning against it with his arm draped very casually on the hood. An ice pick dangled from his free hand.

"Better not." Johns' Adam's apple jumped in his buzzard's neck.

Drake spoke real softly, barely moving his lips. "Wouldn't take but a second." He paused. "That truck rubber cost a lot. And something else, that Ryder is a sharpy with an auto . . . fingers like a whiz, things going wrong right and left; every day in and out of the garage, Hanson's Garage might start charging you parking space."

"Who'll give me thirty dollars?" Tate was backing down.

Johns shook his stick finger under Drake's nose. "I'll press charges."

"On who?"

"On him." Johns turned to look at his pickup again. Ryder was nowhere in sight.

"Who'll give me twenty dollars?" Sheriff Tate did not want to push his luck. "Come on now, where you going to get a tractor for twenty dollars?" No one offered a bid.

"Ten dollars?"

Henry looked at Baskum and shook his head. Baskum did not even try to make a bid. Eddy, back of the crowd, held the Johns boys captive with his card tricks. The fan of cards collapsed into his palm, and he dished kings from the deck into each boy's lap. "How'd you get it?" Elroy asked. "Do it again! Do it again!" the others pleaded.

"Five dollars?"

Buck searched the faces, turning each one over, searching for the rotten egg. The faces were patient, content to wait as long as it took, all the time in the world. Those familiar faces—his family and his tenants—were tight-lipped and bided time. He saw strangers too, sitting out the penny bids, resting on the sidelines in no hurry to see the bank grow richer. And unlike Yohanna Johns or J. J. Baskum, in no hurry to better themselves at the expense of others. No good neighbor wanted Moss Greene's loss to be his gain. Here and there a hand would flutter, a shoulder shrug, a neck stretch, eyes to the sky and down to the ground. Back at the diner someone giggled. Henry looked at Baskum and cracked a big smile.

"One dollar?"

Tate was getting nowhere. Buck heard a soft rustle in the leaves of the oak tree.

"No tractor is worth some lousy Joe dropping a little sugar in the gas tank of your car," Drake whispered. Johns pressed his withered gash together so his lips formed a thin red line. "You and your people gonna pay for this . . ."

"Now you're being sensible." Drake went easy.

"Fifty cents?" Tate lost all hope. Parker Watts, near weeping, put his head in his hands.

"A dime," Sarah Walker called from where she stood next to Drake.

Sheriff Tate leaned over and whispered in Parker Watts' ear, "Well, Parker, looks like you and the C&C Railroad bought yourselves a peck of pennies. Won't make your books look too good. Nothing you can do if the buyers give that machinery back to Moss Greene."

"That's robbery." Parker Watts was livid. The pen in his hand scratched across a ledger page, ruining the neat column in a blue lightning bolt of ink.

Tate turned back to the crowd. "Well let's not be penny-wise and pound-foolish. Do I hear eleven cents?"

Quiet for a moment, but some woman laughed right out loud and several others went, "Shshsh . . . shshsh," giggling in between.

Then a man called out: "You got it . . . eleven cents."

Buck looked for the man. There's one in every crowd. Not from Bone County. Brought his family with him: a dumpy wife saddled with two kids, babies really, little nosepickers. He wore a blue shirt open at the collar. Belt. No suspenders. Workboots with high laces. His hair receded, revealing a broad, high whale's head. Buck took the moment on himself. He sidled up to the stranger and stood close to his ear. The women had left off giggling and quiet returned. And the stranger never noticed. Time to bring him round. "Nice tractor."

"Sure is." The stranger was pleased with himself for holding off.

"Eleven cents?" Sheriff Tate could not believe his ears.

"Twelve!" Sarah put her hands on her hips and glared. From out of the crowd an old soda bottle fell a few feet from the stranger and rolled between his legs. He watched it go, the puzzled wrinkles spreading up his whalehead brow. Then the wrinkles smoothed away. He looked to the church steps and stared straight ahead.

Buck saw Tina creep up on the other side of the man. Ugly stares had no effect and thrown trash rolled right by. Best make things perfectly clear; better draw him the picture and draw it big. "You'll never get that tractor out of Bone County. Promise."

Now the stranger stared at Buck, the whalehead furrowed in deep grooves. Tina poked him in the thigh and he whipped around to face her. "It'll rust solid here. We promise."

Buck was back at his ear. "Just helping out a neighbor. Understand? Find another auction. Buy a tractor somewhere else."

The big brow furrowed deeper. His naggy wife came up behind him dragging a little nosepicker. "Make a bid, you idiot."

Tate was hoping for a score. Maybe jack the ante just a touch. "Do I hear thirteen?"

Wishful thinking. A tin can clattered on the bottom church step and jounced to the ground. The crushed can rolled in a tight circle, wobbling like a drunk.

"Make a bid. Make a bid." The nag yapped at the back of her husband's head. The big brow trembled and he looked around the crowd and recognized no familiar face. Buck saw his father staring at the stranger. Henry, too. Ryder stood in the semicircle near the church steps and folded his arms. Eddy was with him, his Mex eyes cool, like shady stone nuggets. But the nag was desperate for a bargain. "You gonna let that little snot tell you what to do?"

With his hand the stranger rubbed his forehead. He looked at the tin can at the base of the church steps and then he turned behind him and saw the empty bottle lying at his wife's feet. His woman was close and he put a hand on her shoulder.

"Just shut up."
The little nosepicker started to sniffle.

One Hay Rake	4¢
Two Head Horses	3¢
One Grain Drill	1¢
Two Hay Wagons	2¢
Corn Row Cultivator	2¢
One Tractor Plow	2¢
Five Horse Collars	3¢
Ford One-Ton Truck	5¢
One I.H. Mower	1¢

And on and on; Moss Greene's property was sold bit by bit, a horse to this one, a plow to that one. Each family bought a piece and put a penny down. When the auction closed, each family mounted the church steps and stacked their copper under the banker's nose. Total proceeds from the sale: $3.50.

Moss Greene and Liza sat at the back of their gray wooden clapboard wagon. The gate was down and their legs dangled over the edge. The wagon and the two great dappled mares were now Eddy's. Drake Walker's tenant ran a rough palm over his thinning hair. The clapboard wagon, far from new, had most of its parts intact, no gaping holes in the bed, no spokes missing from the wheels, no long cracks on the draft beam. Eddy stood by the open gate and fingered the rough wooden slats. He stepped back from the wagon. His Mex eyes opened wide, frank and honest like a simple prayer. "My wife, she hates these wagons, says they jounce around and hurt her butt." Eddy dropped his hand from the graying wood; this was just a plain fact.

"You really didn't have to —" Moss Greene stopped when he saw Eddy shrug.

"Next time it might be my house, and maybe Walker won't be around to help me out."

Liza began to cry. She wiped her eyes on the sleeve of her dress and took a deep breath. "I was sure they were gonna take it all away."

Eddy looked down at his polio pigeon feet; it was done. Without saying good-bye, he walked over to Drake's truck, climbed in the back and waited for the others to show.

Sarah Walker was the last person up on the church steps to pay for her bid. She placed her dime and two pennies down near the stack of coins at Parker Watts' elbow, and the banker, nearly delirious, dutifully entered the payment in his ledger. Sheriff Tate was sitting now and he leaned back in his chair. "Well Mrs. Walker, what you gonna do with your tractor? Ride it to church?" Sheriff Tate hooked his thumbs into his gunbelt and the crow's feet at his eyes wavered.

"If Moss Greene drives it, and Liza don't mind, then I just might." Sarah came around the table and Sheriff Tate turned in his chair to face her.

"You're a smart man, Sheriff."

Tate's eyes shifted and his mouth turned down a little at the corners.

"Nobody was really sure," Sarah kept on, "just how smart you were. We've heard of occasions where—" she did not finish. Parker Watts had her receipt and he laid it on the table. The receipt was illegible. Sarah took it and started down the steps.

"Mrs. Walker." Sheriff Tate was leaning forward now, his elbows on the table and his fingers interlaced. "I've always prided myself on having an open mind."

"I can see that." Sarah put the receipt in her skirt pocket. Parker Watts was now looking at the Sheriff, confused. Tate was not about to fill the banker in about the temper of a crowd.

"You're a strange bird, Mrs. Walker."

"Why, thank you, Sheriff. I've always prided myself on it. But live long enough and you'll see a good many stranger."

Sheriff Tate didn't like it one bit. He stood behind the door of his jail and pulled the thin edge of the shade back from the glass so he could peek between the bars into the square. The crowd was breaking up now. Baskum had not stuck around for the third bid and Yohanna Johns had rounded up his brood and left by the fourth.

In Iowa a crowd almost hanged a judge—that's what the Walker woman was saying. And even now the National Guard was at the north end of the state, for in the north corner, the corn growers stopped trucks on the road, dumping their cargo or turning them away from the buyers in the capital. Back in May the National Farmers' Union called a strike. Tate gritted his teeth and waited for the shit-storm, but the wind blew cool and the strike never blossomed. Some said that was a good sign—that was good for some people. Not Tate. He didn't believe in signs, good or bad. In July the Farm Price Index went to 83. People talked about a record harvest, about prices coming up way over cost of production. Tate knew people like to talk.

But the main harvest was a ways off and Lepke had not posted any price at all on the county grain elevator. Lepke could post 15¢ a bushel, and then again he could post 2¢. Lepke said nothing; he kept reading the *Sioux City Journal* and pouring coffee in the diner.

Parker Watts was sure all the fuss was because of the Reds. "The Reds!" he would holler. "It's the damn Reds!" But Tate knew no Reds slithered around Bone County, and none were likely to. The first Red who stood on a soapbox would get his ears bitten off. No questions asked. Tate had never seen a Red. Unless Drake Walker and his crew were Red, but Tate doubted it. Walker paid his mortgage every month and when the harvest came he would take in the slack with a percentage of his cash crop, bailing out his tenants and keeping the Eastern Range productive. But Tate was not kidding himself; that auction crowd was the living animal of justice. Drake Walker never asked himself if he had the right; he just went ahead and let the rest follow if they wished. The crowd might just as easily have overbid the Walker group, left them hanging and without a chance. But the crowd followed instead, hating Parker Watts, his bank loans and the Railroad that bore their goods away. The crowd had taken over the show, with a whisper here, and a nudge there, and in the end Moss Greene never lost a fly off his horse's butt.

Tate was not fool enough to try and stop it. No, the Bulls were up by the tracks . . . no point in calling them down to the square so they could stand with their heavy sticks tap-tapping on the ground. A useless gesture. The crowd would not have listened. The best thing was to let the Bulls stay by their rails. Let

Parker Watts pick up the pieces, and let Moss Greene go home.

Ollie Cottle stepped out of Hanson's garage and rested his body against the Model A. He took the blue watchcap off his head and set it down on the roof of the car. The horse-drawn wagons clattered around the oak in the center of the square; some moved west, some north. The overworked pickup trucks and family cars rolled out of town, some off to the wooded reaches of Bone County and some beyond. Cottle stood there by the Model A watching the crowd scatter like chaff and hearing the hubbub subside; the rumble of the autos ran down, fading in the distance. Cottle looked at his hands; they were creased and filthy. He went back into the garage to use the grimy sink, washing his hands before lunch. When he returned to the Model A, looking for his watchcap, his hat was missing. Cottle looked on all sides of the car, under it, and even poked his head through the windows, peering at the seats and on the car floor. But the blue woolen watchcap had vanished, and the square was deserted.

Early in the afternoon a dusty Studebaker rolled into the square. Preacher Simon stepped out of Lepke's Diner as the car rounded the church and circled the green fanned leaves of the oak tree. The car's engine hardly made a sound—this one had a muffler. Dusty as the car was, Preacher could tell that the auto hummed, and was kept well oiled. A blue eagle decal was taped to the left side of the front bumper, symbol of the National Recovery Administration. Three large letters, AAA, were stenciled in white paint on the driver's door right under the window: Agricultural Adjustment Administration. So the promise had been kept after all. The Government was moving in.

The car passed Hanson's Garage, and then the Goods Store. The tires ground dry rubber to macadam on the roadbed, and the car stopped broadside to the diner a few feet from where Preacher stood. The engine died with a purr and the door opened. The Adjuster wore pleated pants and two-toned shoes.

Sweat rings dried in yellow stains under his arms. One of his suspenders was slightly frayed, as was the collar round his neck. The Adjuster's tie hung loose, limp over his chest. He was thirty or so, and his stiff blond hair, combed smoothly back over his scalp, receded at the temples. His eyebrows were blond and bushy; they stuck out like shelves. When the Adjuster spoke, it seemed to Preacher that the voice came not from his mouth, but from somewhere close by, in the air perhaps, or from deep within the leaves of the oak tree.

"The President sent me." The Adjuster held out his hand, broad and smooth, the nails dirty. "The name is Sykes."

Lepke dropped a hamburger patty on the grill and the meat sputtered as it touched the hot metal; fat juice ran bubbling at the edge of the patty and a light cloud of gray smoke rose up into his face.

"An Adjuster!" Hanson croaked. "We don't need no damn Adjuster." He lit a cigarette and inhaled, the smoke wheezing down his gullet. "What's he gonna do? Measure the corn? Kiss the topsoil? Look at the sky? Do a rain dance?" Hanson shoved his coffee cup across the counter.

Lepke left the grill and went for the coffeepot. "Didn't you hear, Hanson, there's a Depress—"

"Beans!" Hanson snapped. "I haven't been depressed a day in my life."

Preacher Simon had left the Adjuster at the curb, and now within the safety of the diner, he watched Sykes park his car properly, get out, and cross from the diner to the Sheriff's office. "We shall work hard and we will prosper." Preacher was talking to himself.

Lepke poured more coffee into Hanson's cup, laid the pot back in its heated cradle and returned to the grill. "What about our unlucky brethren, Preacher?"

Preacher Simon turned his hat over and looked into its white satin crown. "They have sinned and failed to prosper."

Hanson coughed into his cup, sloshing some coffee onto the counter. "Balls!" he rasped. "Baskum's tenants, *Henry* in particular, couldn't plan ahead. Moss Greene bought a lot of machinery he couldn't use. And Drake Walker's two buddies never did a day's work in their lives."

The diner door opened with a groan; two railroad Bulls stepped up to the counter like cowboys at the saloon's brass rail. Hanson frowned and quit jabbering. He was through complaining for now. Lepke moved around the grill like a professional, slow and deliberate. He paid little notice to the Bulls. The bruiser with the big bald head was foreman. Everybody knew him as Simple and Lepke would take his money but could not abide his company. A sliver of pale skin peeked between the buttons on his shirt, pressed open and straining against a large belly that hung over the waistband of his trousers. Simple carried a policeman's billy by its leather thong, and when he put his large hands on the counter rim, the nightstick dangled from his wrist, gently swaying. His nose was broken, out of kilter, and Simple blinked his tender, mousy eyes. Meriwether hung back by the standing fan near the screen door. A revolver was tucked in his belt. The railroad company's third Bull, a young consumptive fellow, was up by the tracks to guard their business.

Meriwether was the mean one. He was forever squinting and touching the revolver; his red hair stood on end, crowning a pinched hatchet face. He was a fidget fiend, unstrung with jim-jams, his eyes darting about, wanton. But still the man boasted a dangerous tick-tack cagey head. You had to move fast, or he would catch you in the act. Meriwether brushed against the standing fan and felt the bulge in his back pocket rub over the metal. He dropped his fingers from the revolver, pushing the blue woolen watchcap deeper into his pocket—out of sight, out of mind. Pushing the cap away from nosy poky noses.

"Say, Lepke," Simple said. "How about one of your swell hamburgers?"

Lepke nodded his head, never turning from the grill, not bothering to answer.

"Say, Preee—cher . . . " Simple turned his big bald head. "You hear? The guv'ment's arrived."

Preacher was still staring into his hat's satin crown. He placed the hat carefully on his head and didn't answer. Hanson drained his cup. "We heard."

Simple turned his head back to Hanson. "Dat so?" He took

his large hand and with sausage fingers stroked his chin. "He gonna ask you folks to plow up a third. Keep your prices up. I promise."

"Since when you been so interested in prices, Simple?" Lepke threw another burger on the grill.

Simple took a deep breath. "Since dis mawning. Bad auction. Watts not feel too good, I bet. No good."

"You were there?" Lepke brought down the spatula.

"Close enough."

Preacher suddenly spoke. "Watts and the Railroad got cheated. So what about prices?"

Meriwether couldn't stand the niggling, the holy man's havoc. "Trouble in Iowa and other points east."

Lepke flipped the patties on the grill. "So?"

"Farm Union men dumping grain on the highways." Meriwether touched the pistol. "Buyers in the capital ready to pay."

"*So?*" Hanson nearly shouted.

Simple parted his legs and squatted on the counter stool. "*So* . . . some Reds damn near hanged a banker in Illinois. Derailed a freight in Ohio."

"Didn't read it in the papers." Lepke slapped the spatula.

"Wasn't in the papers."

"Well then, you're safe. If it wasn't in the papers, you got nothing to worry about." Lepke scraped the grease. "Nobody'll bother your blessed railroad."

"Amen," Preacher added.

Simple touched the thick muscles on his forearm. "I'm always safe." The nightstick trembled when he let the forearm go.

"He's always safe." Meriwether grinned and his ticktack jim-jams simmered, jiggling under his skin.

Sheriff Tate rocked back in his wooden spring chair and lifted his feet up on the desk. Adjuster Sykes pulled a chair from beside the filing cabinet and the chair legs scraped on the floorboards. Sykes sat at the corner of Tate's desk; the Sheriff noticed the Adjuster's sandy smooth combed hair and thick eyebrows, which inspired confidence—bushy eyebrows always inspire confidence.

"So the President sent you."

Sykes didn't answer immediately. "Just a figure of speech. Your Preacher out there looked like he'd never seen a car before."

"Preacher holds his cards close to the chest."

"I've had worse welcomes."

Tate breathed deeply. Like in Iowa, maybe, or in New York State, during the Milk Strike. The law wasn't always popular. State governments dispatched the muscle, while the Feds supplied the brains. Break some ribs, jail, then the AAA comes around to kiss and make up. Sweet.

"Imagine that." Tate tapped his fingers on the desk. "Yeah, I've read the papers."

"Then you know why I'm here."

"Can't say I care one way or the other."

Sykes loosened his tie a fraction of an inch. "That's not a very good attitude."

"Maybe." Tate could admit anything. "But then Pres-i-dent Roosenfeld doesn't pay my salary."

Sykes let go of his tie and dropped his eyes to Tate's desk. The Adjuster seemed prepared to take the Sheriff into his confidence. "The Price Index is up, Sheriff. You and I know it isn't going to stay up. By September this whole part of the country will still be under cost-of-production. Fourth year in a row."

"That so." The Government man wasn't all that dumb.

Sykes looked up at the Sheriff again. "I want to know who was solvent last year, and who wasn't, and where they live."

Sheriff Tate swung his feet off the desk and thrust his head forward. "Why don't you try the banker? His name's Watts."

Sykes got up from the chair and dragged it back against the filing cabinet. The Sheriff cleared his throat. "By the way . . ."

Sykes turned; the Sheriff was still sitting forward. "By the way, you can come and go as you please, talk to anybody who wants to talk to you, you can go to church, eat in the diner, and I'll even introduce you to the local whore. But if the Bulls don't want you by those railroad tracks—you listen to them."

Sykes' eyebrows met. "I'll remember."

Tate nodded. "Try Bart Lowell, the barber—he's got an empty room he's not using upstairs."

"Thanks."

Sykes left and the cord of the pull shade danced through the metal bars of the door, clinking against the window glass.

For a moment Sykes sensed the air in the bank was very still. But two fans turned slowly overhead and a slight rush of air brushed against his face as he closed the door behind him. A dapper man emerged from a dark hallway back of the cage, presumably the vault. The man was dressed very elegantly for this part of the country. He wore a real starched collar and a stickpin in his tie.

"Mr. Watts?"

Watts smiled and nodded as though surprised at hearing his name spoken in a kindly tone of voice; his eyes were glazed. "The same." He came forward to the cages and then angled off, letting himself out of the cash area through a thigh-level swing gate. Suddenly the banker sharpened up. "You're from the Farm Bureau. Mr.—?"

"Sykes. How'd you know?"

"Oh." Watts waved a limp wrist. "From the car, of course. Triple A—that's the Farm Bureau—no?"

"Yes," Sykes said. "Saw the auction poster on the church—how'd you do?"

Parker Watts stopped smiling as if he had inhaled bad body odor or a cheesy fart.

"I see." Sykes almost laughed. "Penny auction. Did you go it alone?"

"No, the Railroad—" Watts halted. "Is there something specific, Mr. Sykes?"

"That depends . . . "

Parker Watts brought his hand up to his chest, caressing the clean shirt, his fingers grazing the tie pin. "Whatever I can do, of course."

Moss Greene heard the tires of a car grind on the dirt road that led to his farm. He climbed down the ladder from his hayloft and walked out the open barn door. A dusty Studebaker stopped when it reached the house. Moss Greene's two great dappled mares looked up from where they grazed, side by side, in a short-bitten patch of grass. Their gray ears cocked as the car door slammed shut with a heavy thud; then the horses went back to their grazing.

The blue eagle decal on the Studebaker's front bumper told Moss all he had to know. The Triple A stenciled in white on the car door told him more. The blond man with the rolled-up sleeves —no pansy, this one. The Adjuster was looking at his farmhouse and then he turned to Moss, standing in the door of the barn.

"Don't want any."

The Adjuster did not move any closer. "Ain't selling." The yard's gravel scrunched under his shoe and Sykes looked back down the road. He clasped his hands together and raised them over his head, stretching.

"You're a lucky fellow, Mr. Greene."

"How's that?"

"You have kind neighbors."

Greene came out of the barn doorway and walked toward the car. "Best kind to have."

"No, Mr. Greene . . . " The Adjuster leaned up against the Studebaker. "They're the *only* kind to have."

Nightwalkers

GIRLS AND BOYS COME OUT TO PLAY,
THE MOON DOTH SHINE AS BRIGHT AS DAY.
COME WITH A WHOOP, COME WITH A CALL,
COME WITH GOOD WILL OR NOT AT ALL.

The afternoon sun rolled into Buck's eyes; he sat in the flatbed of his father's pickup as it bounced down the U.S. Route. He sat shoulder to shoulder with Eddy and Ryder, bumping knees and elbows. The truck slowed and gravel ground under the tires. Drake parked his pickup by the side of the farmhouse, got out of the cab, and loomed around the side of the truck as Buck lay on the flatbed. His father seemed to have grown since the auction. The hair stubble on his shaven face was bluish and rough.

"Where'd you say that Moon dame was camped out?"

"By Lepke's grain elevators."

Drake really seemed larger, like swollen knuckles after a fight. "They gonna be there all night?"

Buck stood up and now rose above his father, looking down at the big man's shoulders supple under his shirt. Around Buck the tenants stood up too; one-eyed Ryder dropped the truck gate like a lazy sailor weighing anchor. The tenants got down and left Buck standing alone on the flatbed, close to his father's shoulders. "Yeah, I suppose . . ."

Drake brought up the gate and latched it, the metal clanging close to Buck's shins; his father was almost smiling, like a man with a secret. "Well, then you can have them stay here tomorrow."

The tenants left the Walkers and wound their way across the fields to their own homes. And the day inched by for Buck under the tedium of his father's commands. Garden set to rights. Fix up the water wagon for tomorrow's irrigation. Clean up the stalls. The jobs were endless. Drake had made up his mind about the Moon woman and so that was that. On with the rest of the day.

The sun hung low and more than once Buck was sure that an owl wheeled above him in the sky, but even squinting his eyes and searching the wide blue crown, he saw nothing. No hint of flapping wings, no hint of a lonely scavenger circling the riverbank, marking the spot where the dead man drifted from Bone County. The Bulls' snickering laughter was all the wake left for the floater's last witness.

Soon Buck smelled his mother's cooking. But even this was no distraction. And so dinner for Buck was short but tedious and the sun set in a ball of red oblivion. He couldn't sit still, his butt squirming in the chair. The soles of his feet itched like he had stepped on a prickler. And he had nearly been reprimanded. But Buck finally managed to hold it all in, clean the kitchen with Tina —then bolted out the door into the night where the darkness would let him think. First, he wanted a cigarette. No doubt Ryder by the tracks would fork one over. He headed out in the night, using a tractor path by the fields that led to the tenants' houses.

Vague rustlings, deep in the corn, broke through the air across the path. Crickets most likely. The reet-reet insects played out before his footsteps and directly behind, but just where Buck walked, they fell silent until he had passed. Their high-strung chirping, somehow pointless in the night air, opened around him and he pushed the bubble of hush as his feet struck down the gravel path. The stars were very bright. They seemed close as though dangling in a dark vault, held motionless by invisible wires in a deep cavern. The stars had names that Buck never understood; sometimes he made up his own names for their design: the Candle, the Hand, the Owl, the Woman . . .

The tenants' houses were lit up orange like jack-o'-lanterns.

The windows were bright, flickering with the glow from coal oil lanterns. Hung on the eaves of each porch, two other lanterns burned, one lantern to a porch, two porches, two lights glowing away out in the darkness. One porch was empty, but on the other chairs were set out. Ryder and Eddy sat on the cane-back. From out in the darkness Buck could tell Ryder's cane-backed chair was busted, for his bottom was squeezed into the frame and he looked almost as though he was sitting on the crapper. The dull red ember of Ryder's cigarette hung from his lips. Ryder took a drag and the ember glowed brighter. Buck figured they could not see him that far out in the field. But then Eddy called from the porch, his scratchy voice clean in the night.

"Come and git it, Bucky . . . we know yer slinking around out there."

Buck was breathing heavy and deep. He approached the lanterns' glow and tried not to pant when he spoke. "How'd y' know?"

"You made a racket." Eddy's Mex eyes narrowed. "Grunting and groaning up the road, talking to yerself—what do you say out there in the dark?"

"Didn't think I was talking." Buck hopped up on the porch and sat down, dangling his legs over the edge.

"You were." Ryder palmed his cigarette over his knee and scratched his face under the eyepatch.

"Just naming the stars, Ryder."

Eddy's raspy voice cracked in, "They already got names." Eddy dropped his own cigarette on the wooden floorboard; the ember shattered in the whorling shape of a burning rose. Eddy rubbed his boot over the coals, and they died, blackdust. A chair creaked. The smoky glow from the lanterns fell over Buck's shoulders and the lamplight ranged like a tent, pushing the darkness back into the fields. A mosquito hummed, droning in the wick's heat; the no-see'ums tickled and bit. More than once each man slapped his skin. The tent of light glow faded to black a few feet from the porch. If there had been someone out there, you could not have seen him, but you would hear that somebody in the silence of fright, in the silence of dread-struck crickets. A foot crushing a clod of dirt—that you would hear, or a twig snapping . . .

Eddy coughed. "Quit mooning, Ryder—git the jug you're hiding."

Ryder pulled his bottom unstuck from the cane-back chair. He put a thick hand on Buck's shoulder. "Come with me, Bucky. You don't seem afraid of the dark."

"I'm heading for the grain elevators." Buck slid off the porch edge and stood up. Ryder was already shrouded in the murk, walking off along the tracks, toward the Railroad's property.

"Well, maybe . . . " Ryder hissed, "we're going in the same direction."

It sure looked that way. Buck jumped quickly, catching up, and kept close to Ryder's heel as they walked along. "Don't keep so close." Buck fell back a couple of paces. Ryder was right. Parts of the railside were laced with barbed wire in places, and if he stumbled into any, Buck on his heels was sure to follow.

"We'll come up like prickly pears." Ryder's horsy laugh capped it.

"Ryder, lemme have a cigarette."

Ryder stopped and Buck, too close, walked right into him, bumping his chest on the tenant's bony shoulder.

"Here." Ryder held the pack under Buck's nose; the thick scent of fresh-cut wafted around the pack. He drew out a Lucky Strike and pressed one end with his fingernail. Ryder whipped out his cigarette lighter; he flipped back the cap and struck the wheel. The Zippo flashed and a small blue-yellow flame burned over the windscreen. Ryder was proud of his Zippo. Said he owned it for over ten years, same one. Said it was the last thing he owned outright. Said he always polished it on his birthday. Buck even saw him polish it once.

Buck stuck the Lucky Strike between his lips, bringing his nose to the flame. He dragged; the Lucky burned. Ryder snapped the Zippo cap, snuffing the flame. The cigarette glow remained, enough light for Buck to make out the tenant's hawk nose and the wrinkles at the corners of his eyes. Buck drew deeper on the cigarette and the ember crackled; he filled his cheeks with smoke, bulging, quick: cigarette plucked and he took a breath. The smoke filled him down inside and Buck exhaled through his nose. The darkness swallowed up the smoke and his nostrils hissed.

"Like a real professor." Ryder was walking again. Buck hurried to catch up; he held the cigarette with his thumb and forefinger, and the ember warmed his hand. Rich and sticky, the tobacco raced through his blood, and the sky went dark velvet. The nicotine balanced in his veins and Buck's head cleared. They were near the Bulls' workhouses. The houses were dark; a tight knot grew like a tumor in his throat.

"Ryder." Buck kept his voice very low. "We oughtn't to be up this way."

"Quiet." Ryder knelt down. "I keep the jug up here, case anybody finds it—they'll think it's the Bulls'."

"What's wrong with store-bought?"

Ryder spat on the ground. "Weasel piss." He was moving real slow now, taking each step so he would not make much noise. They kept close to the edge of the fields. Buck thought he was making less noise than the tenant. The crickets' chirping soared around them, as though the insects did not mind the bodies' closeness. One was singing right next to Buck's foot and when he touched the ground it skittered away, but did not fall silent. The bug went *reet-reet,* and three more called *reet-reet-reeet.* Then two dozen across the way near the workhouses sang back *reeet-reeet, reeet-reeet.* Back and forth, around and around.

By the edge of the field, Ryder dropped down on his knees again; he came away from the field's edge with a big round canteen. "I put the jug away last time, so I go gets it." Drunkard's logic. "Eddy'll put it away after we're through and next time he go gets it." Pretty clever; only one guy would know where the jug was, and if any was missing between pass-arounds, the other would know the keeper had been dipping in without permission.

"Got to protect the sauce." More logic. Some soft noise came from the Bulls' workhouses. "Let's git," Ryder whispered. More crickets went *reet-reet.* Buck felt his own breath and he dragged again on the cigarette.

"Not yet, Ryder—I got an errand."

Metal struck stone: the noise had not come from the workhouses. Down beyond the railroad's water tower and coal tender, and beyond Lepke's grain elevators, a small fire was just starting up. A campfire: the light was bright and cozy through the tangle of railroad machinery, through the spars of the towers, and a dull light reflected off the silver-painted grain elevators. Beyond the campfire Buck could just make out the railroad bridge that spanned Yellow River and the narrow, single wooden access lane that ran alongside, bolted and nailed to the railroad crossing. The access road ran to the back of the workhouses and hooked up with County Road 6, on the far side of Yellow River.

Buck stood up real straight like he was facing up a bully; he pointed to the campfire, the shifting light unsteady in the darkness. "That's where I'm going." He ran off softly toward the flicker, disappearing into the shadows of the water tower, which loomed like an ogre over their heads.

Buck heard Ryder light off after him, the tenant's big footsteps scampering faster in the trail of his own. Under the water tower and out, the silver grain elevator soared into the night. Buck leaned against it and caught Drew's face in the firelight. Ruddy, with a Persian glow, Drew's dark eyes pinned him against the elevator, dumb with his own heart beating. Then Ryder snapped out of the shadow and came to Buck's side. "You know them?"

Ryder's hiss melted into the darkness. Drew's Indian scout eyes were steady and Buck walked toward them, the campfire growing larger at his feet. In the circle of light Buck stood over Drew and felt the girl's maiden heat again. Coal-eyed, her lids were heavy and half closed. She did not seem surprised to see him.

Lomax sat cross-legged, his face dark; no light glistened off the wet muc-muc, no pink gums dripping with saliva. Lomax sat quiet. Mrs. Moon was standing up; her body came into the light and then she withdrew into the shadow.

"I didn't expect there'd be a next time." Buck's breath came fast and he touched his beltloop.

Drew dropped her eyes from him and glanced at Ryder. Wary in the seconds' hesitation, she stared into the fire. "Our car broke down. We almost got walked outta here. They let us stay till tomorrow."

Mrs. Moon was bent over a ragged tent which she had staked to the ground as it lay flat. Livable junk from the Model A. She slipped a wooden pole under the canvas. Her behind spread as she bent and Ryder took a finger to his hawk's nose, but stopped himself and let the hand drop.

Mrs. Moon straightened herself and gave Ryder the once-over. "Are you Simple?"

That's why Drew was wary; Simple's smell had spread around.

Ryder was almost preening, but he held himself well. "No, I'm not Simple." He stood his ground in the circle of the fire's light and held the canteen with both hands. "Watch out for him, lady. He's jealous of his territory."

"I got a note." Mrs. Moon moved around the flat tent, checking the stakes. "From the Sheriff."

As the man in charge, Ryder nodded and solemnly unscrewed the canteen cap. In honor of the moment, he took a pull. "Too bad . . . " He took another pull. "Aaaah . . . Simple ain't the brightest fellow. He don't even read the funny papers."

Ryder wiped his lips on his sleeve. He left the canteen uncapped, his eyes still on Mrs. Moon. He held the canteen out and nudged Buck on the shoulder.

"Go ahead, Bucky." Buck faltered, not taking the canteen. Ryder was not even looking at him.

"Go ahead." Now Drew had the two of them in the fire's heat: the man and the almost man . . . and the almost man was hers. Buck took the canteen, gripping it hard so it would not slip.

"I'll see you don't put yourself under." Drew's eyes were wide, the lids now open full. "I'll see you get home, with your folks none the wiser."

Buck pulled on the canteen, the alcohol burning its way down his throat, roaring into his belly, churning slowly—warm and comfortable.

"So Simple can't reeed, can he? Is that what you think, Ryder m'boy?"

Ryder spun around, his back to the fire. Simple's huge bulk stood in the shadow. Next to him, Meriwether clung like a bad smell, his thin body ripping the air electric, crackling to move, to do something—anything. Buck's knees were stiff. Without looking, Buck capped the canteen and let it down to the ground by the strap. Meriwether edged away from Simple and a silver glint, a sodcutter blade, caught the firelight. The knife, growing from Meriwether's hand, flowed with his body.

"Hey boy." Meriwether was not smiling; he passed the knife from hand to hand.

"Hey boy . . . I'm talking to you."

Buck stayed still. The nightcrawlers falling to the ground and scattering in all directions. Except one, dangling bloody, cut in half.

"Hey, Walker boy, you fish this morning?"

Buck's mouth was dry and the body floated like a log face down.

"Hey . . . I'm talking to you. You deaf? I asked you if you went fishing?"

The Bulls' morning laughter tickled the dawn. Buck had lost the worm can somewhere when he ran. "No, Meriwether. Everybody knows fishing's lousy that part of the river."

The knife hand twitched. "You a wise-ass . . . ain't you?"

Meriwether crouched, the blade up high.

"Ain't you?" His red hair was standing up on end, like a wind had blown it stiff. "You think you got us foxed?"

Meriwether was moving in the fire's light. "Hey boy, bring me that canteen. Open it up and set it right here for me." He held out his hand.

"C'mon." Meriwether was smiling; a tooth was missing, one black gap under his pink lips. "I think you're a little barnyard hen, Walker boy. That's it, just a barnyard hen. C'mon, bring that canteen over here. Bring it here . . . or I'll come get it."

"I have a note." Mrs. Moon slipped up to Simple and held the scrap of paper in his face. Simple smiled broadly, his eyes vanishing in a fold of flesh. He took the scrap and gazed at it in the light. He thrust his hand out toward Meriwether, who stopped circling the fire. "Reeed it."

Meriwether crept back to Simple and fingered the scrap. Peering at the paper Meriwether squinted his eyes, moving his lips. He read it through twice and then started aloud: "It says, 'Simple—doan bother these people t'night—Tate'—that's what it says."

"Which people?" Simple looked around.

"Anybody—" Drew broke in.

Meriwether dropped the scrap of paper to the ground, and it fluttered toward the fire. "Tate doan have no jury's diction over here." Meriwether circled the fire again, the sod-knife down, catching a dull reflection from the burning branches. Buck heard something moving in the cornfield behind him. No animal. Meriwether heard it too and stopped still. The crackling of cornstalks caught Simple's attention and he looked toward the dark field.

Eddy swept aside the cornstalks and came into the sandy patch of campsite. The firelight burnt Eddy's dry red cheeks rusty brown; the cross-hatched creases under his Mex eyes moved as he came close to the fire. Eddy carried a broken-off hoe handle, smooth with use. The stick was four feet long and snapped to a jagged point where the blade once was. Eddy also carried a short sickle tucked in his belt. He passed the broken hoe handle to Ryder who took the long wooden pole and held it firm. Eddy stood silently at the edge of the field, watching Meriwether over his jutting moustache hairs. The cross-hatched creases under his eyes shifted like a fan in a cardplayer's hand. From the campfire's flames a red sheen slashed bolt lightning across Ryder's eyepatch. And then the black patch settled like a big black egg over his eyesocket. You could tell the hoe handle felt good in his hands.

Eddy came over to Buck and picked the canteen off the ground. The tenant's body heat seemed to radiate from his belly, stronger than the campfire. Eddy held the canteen in one hand and with the other uncapped it. Staring at Meriwether with his flat Mex eyes cool as a shady tree, Eddy brought the canteen to his lips and took a long pull. The tenant's Adam's apple bobbed twice; he never took his eyes off the thin jimjam Bull.

The scrap of paper, Tate's note, fluttered again and Buck nearly lunged for it, but he kept still. And the scrap was swept into the small fire. The flare from the burning paper lit the circle yellow for a moment, then died. The paper ash, laced with afterburn sparks glowing deep red, was caught in the embers' rising heat; the spark-laced ash soared into the air, carried in the rising current. The ash floated for an instant in the warm updraft; the red flecks within burned out the remaining fibers, and then the ash flew away, engulfed darkly, drifting invisible into the night.

"Where's your pistol, Meriwether?" Ryder pulled his long hawk's nose and leaned on the hoe handle.

Meriwether closed the sodcutter blade and sidled up to Simple. Wherever the gun lay was not close enough. Simple could call the other Bull; that would jack up the score some, jack it up completely if he brought the gun. Buck held his tongue on that, but Ryder was thinking fast. "I wouldn't. It'd positively be two to one by the time he got here."

Mrs. Moon, in the darkness, pulled a string, and the tent, which had lain flat on the ground, came up full and taut. The tent's sides were patched; one of its entrance flaps was missing. Her back, turned to the fire, was brightly lit: the print of her dress was flowered blue. "You could still call your man, Mister Simple." She did not bother turning around.

"And there's no note anymore." Drew laid down the glove, daring him to go. But Simple did not take the dare. He looked at Drew for the first time. Oddly, he cracked a smile.

The fight seemed to ebb from Meriwether; distracted, he looked over his shoulder to the workhouses, as if he had forgotten something. Simple moved first, very slowly, backing off down to the water tower and the workhouses. Buck heard the big man walking away. In the darkness Simple whispered, "Sleep tight . . . " Meriwether still stood alone in the circle of the firelight. He was not looking at Mrs. Moon or the tenants; he stared after Simple until the foreman's footsteps faded away. As if jerked on a leash by a large dog, he trudged after his foreman and shortly disappeared under the water tower, following the now silent footfalls.

The fire burned low and Drew chucked a few dried cornstalks on top of the coals, then some rail-tie slivers; the cornstalks smoked and caught, and the circle brightened. Tar on the rail-tie kindling bubbled, and the oily smoke was swallowed in the air. Everyone loosened up a bit. Ryder moved over to Eddy and took the canteen.

Mrs. Moon whisked away from the tent, brushing past the circle of light, her dress flowing. She plucked the sickle from Eddy's belt as she passed into the shadow.

"Be still."

Buck was crouched, and froze again as if waiting for another onslaught.

"Hush."

Mrs. Moon was down on all fours now; lightly, with her fingertips, she felt the dirt where Meriwether once stood. "More fire." Drew threw more cornstalks over the fire, and they flared yellow and brilliant. Mrs. Moon looked closely at the dirt and then she stopped, finding her mark. In the harsh light from the fire, Meriwether's vague bootprint, a phantom impression, was left in the dirt. So faint was the mark that Buck could barely see the bootprint outline. Mrs. Moon hovered over it for a moment, eyeing it for the final calculation. She swung the blade in a fast arc striking the ground, the sickle's point jabbing the bootprint arch. She let the sickle handle go; plunged in the dirt it wavered, trembling over the track. "You leave it be," she ordered Eddy.

"But my—"

"Leave it." She rose and made her way back around the firelight. The older men did not like this at all. Mrs. Moon addled them and Buck knew their throats were dry. Before Ryder could take a swig from the canteen, Eddy grabbed it back. He took a pull and swallowed hard. "Well, I never . . ."

Ryder took the canteen before Eddy could have another go. He took a pull and looked at the other man. "Lucky thing you showed when you did."

"You were a long time coming back." Eddy held his hand out for the canteen. "I just set after you. Saw Simple standing up here and circled around. Bad place to stash it," Eddy reflected. He looked back at his sickle thrust in the ground.

"It wasn't such a bad place." Ryder seemed a little insulted. "We just saw the light from the fire and came to take a look. Bucky says he knows these people."

"Helped my dad today." Buck found that Drew's eyelids were heavy and half-closed again, leaded hoods against the night. Ryder with his one good eye shot a knowing glance in Buck's direction, one arched eyebrow and slanting smile. The others noticed. Mrs. Moon too. Saying nothing about it at all, she brought a cushion from the tent and eased her bottom down onto the ground. "Have a seat, gents." The fire crackled and she waved the men into its glow. "You're the first protection we've had in a long time."

They sat, but Ryder acted slightly ashamed. Simple had caught him unawares. He hung back a bit, shoulders slumped. Now and again he looked toward the workhouses and the water tower, like an Army guard. They passed the canteen around; each man took his turn reaching down for the jug. Ryder had that Zippo out again and another Lucky Strike. Mrs. Moon did not drink, but she did not seem to mind if the others did. Drew fed the fire with little twigs and never took a pull. The thin smoke from the burning wood caught up in Buck's nostrils, sharp like mustard seed, the burning scent drawing him back to the canteen again and again. On the next pass to Ryder, Buck grubbed another cigarette. The nicotine warmed him up; the skin on his face, tight as leather, grew hot. The fire clawed his body with a child's eager fingers; he felt Drew next to him, but he couldn't bring himself to look at her, as though by gawking—or even just caught in a fleeting glance—he'd tip his hand.

Buck stood up from the fire, leaving a hole in the passaround circle. The air out in the darkness was cooler, but his body was like Parker Watts' wood stove in the winter, stoked and roaring, warming the air in a corner of the bank. He wandered down along the railroad tracks and when he got away from the firelight, standing still, the crickets started chirping again, close enough to touch. Soft footsteps padded on the gravel and the sound followed a few feet behind him. Drew.

She stood for a moment and they both looked back at the glow and the people huddled around. "You don't drink often."

"Not often." Admit and succumb. The crickets sang in the darkness of the field. "Only once before. When the carny was here —Ryder gave it to me, but the others weren't there."

"I don't drink at all."

"No, I didn't see you take any."

Her face was very close, so close Buck could feel her breath, a warm gentle feather on his lips. He could hear her deep breathing, the sound of a gulp when she swallowed in her throat. "Thanks for the water, today—this morning."

"It didn't get you too far."

"No," she shook her head and her hair grazed his face. "But when the car's fixed we won't need water."

Buck sat down on the slanting gravel bed of the rail tracks. He looked up at her. The moon had risen and it arched over her shoulder, casting a blue light over the fields.

"About my dad . . . "

She looked down at him, her rosebud swell rising and falling as she breathed. "Get up."

"What?"

"Get up."

He stood up, brushing himself off. Drew put her face right to his and touched his shoulder. "There's a river." Whispering in the wind.

He could barely talk. "Yes."

"Take me to it."

"But it's only a little river."

"Yes, take me to it."

Her hand was on his shoulder; it melted through his shirt, sinking into his skin, deep through his chest and running down the side. He wanted to touch her . . .

"Take me to it."

Simple struck a match and lit a coal-oil lantern. "I don't like it at all." His great dome head shone in the sickly smoky wick flame light. His eyes, hot pinpricks in the folds of flesh, darted over the bunkhouse walls. "Not at all." One man snored; Simple paced and Meriwether sat on his cot with one boot off, his foot curled in his lap.

"Jesus, Jackson, Jalopy, Jonah!" Meriwether massaged his foot. He kneaded his heel, thumb and finger, pressing the skin, searching for the jab. "Didn't see the damn wire. Barb went right through the damn boot. Damn boot. Right through the sole." He stabbed his finger at the worn leather boot, lying on its side, laces tangled, tongue out like a sleeping dog.

"Look at that damn foot."

Simple kept pacing, his hands clasped behind his back. But Meriwether wasn't watching the foreman; the skinny widget, foot curled in his lap, squeezed the sole's tough flesh, probing for the barb. "I think I still got a piece under the skin. Damn boot."

The other railroad Bull, still under the covers, sacked in the sack, snored.

"Damn boot."

"I don't like it at all." The large skin dome tilted in the light. The railroad bunkhouse was dark even with the lantern, and stuffy. The smell of bird droppings and termite eggs had sunk into the wooden frame. Little flecks of tar from the gang-work were smeared on the walls, congealed and tumorous; so speckled were the walls with tar spots that it was impossible to tell what was wooden smooth and what was sticky to the touch. The whole bunk was wormy through and through; rotten insects in their tiny tunnels devoured old wood, and the building sagged, diseased to the core. Meriwether, on the cot, pulled out his sodcutter, ready with the blade to go poking for the fragment. "Don't think I can get it. Damn boot."

"First the auction." Simple counted off his fingers. "Now this business." He ticked off the two extended digits, fat as sausages. "Things are getting out of hand. Yes, they're getting out of hand."

"It's stuck, all right." Meriwether held the blade point to his sole. "Gotta let it work hisself out." He got off the cot and limped to the lantern, twisting the screw to brighten the flame. "Damn Judas boot."

Buck walked down the tracks heading for Yellow River. Drew followed, her soft tread behind him, stroking the ground close to his heels. Where the barbed wire tangled in loops by the railbed, Buck felt his way slowly. He took her hand and led her into the fields. So they hiked around the cornstalks, circling back to the clear path by the rails. More than once they came close enough to the barbed wire for Drew's dress to snag, but somehow she passed around the metal barbs as though her edges dissolved in smoke, coalescing firmly once safe beyond the wire gauntlet's grasp. The rail line and service road crossed Yellow River over a rusty iron trestle; the river was bounded by trees on either bank. In the wandering moon's glow, Buck could just see Preacher's church steeple over the trees on the far riverbank. He led her down to the nearest row of trees, away from the trestle, looking for the place where the barbed wire broke. He found the place several yards down. Drew squeezed through the thicket, grabbing the branches of trees, falling the last foot to the stony bank. The moon was high now, and the water glistened as it rambled over the rocky bottom. Where a twig poked out of the water, the snag parted the current, and the ripples of the V caught the silver light, making it impossible to tell whether the snag caused the ripple or the ripple parted for the snag.

The bank was flat shale rock, and in the cracks of the shale, sand was tamped down as if with a spoon. In better times when the creek was swollen and threatened to spill over, the trees held the water like a girdle. And once during the season's flow the rushing current pulled a timber down, a cracked stay in a whalebone corset. Now that the river was low, the trees' roots were exposed in a tangled mass, sinking down through the moss and shale to the soggy soil below. As the dry spell lingered and the river fell away, sand appeared in the cracks of the shale. Already many of the exposed naked roots were dried and cracking, but deep in the bank the earth was still soft and moist. The corset held; the trees were fighting back. Buck looked up at the sky and the stars that hung by threads in a dark vault now were dimmed by the silver plate with the pockmarked face.

Drew knelt down and touched a dark edge-pool on the riverbank. As she skimmed her palm flat, the moonlight raced across the tiny darkened backwater, a pearly invader in the sluggish pool. She touched the dark water again and when Buck looked up, he noticed that the tree that shaded the backwash now seemed to bend back away from the riverbank, letting the moonlight fall on their shoulders and casting shadows on the pool.

Drew took her finger from the water and held it to the moonlight. The drops ran down her hand and arm, quicksilver slick. The edge-pool glistened now, and the silver moonraking ripples trembled across the water, sucked to the faster current, catching on the snags and ripping over the rocks.

She dipped her finger in the moon pool again, turned and shook her finger toward the roots at the bank. The water droplets flew off her fingertip, vanishing, silver fire snuffed into tangled darkness. She shook her finger as if scolding, but nothing in her manner seemed angry as she shook the water off her finger. She could just as easily have wiped her wet hand at the bottom of her skirt. The droplets flew and vanished, claimed in the tangled roots of the hot riverbank.

She smiled; those know-all amber Persian eyes stalking him . . . daring him to come and get it. Buck was fevered and wanted to say something; he wanted her to talk. He opened his mouth. She touched his cheek with her glistening finger and the coolness of the river flowed into his pores.

"Shshsh . . . " Her finger fell from his face. The tree bent back as if pulled and tugged with rope, at a silent command; the roots in the riverbank stirred. The tree was an old one, its branches full, the leaves broad, almost black and very still. Her lips were at Buck's ear. "Listen."

From up beyond the trestle he heard it. Very faintly, a frog croaked, and the sound drifted with the water, hung over the glistening edge-pool and passed on down the flow.

"She's lost her lover," Drew said. "Lost him before you were born." The canteen hooch burned in his stomach; the frog croaked softly twice more and then stopped. The river flowed on, past the sleeping town, its houses' shutters drawn against the night, lanterns cold.

The roots along the riverbank seemed to squirm and come alive as though shivering in delight, stirring awake in the summer heat, moving in the moonlight where night's steam rises from the bank and the darkness. Up the lip of the riverbank one twig scraped against another, the sound of two thin bones rubbed together. Buck looked for Meriwether's dry eyes, the moonlight catching them as they peered between the bramble's thick leaves; his sodcutter blade held low between his knees. Buck's hands were sweating as if the Bull were about to rise from the brush and saunter toward him, knife in hand, to whistle down his neck. The hooch pounded in his arms and the ground shifted under his feet like soft sand.

A branch full of leaves rustled hard, as if blown by a stiff breeze, but the air was still and nothing moved. Buck looked to Drew's eyes to see if the twig's broken snap, the rustle, the sound of a stranger only paces away, left any mark upon her. But her eyes were dim and forgiving, her ears deaf to the sounds about them that refused to keep still. She moved again and took one of his disgruntled hands. Her fingers were very warm and the lines in her palm were soft and complicated, and he tried to trace them. Her lips were very close; the knots in his throat went slack and fell away. Drew's eyes were wide and her eyebrows seemed so fine, like cornsilk woven together by tiny fingers, only dark brown and smoother by far than any cornsilk. The canteen hooch blew his head up like a grand balloon, the pressure swirling behind his eyes ... He closed them under the simple dread of silent staring eyes hidden in the riverbank bramble. And then he felt her lips. Her mouth was very soft—she parted his teeth and her tongue darted over his gums, warmly full.

A thin sapling snapped, green bark torn open; leaves rustled again; the thickets trembled and then went still. Buck's tongue lay dead in his jaws. Drew's eyes were open and she looked him in the face. Dry leaves cackled and then were smothered under a footstep. Drew's eyes were soft as lead; he broke from them. "Wait here."

"Hold on."

He paused, half-crouched in the darkness, waiting for Meriwether's thin voice to come slithering out of the bramble. Nothing yet. Drew came up beside him; she held a broken branch in one hand. The branch was stripped of leaves and bark, smooth; she held it like a club.

Buck took one end of the branch and circled his fingers tight around the wood. "No, stay here."

His grip was stronger and she let the club go; and then Buck melted into the night, crawling quietly up the bank. He would circle around, coming up behind. The tree branch was light but sturdy in his fist. The canteen hooch pressed across his neck like a yoke; Buck shook it off and took each step with care, touching down lightly with his feet, testing for a crackle or snap, then resting his weight before taking a new step. Thirty paces out in the bramble, Buck turned and stopped. The river water gurgled like a hapless child; the woods were silent and Buck held his breath.

A mosquito hummed in his ear and then landed on his neck. It speared its tiny needler in his skin, a venom flame burning one pore. Slowly his hand crushed it against his neck.

Toward the riverbank and the running water beyond, a spray of leaves trembled like a small rush of applause. Buck took two steps, and a large oak leaf brushed against his face. A tree limb towered over him in the dark, but he could not find its trunk. He heard Meriwether's breath somewhere out in the darkness, eager sighs fouling the air.

Ten more quick silent steps and Buck could see the river's glint over the bank's bramble. Another twig snapped like a breaking bone. In front of him a bush grew up out of the bank like an enormous fat woman guarding the way; surrounding her were smaller bushes, like children hanging on her skirts. Meriwether was not standing up, but he was there. He was crouching close by. The air was dead still. A shoe scraped against the ground, and the fat bush trembled under its weight.

The tree branch was light in Buck's hand and he beat the bush, driving the wood deep into the leaves. Tiny twigs broke and cried, tearing down their stems. A shriek ripped out from the bramble, wailing high in the air. "Stop it! Stop it!"

Tina fell out onto the bank, bringing snatches of thickets snagged in her clothes. Her dress, hiked up around her thighs, was torn, her hair in total disarray.

Buck saw his sister's pale white shoulders and he shuddered, his stick hand leaden. He let the branch go and stared down the bank, very hard for a moment, making sure Tina was not limping or worse. "Jesus, Tina! I coulda broke your head!"

Tina just stared up the bank and glared at Buck. Down a little ways Drew emerged from dark bramble, a single leaf clinging to her hair. "Not hurt, are you?"

"No, just lucky." Tina held her hand out, ready to shake. "Nice to see you again, Miss Moon."

Drew took the smaller girl's hand. Buck let himself gingerly down the lip of the riverbank. Tina broke off the handshake; her knees were gangly and calloused, but scraped from her fall. She brushed them off and in the darkness she touched them with her fingertips to see if the skin was broken.

Buck crouched down low to get a better look. "No iodine. Promise. We'll get some peroxide, minute we get home."

The candy cane melted and the pixy pouted in Tina's lips. "It's all right—you just scared me is all. I didn't think you'd heard." Then she stood on her toes and whispered in the older girl's ear. But Tina whispered loud enough for Buck to hear. "Don't worry. I know you came down here to spoon around. I won't tell. I'll keep a secret."

Buck rubbed his knuckles. "You better." The sprite might sport a shiner yet. Tina glanced over her shoulder and then went back to Drew's ear. She whispered low. Drew nodded very seriously and Tina giggled.

"Well?" Both girls looked at him, laughter in their eyes and the fun-house door slammed in his face. Drew took his hand again.

"Never you mind." Her woman's eyes, Indian scout's honor, capped his question mark; he never asked again. She was not smiling and her face came forward and she kissed him on the mouth. If Tina's presence did not bother her, it did not bother Buck. He kissed her back; her tongue slid and he tasted it.

"Oh my . . ." Tina dangled on the hook. Buck was not looking, but his sister sounded pleased and slightly awed. Drew broke the kiss and turned to Tina. "For your edification."

"Thank you." Tina stood there watching them and Buck realized that his sister was not long off for this. As if surmising much the same, Tina thumbed her nose at him and scrambled to the roots of the riverbank. She reached the steep bank and gripped her hands into the tangled soil, then jumped back as though she had touched the cold face of the dead. She squatted down low and peered on the dark smooth shale of the riverbank. Buck saw something at her toes and came close, gently edging his sister a step away so the moonlight fell full at their feet.

A pretty green garter snake, silvery in the moonlight, lay partly curled on the shale bank, belly up, its arrow head twisted at an angle.

Buck looked up at the tangled roots to where the trees grew thick in the bank. Pieces of twig and leaves were still in Tina's hair. "You must'a brought him down with you when you came crashing through. Looks like his neck is broke."

"Oh, Bucky, he's lovely . . ." Then the thought of it ran through Tina. "We *killed* him. But we never meant to." She looked at Drew who was now standing close, eyes down to the snake.

"Drew, I didn't *mean* to kill him. Is it bad?"

Drew was very serious. "That's a matter of opinion. Some people, they say it's bad luck. As for me, I never like to see a wild thing die that doesn't have to. These garter snakes are wily critters; they're awfully good at playing dead."

Drew fished in the pocket of her frock and pulled out the stub of a candle, not even an inch of wax. She blew the lint from it and pinched the tallow around the wick. From the same pocket she pulled a match. She held the wooden match between her fingers and looked at the blue-and-white tip. "My last one."

Then she gripped Buck by the wrist, her fingers tight around his skin. Drew pulled him down to his knees, shins against the cool shale rock. The dead snake lay between them. "The Devil don't know all the tricks."

The matchhead flared against the shale and sputtered sulfur, smoking yellow. The tallow on the pinched wick ran and the candle caught. The candlelight glowed beyond Drew's fingers, fighting back the moon. Tallow gathered at the base of the short wick, a tiny cup of waxy tears.

"Here." She held the candle stub out to him, and he took it between his fingers, careful not to drop it. Drew shifted the weight on her haunches.

"Come on now, stop fooling. We can see you're just begging for our sympathy." She was talking to the snake, her head bent close, as if the dead thing could hear. Buck's arm was stiff, awkward as he held it out, gingerly holding the candle above the ground. His knees were cold against the shale bank and his fingers trembled, letting the silver wax run over the lip and fall tracks and helped them slip along. When he touched Drew, she looked over her shoulder and made the noise to reassure him. They came to the campfire. The fire had dimmed and Mrs. Moon was alone, building it up herself. After a few sticks flared on the coals, Mrs. Moon crawled into the tent. Lomax, nowhere to be seen, was apparently in the tent as well. Tina stood off down the sandy patch, just out of reach of the fire's light. Buck touched the cleft of Drew's buttocks once more and she turned to face him. Pressing her thighs up against his, she kissed him again. Tina began to walk home. "Pa said it was all right for you to camp at our place tomorrow." Tina wandered away.

"It's safer." Buck touched her thigh.

Drew kissed him again. "Tomorrow."

Tina and Buck slipped quietly under the water tower and away . . . creeping past the Bulls' workhouses and toward their father's farm.

A screech owl, ruffled red and brown, dropped out of the darkness, behind them in the quiet of the nighttime land.

The owl swooped down along Yellow River, its shadow passing over the silver water and the dark ochre of the riverbank grass. The owl pulled its wings, dropping to the bank by the U.S. Route and the bridge that spanned the river. The owl hobbled down the steep bank and vanished in the shadow of the bridge's ironwork where the dead man floated, snared on a concrete piling, his eyes closed like snuffed lanterns, his limbs soggy with the water. The faraway rattle of a living man limping fell on the dead man's plugged ears and the owl rested under the bridge. In the shadow two amber beads glowed like tarnished pearls and then vanished. The owl closed its eyes.

Moss Greene's farmhouse was quiet and asleep. No lights burned. The clapboard wagon was parked in the middle of the yard and unhitched. Moss Greene's happy black Labrador with soft fur behind the ears slept on the porch, snoring deep and sound. He still snored as his skull was crushed with a crowbar. The bone caved in. He died and blood ran down the porch. Dog blood. Red.

Gasoline splattered on the dog's fur and ran in the wound. Splattered along the porch, in the door frame, the windowsills, splashed against the clapboard. The air reeked, soaked volatile: gas. And a match.

Flared, thrown dancing, lighted. Caught. Fire-devil running. Caught. The windowsills leaping. The door frame burned in a square hole. The dry wood crackled. The house was still waiting, quiet and asleep. The porch was gone in a wave, the dog carcass black under the flame, skin smoking, but the house was still silent. The wood smoke drifted in a cloud across the front yard and wafted against the barn wall, seeping through the clapboard cracks.

Inside the barn the two great mares jolted in their stalls, the wood cracking. Bit pieces linked to reins fell from hooks in the timber, catching across one mare's neck and shoulders. The two horses splintered their stalls' sides and more tack fell, open headgear and tangled traces. The wood joints broke and the stalls collapsed and inside the barn the two dappled mares cantered in the smoke, braying. One was tangled in traces and headgear, the other had bit and reins slung across her shoulders.

Fire smoke drifted into the barn through an open crack in the sliding door. The mare with the bit and reins jolted her way to the open crack, hoofs pawing at the wood. She nosed the door with her great head and the siding slid on its rails. She cantered out into the yard, the fire heat hitting her in a hot cloud.

A man rushed across the light of the flame and she reared, and then her sister bolted from the barn, the head tack and traces flying from her shoulders like phantom whips. The two great mares turned on the man and backed him toward the burning house. They reared at the heat and swung off, galloping into Moss Greene's fields.

The house's roof shingles bent in the heat. Footsteps backed away, limping. A blue woolen watchcap dropped to the ground. The footsteps fell again, one after another, fell limping into the night and were gone. The roof caved in and the fire soared, billowing black smoke, laced orange and rolling into a lit sky. Window glass melted—the dog carcass charred, glowing. Off in the night air across the fields two horses neighed and galloped, their hooves' heavy rumble on the ground. The blue woolen watchcap lay in the dirt, smudged with grime, innocent and blindly silent.

Under the Bedclothes

IF YOU LOVE ME AS I LOVE YOU,
NO KNIFE SHALL CUT OUR LOVE IN TWO!

"Fire!"
"Fire!"
"Fire!"

Lepke was the first to see the smoke rising in the distance, north of his grain elevators, an evil smudge against the blue dawn sky. He stood in the screen door of his diner. "I said *fire*, goddammit! *FIRE!*" Sheriff Tate came from his house near the square, buckling on his holster and buttoning up his fly. "Where?"

And then he saw. "Lepke, wake up Hanson. Git Lowell." Tate dashed to his car and turned the handle on the siren bolted to the passenger door. The siren howled in the morning. Someone shouted in the rooming house. Preacher appeared. The Adjuster Sykes came downstairs, hiking up his suspenders. Eve hung out her upstairs window. Tate kept the siren going, wailing away.

The first carload of the Blue Vista Flats Volunteer Bucket Brigade hauled off in Tate's car. The second carload followed in Adjuster Sykes' Studebaker, throwing dust in the air as the rubber squealed. The Studebaker jolted down the dirt road, bumping over the railroad tracks. Sykes saw buckets dangling out the windows of the car ahead, axes bristling, clanging against the metal doors. Sykes slammed on the brakes and swerved around the Sheriff's car, stopped in the farmhouse yard. No one got out of the car. The sky was misted with smoke over the rubble. Little flames still licked among the charred remains. There was not so much as a skeleton left of Moss Greene's farmhouse. The ruin, beams tipped and walls collapsed, still gave off the acrid gas stink. Grass was burned and charred around the edges of the house. Sheriff Tate got out of his car. The others followed. Too late, they stared at the embers.

Then they saw the bodies. Four bodies lay behind the house. Their skin was sooty but unburned. Not a blister raised on the flesh. Sykes crept close for a better look. The ogling was indecent, but Sykes stared bald-eyed all the same. Moss Greene, twisted on his side, clung to the ground, a clump of field grass clenched in his dead fist. Liza, his wife, lay on her face. One child, a little boy, had his eyes squeezed tightly shut; a tear had long since evaporated in a streak down his face. The last child, a girl, stared straight up to the sky, her blue eyes plastered open, gazing. They were dead all right. But unsinged, unscathed; their flesh was waxen, but not burned, asleep without breathing—not death. Sykes hated the stillness of the bodies; it could have been the smoke that killed them, not the fire. On their last breaths they could have crawled that far. Maybe.

"Git the bodies." Tate put himself in charge. "And wet down whatever's still hot." Some men went with buckets over to the water pump. Sykes got in his car and backed it up closer to the bodies sprawled on the ground. Preacher stood next to the driver's open window. "You'll want company for the ride to town."

Preacher understood. Sykes nodded. His stomach turned at the thought of driving in a car full of stiffs, no matter how well preserved. A human bucket chain started dousing the charred remains. Clouds of steam hissed up from the ruins, swirling with the smoke.

Sheriff Tate supervised the dousing and glanced at Moss Greene's barn. The structure had not even caught or blistered. Hay rake, tractor and hay on the auction block not a day before; Moss Greene granted a reprieve from the banker's levy; and now, suddenly, the reprieve cut short, charred and broken in a summer's fire. Tate rubbed the skin under his nose. Some reprieve. Not a goddamn day later and the real taxman shows up, the one with no face who comes in the night. If yesterday . . . if yesterday he had brought the goddamn Bulls down to the church and run a real goddamn auction with no penny this and no penny that, nobody'd be dousing the goddamn house. Moss Greene would a been on the road, but he'd be alive. Tate took a deep breath. Christ . . . he could run a second auction tomorrow, half the people would show up with Yohanna Johns and Baskum first in line, trying to get their mitts on what they missed the day before. Wouldn't be the first time people bought the same goods twice. Tate took another deep breath and tried to let the feelings pass.

Round the side of the barn near the edge of Moss Greene's field, the black Labrador crept out of the cornstalks. Tate saw the dog, its muzzle wet and glistening in the sun. He walked toward the barn's corner with half a notion about finding the Greenes' dog a new home—Drake Walker might take the hound in. Tate stopped cold ten paces from where the dog sat at the edge of the cornfield and blinked its eyes. A crazy matted crease cut across the dog's skull. A wound cracked bone, not open and running, but closed and healed, a seam holding the black Labrador's brains in place. Tate took another step, hand out, giving the dog a good sniff as he approached.

The dog snarled, its black lips curling, white canines exposed. Its mottled gums were running wet and the dog's mean throaty rasp seemed to run right up Tate's outstretched hand. Tate pulled back his hand right quick. The dog's growl rose to a higher desperate pitch. Tate let it be and slowly took two steps back from the cornfield's edge and the corner of the barn. The dog's jowls twitched high up over a fang and one paw scratched at the dirt. Tate touched the gun butt of his holster.

"Sheriff? Hey, Sheriff!" Lepke was walking away from the smoking farmhouse ruins. A cigarette dangled from Lepke's lips. "Found this in the grass."

Tate left the corner of the barn and met Lepke halfway. Lepke held a blue woolen watchcap; he twisted it inside and out, stretching the knit. Tate took the cap from Lepke's hands.

"We got a crazed dog on the loose. Put out the word. Might have to shoot him."

Lepke was still staring at the watchcap. "Dog?"

Tate looked back to the cornfield, but the snarling hound was gone, its paw marks scattered in the dirt.

In his Goods Store a cloud of cigarette smoke swirled around Hanson's dry prune face. He dropped the butt and ground it out on the floorboards. Most people made their own coffins; of course relatives were called in at a moment of need, supplying their handiwork. But Hanson had bought four coffins from a traveling salesman some years back and had stashed them under more immediate goods somewhere in the further reaches of his store. He seemed to remember buying two adult coffins and the salesman throwing in two children's pine boxes into the bargain. When he finally unearthed the pine boxes under a stack of corsets and brassieres he recalled the salesman's pitch.

Finest wooden overcoats in the state. Guaranteed for life.

Heh. Heh.

Keep out the ground sweat—lacquered inside and out. Not to mention our special feature.

Special feature?

The knell, my good man.

On the two adult caskets death bells were fixed. A wire ran inside each box. *"You twist the wire round the pinky of the dear deceased."* Salesmen love to explain. They'll explain anything.

"Just in case you've made a mistake. Heh. Heh."

A mistake? What guff was this?

"Why a spasm of nerve dropsy, my good fellow. Scourge of fainthearted women, epileptics, neurotics, common in France and points farther east, paralysis of mind and body, a nervous disorder."

So what of it?

"Dammit Mister! They wake up six feet under."

Hanson knew a good thing when he saw it. "I'll take it. And the others, too." And so he did. Hanson dragged the first casket out into the middle of the store. The screen door opened behind him. Ollie Cottle stood watching the Goods Store owner struggling with the bulk. "I think, Ollie," Hanson dragged another casket out, "we've finally found a use for these."

"So Ah heard."

"Maybe I'll even get the county to pay for 'em. I did pay for them once, you know."

"Ah remember."

"Do you?"

Hanson pulled the wire and the bell rang over the coffin lid, bright and rich. Hanson looked at Cottle as the bell died away. "Scourge of millions."

Cottle left Hanson tinkering with his bells. The sight of the coffins, especially the little ones, made him tight in the chest. The air in his windpipe was harsh like smokestack discharge, venting in the sky. When Cottle entered the garage and laid his hands on the Model A's engine hood, he breathed easier, and the fumes from the oil spilled on the concrete floor seemed sweet and fresh, better by far than Hanson's stuffy Goods Store.

The Model A's engine was a mess. Sludge and grime were thick and grainy all over the casing. Some of the wires from the distributor cap were cracked, the metal shining through. First things first. Cottle slid in the driver's seat and got ready to push the starter. If the battery was dead, time to give it some juice. He jiggled the stick shift into neutral. Cottle noticed a small metal sleeve, three inches by two inches, with a clear plastic window. The metal sleeve hung by a cheap metal chain under the dashboard near the steering column. Cottle touched the metal wafer and looked through the plastic: the Model A's registration.

DEPARTMENT OF MOTOR VEHICLES OF THE STATE OF DELAWARE

Car #: 542113 Registrant: Mrs. Landau Moon
Vehicle Type: A, Ford
Seats 4 Passengers
Fuel: gasoline/gasahol
Signature:
A. Landay Moon

DATE: Oct. 11, 1927
EXPIRATION: Oct. 10, 1928

////////////////////////
//   //
// AUTHORIZATION   //
//   //
//   Dept. M. V.   //
//   DELAWARE   //
////////////////////////

    Cottle fingered the metal sleeve, rubbing the spot where the expiration date showed through the yellowing plastic. Five years had passed since anyone had bothered getting the car registered. Not very wise. The law was getting touchy about those things. But that was Sheriff Tate's business. If Tate wanted registration, he could damn well ask for it hisself. No point in bothering Mrs. Moon about it. Only Sheriff Tate really bothered about that law. And his law didn't seem to bother Mrs. Moon much anyhow. Cottle pressed the starter button and heard the click-click of the generator. The car's battery was dead, its juice drained overnight.

    "How long will it take to fix it?" Mrs. Moon, in the darkness of the garage, gave Cottle the willies. Her eyes were big as fried eggs and they followed him whichever way he poked around the Model A.
    "That's hard to say. You got a touchy sit-too-ayshun." Ollie Cottle glanced at her for a second, meeting her eyes, and then closed the hood over the engine. The garage was cool seclusion; the daylight burned the air outside. Now the cocoa man with oily hands stroked the metal hood. "Needs a new part."
    "What part?"
    "A gas-get."

"How long to fix it?"

"Dat's de thing, you see. Ah put in the part, but your car, she still be dead. No fixin' and no good."

Cottle would not look at her. Oily hands rubbed against his bib-jeans. He had money on his mind.

"How much?"

Cottle brightened a little. "Well, you gimme ten dollars now and Sheriff Tate won't bother you."

"How much later?"

"Double sawbuck, if she feel like being fixed. If de car wanna stay dead, we sell it for scrap."

"And what after that?"

Cottle patted the Model A, feeling the metal—knowing how it could run—what made the jangle work. "If it get well ma'am, you drive outta here. But, if she go for scrap, you get half the sale."

"Pay him."

Drew, her skin's heat rippling off her body in a wave, came into the garage out of the light. From out of a brown leather purse she handed Cottle two five-dollar gold pieces.

"Where you get dat?" Money was money; it had a look, a taste and a smell. Gold never walked in the same parade. Cottle held the coins in his palm. "I ain't seen pieces like dis since de Army—dey all supposed to be wid Uncle Sam."

"Ain't you heard?" Drew was cool as cream, the skin of her throat drawn from butter. Cottle's eyes suddenly gleamed, sparkling with amusement.

"Yeah, Ah heard. Fools rush where d'angels a-feared to tread."

Hanson appeared in the garage door, his hands thrust into his pockets. His wrinkled face seemed wrung like a dishcloth into a leer. "Fools and angels . . . such philosophy . . . " The wrinkled dish cloth dripped as he looked at the money and then at Mrs. Moon. "Those are very pretty coins."

Buck drove the Walker pickup onto Hanson's Garage ramp, and Tina hopped out the passenger side. Buck idled the car and leaned his arm on the window; the window ledge pressed the muscle and it corded up his shoulder in a nice sweet flex. Drew came out of the dark garage. The morning light turned her skin to honey. Buck popped the flex a little more. "Where's Lomax?"

"Back at camp." Drew brushed a wisp of hair from her forehead, the strands turning translucent in the sun. "He sleeps late."

Buck motioned for Drew and Mrs. Moon to get in the cab. Mrs. Moon sat up front with Buck. Tina and Drew climbed in the truck bed.

Lomax was awake, sitting by last night's burned-out fire. He seemed unconcerned about being left alone. His blank round face was passive; he sat like an Indian chief, cross-legged, staring over the dead campfire, past the tracks and into the endless fields to the north. He did not even turn his head when the truck ground to a halt.

After Mrs. Moon had struck camp, collapsed the tent, and thrown the bundle in the back of the truck, Lomax uncrossed his legs and stood on his feet. Drew took her brother's hand and led him to the truck; Tina, all gangles and gawks, scampered into the back, trying to help, trying not to get in anyone's way. Lomax helped himself up beside her and sat with his legs stretched out, quiet as before. Drew, back to the gate, slipped her bottom over the palms of her hands and shimmied onto the truck bed. Mrs. Moon sat again in the passenger seat.

"Damn this place," she hissed in Buck's ear. He turned to look at her. The animal in the woman's eyes was dripping out like a running sore—forehead furrowed, a snarl curling over her top lip like smoke from a dying cigarette. "Those Bulls would've got us tonight for sure. Friends or no friends. Note or no note."

Buck turned away from her face and made no comment. He started the pickup and headed back over the trestle for the County Road. Mrs. Moon now relaxed beside him, her anger dissolving in the air. Buck's spirit lightened and then his stomach groaned, an empty squeeze for lack of bacon and eggs. Out of the corner of the pickup's windshield, he noticed a black smudge in the early-morning sky over Moss Greene's place, and Buck wondered what Moss was having for breakfast.

Adjuster Sykes stopped the Studebaker at a mailbox on the U.S. Route a mile west of Blue Vista Flats. The rusted metal flag was down, the box empty and the name painted on the side was barely legible: J. J. Baskum. Sykes turned in the dirt road off the main highway and drove in first gear to keep from denting the car's chassis. The road ran straight into the fields where a small wooded cluster engulfed the rutted track. On the far side of the trees was Baskum's house. More fields, and off in the distance another wooded area at the back of Yellow River's flow. Sykes cut the engine and in the leaves overhead a cicada shattered the silence, razzing like a buzz-saw.

J. J. Baskum owned a two-story house, shingled and proper, painted white and in need of another coat. The shutters on each window were thrown open and the windows raised. White curtains hung over the sills, pulled from the house by its own draft. Sykes looked at the corner of the farmhouse and then realized the startling difference in this house and Baskum's dirt road. Every fifty yards back to the U.S. Route wood poles fifteen feet high were driven into the ground. The last pole was driven in by the corner of the house and tilted in the soft dirt. Black cable snaked through a hole cut in the corner of the building. J. J. Baskum had electricity; not only that, he owned a telephone. Sykes had seen the telephone poles with their power lines on the U.S. Route, but he hadn't noticed that none of the dirt roads carried power. Baskum's was the first.

The Sheriff's office had power. So did the First Blue Vista Flats Bank. But then they were housed in the same building. Lepke's Diner had power and so must Hanson's Garage. But none of the houses had power and that seemed natural, but Baskum's house did have power, and that did not seem natural. So, J. J. Baskum needed a phone. Who the hell did he talk to?

As Sykes stood under the grove of trees and listened to the humming of the insects, Baskum's front door opened. In the darkness of the doorway a man was standing with his back turned. A woman shrieked, "Never! Never in a million years!"

The stout man with the dirty white tie spun around and took one step from his door to the ground. Something flew out of the open door. A mophead. The mophead hit Baskum on the back of the neck. He stumbled down the stoop, and fell like a fat saddleback porker, sprawling in the dirt. The door slammed shut with a final bang. Sykes stayed in the shade of the trees. "J. J. Baskum?"

Baskum looked up from the ground and pulled the mophead from around his neck. He stood, dusting off his clothes. A gold tooth flashed when he spoke. "I'd introduce you to my wife, but I guess that's about as close as you're likely to come." Baskum shook some dirt off his tie. "For today at least."

"Hell hath no fury like a woman."

Baskum took a step forward and came toward the trees. "You may have a point. . . . " He stared at the blond man for a moment, and then at Sykes' Studebaker. "Farm Bureau, eh?"

"Agricultural Adjustment Administration. My name's Sykes."

"Yes, I'd heard. Didn't know your name though. You come from town? Hell's bells was ringing."

"There was a fire."

"That so? Who?"

"Moss Greene's place."

"Any damage?"

"They're dead."

Baskum looked at the ground. Up in a tree a woodpecker went tektektek . . . He hiked up his pants and shifted from foot to foot. He rubbed the back of his neck. He glanced back at the house as if he'd forgotten something. Then he looked at Sykes, his gold tooth flashing. "What the hell do you want?"

Sykes took a step out of the grove and a shaft of sunlight fell over his shoulders. "That depends, Mr. Baskum. You broke even last year, with a little left over. You overproduced and that's not uncommon; the prices dropped and you just barely made it. What about this year? You feel like making money?"

"Now you listen, Mr. Adjuster. I'm not with the National Farm Union, or any of those Reds. And there ain't a farmer alive that don't wanna make money. I'm not sitting on my ass waiting for relief, and I almost got my hands on another thresher, but the goddamned Eastern Range bastards fixed a penny auction for their pal, Moss Greene. If Triple A can get me a goddamned thresher, maybe we can talk."

"You got loans, Mr. Baskum."

Baskum waved his hands in the air. "You're damn right I got loans. I got loans coming outta my ears. The only reason that little shit Parker Watts doesn't close me down is 'cause I pay up on time. If I miss once, the shit-picker and the goddamned insurance companies'll close me down, throw my tenants off the land, and pull out the goddamned telephone." Baskum took a breath and looked back at the house again. "Quite frankly, I wouldn't miss the goddamned phone."

Sykes stifled a smile. "I was meaning to ask you about that. Not too many people out here own a phone."

Baskum kicked the mophead and it jumped from his foot, landing in the middle of the yard. "Aw, it's my wife's. She wanted a phone, in case I drop dead somewhere, they could call her up and tell her." He rubbed his face with his hands. "Now since I haven't dropped dead, she just calls me at the diner."

"You have insurance?"

Baskum sighed. "Five years ago I had all kinds of insurance. Equipment Insurance. Fire Insurance. Life Insurance. Livestock Insurance. You name it. And it's all been put up, like everybody else. Collateral." Baskum paused and took a breath. "But maybe if the Farm Price Index keeps going up, I'll have more at the end of the year."

The leaves in the trees rustled like rushing water. Baskum shifted his foot over the ground and overturned several small pebbles, brown and black. A cloud passed over the sun and the shaft of sunlight fell from Sykes' shoulders, the color dying in the fields. Baskum looked at the sky, searching for the wisp of cloud which threw the shadow. "When's the funeral?"

Sykes wasn't about to give up on J. J. Baskum. The fat farmer might yet see some sense. Yohanna Johns was going to be the tough one. Johns' farmhouse was very large. Ten rooms at least, with a porch that ran around the entire building. Clotheslines hung from the porch posts, and laundry swung from the clothespins, dangling helter-skelter, shirts by their cuffs, pants from their beltloops, long Union Suits (wrong season) pinned by the flap in the rear, as if some strange demented housewife had thrown the clothes every which way, a laundry circus, tightrope walkers slipping on the wire and plunging headlong.

Two of the windows in the front of the house were broken. The porch leading to the front door seemed battered in, trampled by a platoon of muddy boots, the floorboard paint worn away. Cow flop was strewn between the house and the barn; Sykes could see a moist seepage from under the door of the milkhouse. The milkhouse door opened and one of Johns's sons came out, swinging an empty pail. The young man was wearing knee-high rubber boots, the kind you wear without shoes. He stopped and looked at the Studebaker.

"How do you do?" Sykes was all smiles. "I'm from the Farm Bureau."

The young man looked at Sykes and then looked at the car. He stuck his toe under a cow patty and, with the grace of a football place-kicker, lofted the pancake into the air. The cow flop sailed over the hood and splattered onto the Studebaker's windshield. Parts of the dried patty broke off, but the wet center clung to the glass and dripped onto the windshield wipers. The young man passed the car, ignoring Sykes, dropped the milk pail on the porch and kicked off his boots before vanishing into the house in his stockinged feet. Sykes looked at his car as the cow flop settled on the windshield. At least the kid had not fouled the driver's side.

"Who the hell are you?"

Yohanna Johns. The geezer stood in the door, his back somewhat curved. Behind him the shitkicker grinned ear-to-ear.

"I'm from the Farm Bureau."

Johns took a step out on the porch and let the screen door slam in his son's face. "I can see that." He looked at the Studebaker. "You got shit on your car."

"That's true." Sykes was ready to admit anything. The cow flop settled nicely in the thin gutter that rimmed the bottom of the windshield. "Like it fell outta the sky."

Yohanna Johns did not smile. "You can save your breath, Mr. Sykes. I ain't plowin' up a third on a promise."

"You knew my name."

Johns turned to the screen door and opened it. His son backed off into the shade of the house. "Knew it yesterday." The screen door slammed.

Sheriff Tate heard about the Moon coins soon enough. Lepke told him. Lepke had heard it from Hanson, and Hanson had seen it with his own eyes. Two five-dollar gold pieces, paid in cash, coin on the barrelhead, indisputable, hard as nails, clean as a virgin, negotiable as whiskey, for all debts public and private. Ollie Cottle took the money, smiling, handed it directly to Hanson and broke out a new gasket.

"Where are the coins now?" Tate was sitting in his office. Lepke was still expansive, elastic with the news. Tate was bored in those early-morning hours. With the bodies resting in Preacher's church, he had nothing to do. The blue woolen watchcap dangled from a hook on the coatstand.

"The bank." Lepke was breathless. Sheriff Tate lifted himself out of the swivel chair. The chair squeaked, almost wheezing. They adjourned to the bank, Lepke on the Sheriff's heel. No doubt Lepke was slightly disappointed. Any order of the boot was canceled. As long as the Moon woman could pay, she could stay.

Upon Hanson's request, Parker Watts had opened the bank early and had counted the coins in a slow but deliberate manner. One coin. Two coins. Five dollars each. That's ten dollars. Parker Watts had scratched out a deposit receipt. Hanson still stood before the teller's cage as Sheriff Tate and Lepke entered; the Goods Store owner held the deposit slip. The paper was now creased and slightly moist as the perspiration from Hanson's hands did its damage. Parker Watts sat in his teller's cage, a jeweler's lens screwed into his eye; he examined the coins under the light of a green-shaded desk lamp. Hanson worried the deposit slip with his fingers, ruining the paper document, heedless of the fact that the money record was an important item to preserve. Hanson sensed that Parker Watts' scrutiny of his coin was a little out of the ordinary and that perhaps a pronouncement might be forthcoming from the banker's lips, that in fact the coin was a fraud, fool's gold, paid to a fool nigger, handed over to the fool nigger's fool employer, and ultimately passed along to the only fool remaining unfooled: the banker, Parker Watts. Hanson worried the deposit slip some more, and the paper began to disintegrate in earnest.

Parker Watts coughed, dropped the jeweler's glass from his

eye and noticed Lepke watching Hanson, Hanson shredding the deposit slip and Sheriff Tate, a step back, watching it all.

"Is the money good?" Hanson croaked.

Watts leaned back in his tall teller's chair and looked at the Sheriff. "Oh, it's good all right."

Hanson seemed pleased.

Lepke was in a dither. "What's with the microscope?"

Watts did not reply. He took one of the coins in his fist and flipped it into the air. He caught the gold in his palm and slapped the back of his hand. "Heads or tails, gents? Heads or tails?"

"Git on with it," Hanson snapped.

Watts dropped the coin on the teller's ledge and it clattered with a high sweet sound against the other money. "You didn't bother to look at the coin's minting date, did you, Hanson?"

Hanson wasn't sure precisely what a "minting date" was; he reasoned that in this particular case, a "minting date" had little to do with confectionary products. He was not about to hazard a guess and risk looking foolish. Watts seemed pleased with himself.

"This five-dollar gold piece was minted by the United States Treasury in Washington, D.C., sixty-six years ago. The date on the coin's face is 1866, one of the first mint-runs after the Civil War. I think it would not be unreasonable to assume that we've all heard of the Civil War. I frankly," Watts paused, "I frankly have never seen one of these."

The fan blades spun slowly overhead; their barely audible whop-whop stirred nothing but the flies.

"Is the coin valuable?" Tate was catching on.

"Valuable?" Watts shrugged. "That depends on how you look at it. Value is based on trading. This coin," he held it up for everyone to see, "was traded for a gasket and as a down payment for services to be rendered. On the other hand, the coin might also have been traded for the C&C Railroad, the land around the railroad, the railroad's operating personnel, its corporate headquarters, its liabilities, its available cash, and the Chairman of the Board's cufflinks. Moreover, as the good Sheriff is well aware, even the possession of such a trinket is a crime."

Watts smiled; the buttons on his vest seemed to glow as though polished by a drill sergeant and his tie plumed stiff and proper. The peacock in Parker Watts posed for a photograph, but his mouth kept moving. "However, Hanson here bought a gasket with it."

"Damn!" Hanson cawed. Tobacco saliva speckled on his lips. "Give it back here." He thrust the wilted deposit slip through the hole in the teller's cage and waved it in Parker Watts' face.

"Not so fast," Watts said. ' This coin is now in the custody of the bank and on principle has to be turned over to the United States Government."

Lepke gaped, tapping his toes. Hanson reared himself to his full height. "We have some law in this country, and I say you have tricked me."

"Yes, the law, the law," Watts agreed. "There is indeed a law. Somewhere. The coin is now tendered at its face value of five dollars. Two coins. Ten dollars. If I were to proceed with an appraisal of this coin, I would go through the bank's channels. They would order me to proceed to the capital where an appraiser would meet me. I would get my traveling money and expenses for the trip. Total cost, maybe thirty dollars. I would then get a pat on the back, maybe an office at the company's flagship branch in the capital, and possibly even a new suit." Watts paused and listened to the other men breathing.

"Hanson would no doubt get himself a lawyer, if he could afford one, and begin proceedings. In this case a lawyer might even be retained on contingency. The bank, using its own lawyers in defense, would pay them from the interest collecting on this coin. More than sufficient. There's an even match for you—the proceedings would last for years and years, and all I'd have was a pat on the back and a new suit. However—"

Hanson's eyes brightened. Watts continued, "However, if we were to . . . forget about this initial deposit, and . . . if you were to open a safe deposit box with this coin and . . . we were to put its unknown value in escrow, so to speak . . . we could get ourselves a very discreet appraiser who would find us a very discreet foreign buyer, and quite possibly we could discreetly retire in the fortnight."

"We?"

"Yes, Hanson. We. The four of us. Only we four now know of this coin's potential value. By making this offer I am committing the illegal act of conspiring to annul a legal deposit and to defraud the company's Blue Vista Flats Bank. I therefore require a percent of its value. Sheriff?"

Hanson, Watts, and Lepke now looked at Tate. The Sheriff

said nothing. Watts tried to clear up the matter. "Sheriff, you may now arrest me on conspiracy and fraud with intent to embezzle the Blue Vista Flats Bank and the Republic Banking Corporation of America and the United States Treasury of an unspecified sum. I'll go quietly."

Lepke exploded. "Like hell you will!"

Sheriff Tate stroked his chin for a moment and looked at Hanson. "It's up to you, Hanson. Do you want a lawyer?"

Hanson shuffled his feet. "How much did you say that was worth?"

"I was just guessing," Watts replied. "The coin is definitely worth more than a gasket."

Hanson stared hard at Lepke. "I ain't worried about Watts or Tate." He wouldn't take his eyes off Lepke. "But Lepke, you better keep your trap shut."

"It's shut," Lepke croaked. "It's shut."

Watts was pleased and got down to business. "We split four ways. I'll arrange for the appraiser. I know a man in New York . . ."

Sheriff Tate had walked to the bank's window and was looking out into the square. He saw Preacher Simon go into his church. Four women, his wife among them, were standing in front of Hanson's Goods gabbing to beat the band, obviously waiting for Hanson's return. No one in the bank spoke. He heard some foot-scraping, and Lepke coughed. Tate could see his wife's animated face; her hands fluttered when she talked. If the coin was half as valuable as Watts thought, there was no doubt about it, June Tate would lose a husband and Blue Vista Flats would lose a Sheriff. "There's something you forgot." Tate tapped the glass window. "Don't any of you care where in hell that Moon woman picked them up?"

Adjuster Sykes drove into the Blue Vista Flats square with a swarm of flies buzzing around the car. The flies had followed him all the way from Yohanna Johns' place. They were everywhere: on the windshield, both sides, buzzing around his head, talking in his ears. He tried speeding the car on the open road, but the flies just fell back to the rear windshield and waited for the car to slow. He parked in front of the barbershop. The square was nearly empty, except for a few women, suspended in their gossip, chatting on the Goods Store porch. Hens. Cluck. Cluck. From behind the screen door of the barbershop he heard a woman's voice.

"What happened, Mr. Adjuster, you run into a shitstorm?"

Sykes got out of the car and stood several paces away; he watched the flies hover. He saw the vague outline of the woman behind the screen door. She lived upstairs. Across the hall from his room. Her name was Eve. She was somebody's sister-in-law.

"That's not very funny."

"I know . . . I know." Eve pressed the point. "It's a brand-new government, and that's the brand-new government's car."

Sykes went back to the Studebaker and rolled up the window on the driver's side, trapping the flies within.

"I think what you need," Eve added, "is a bucket of water."

That much was obvious. "And maybe a new interior."

Eve opened the barbershop door and leaned against the door jamb. "Sprinkle the inside with booze." Eve did not look as if she belonged in the broad daylight. "Flies hate the stuff."

Maybe she was not half-bad after all. "Didn't know that." Sykes was open for any suggestions.

Eve shrugged and the strap of her dress fell down her shoulder. "Maybe I'm wrong . . ."

Sarah Walker looked down at the tin basin nailed to the wooden counter in her kitchen. A tiny centipede struggled out of the standing water and over the lip of the counter. Sarah took a broad potato peel from the pile at her elbow and crushed the small spiny worm as it ambled along. Two of the centipede's legs still waved, and Sarah shuddered, the tremor running down her legs. With a paring knife she scraped the potato sliver, the bilous guts, and wiped them off onto the peelings. "Eat good." The centipede's legs trembled again. "Eat good in heaven."

Moss Greene. Owner.

Liza Greene. Wife of Owner.

Moss and Liza Greene. Dead. The tenants had come after Buck and Tina left to fetch the Moons. Drake had been in the barn and came outside to see his two tenants standing by the garden, waiting. Drake spoke with them for a moment. He listened as Ryder talked.

Sarah did not hear the words. She watched Drake come in. Burned alive and dead in heaven. Preacher to lead the congregation, then interment. Then back home and supper. Easy. Sarah peeled another potato.

The centipede's twitching leg moved once more. Then it stopped . . . the sad low song of the spiny worm dying. When she walked back of the house and passed the barn, Sarah could stand at the edge of the fields, and look west toward town. Hearing the engine of a tractor rattle out in the tamed fields, how easy the choices seemed to be. Love your husband. Love your children. Work when you have to, rest when you must, work again, neverending.

Over the tamed clods of dirt, that was where they toiled longest, not warm in Drake's bed, just a quick release, no frantic groping, that familiar satisfaction, back to work again, die in the end. What other choices? Take a stick and walk to California, past Moss Greene's smoldering ruins, waving good-bye to the blackdust smudge in the air. Drake would wake in an empty bed; he would hear Buck begin to stir, and then Tina, first up, would find no breakfast waiting, no milk from the cow, no mother coming in from the barn, only a swarm of flies hovering beyond the screen door watching. Where is the woman, child? What have you done with her? She is late.

And down the road—how far can you go once you've left? Take the last nice dress; look for work; find no work, except at a rich man's hands, but more likely not so rich. More likely a wage slave, spending that last dollar, that last piece of change, on just another piece of change. In the big cities where the girls stand in the street, watching the passing cars, saying hello to you sir, good evening. Are you a Christian? It doesn't matter. But please give Christian charity when you touch my thighs and say hello.

Nice to meet you sister, been here long?
Take a ride?
Live near here?
My wife, she's fat. You're not. You're nice.
Thank you, sir. And what's your friend's name?
You do that very well.
I learned fast. I pull, you breathe. And again. And again . . .
So what about Drake? His palms are cracked where the flesh meets the fingers. And he sticks up for his tenants. Yes, like a

Christian. But more like a man. The phantom Christian with just enough to spare, holding against his own mortgage and two others, cutting into the cash crop, eating more potatoes, hoping that the rabbits won't kill the garden. Sometimes too tired from the day for love later.

And later, he wakes from a blue nightmare, sweating in the dark house, hearing a cricket still awake. Worried in the darkness, maybe crying, laying awake never talking, not even saying that sleep is far away.

Tina. Whose blood is hers? Always watching. Will she grow black hairs at the edges of her nipples, just like her mother? Will she pull them out when she looks in the mirror? Will she let them grow so the hairs curl around her breasts? Will she wonder what a man thinks and why it's so important? Will she throw him out, if he forgets her? She was forged, like a weld. She'll stay forged even after love tears her slit. She will stay forged till a child breaks her apart like a melon and they make her eat a bit of herself. She'll eat a bit of afterbirth because the women say it's good for you. Then she'll know that flesh isn't metal. She'll be strong, but what about him?

Buck. Not a man. But soon. Firstborn, hurting much more than Tina, coming out feet first, but not entwined, not hung by the blood cord. And now he sees with almost-man eyes. Hears with almost-man ears. Speaks with almost a man voice. Sins with almost a man vice. Waiting for the proof. For the power. Manhood. To bend another over his muscled arm, to hold a woman close, till the breath is caught in his first bitch's throat.

"Ma, your lips are moving." Buck was in the kitchen. His arms were folded across his chest; Sarah noticed the muscles in his chest shifting unconscious under the skin. Through the kitchen window she could see the pickup truck parked outside. Tina was scampering in the yard making a disturbance out of nothing at all. The Moons were descending from the back of the truck, handing down the tentpole stakes and their campfire grill, passing out the what-not of their luck. Outside, Tina was a whirling nuisance but Mrs. Moon never waved her off. Inside, Buck was staring, arms corded, with wide goat eyes.

"Moss and Liza Greene are dead, Bucky." Sarah dropped the paring knife. "The children too."

Sarah watched her son's eyes narrow, so that Buck's whites were like sickbed candlelight creeping under the bedroom door.

Moss Greene. Moss Greene, dead. The notion sank between his eyes. It would be a while yet before the message settled. Sarah brushed back her hair and left Buck standing in the kitchen. She went outside into the bright daylight and stood in the shade of the back porch. Mrs. Moon threw the folded tent canvas over the truck side. The canvas fell to the ground like a heavy slap on the butt and the sound was swallowed into the dry air.

"No point in taking up yard space. The hayloft ain't bad; it's softer than the ground, and it ain't damp. Hasn't been for a month." Mrs. Moon didn't argue. A hayloft doesn't smell too bad, unless it's damp. Then it stinks; the ammonia, sweet ticklings of rot —the hay moves a step closer to manure without a cow's digestion. Like hay. Damp hay.

Sarah stepped down off the porch and started walking. She passed Mrs. Moon with a nod, passed the truck, and went along the edge of the field toward Yellow River. Sarah couldn't say she'd condone bringing people on her land without a proper welcome; no, she'd never let the children get away with it. But the Greenes were dead and the Moons were living; and sometimes the dead, still as they were, could walk all over the living. She couldn't explain to Buck, and Tina couldn't yet know the difference between crying and sobbing. But the Moon woman might and there was plenty of time to talk. The dead were walking and Sarah was leading them on, leading their ghosts like innocent children to drown them in the river.

Sarah found a place on the riverbank that was cool and dark, a tree overhanging, leaves broad and full. The bushes were tangled and thick, and she parted their stiff branches and stood on a slab of shale, the water flowing inches below. Shoes off. Dress unhooked and fallen. Brassiere gone and underpants forgotten, she sat, her warm thighs on the cool shale, and dipped a toe in the water. The water flowed brushing her toe, caressing as it kisses everything. The river air was in her head. A dragonfly appeared with big green eyes, lightning wings, veined and furious. It darted down the river and vanished in the shadow of the U.S. Route bridge that hung like a visor over the running water. The concrete pilings were damp and cracked at the waterline. The dragonfly appeared again and then shot to the sky.

The water flowed around her body and she felt it flow around her skin like a ghost of anguish. The water was wet, the grief still wetter . . . Liza Greene her face a ripple in the water, angry at the robbing fate that stole her life away, that let her sleep and never roused her to a burning house. Sarah watched the ripples in the water, watched it rinse her skin and the Greenes' nagging memory away. Man and wife were dead. Love them if you must, leave them now in the water's running . . . leave them now, and gone forever.

Over Sarah's shoulder the bushes moved, but she did not hear them. Simple's big bald head and mousy eyes were hungry at the day. He touched Meriwether's shoulder and kept him silent. They waited and watched, saw Sarah's pale skin in the daylight, watched her bathe, and hid low when she headed back to the farm.

Buck came out to the porch. Drew was holding the windchimes gently by the bar. Old Moss Greene would not let go. Buck could not shake him loose. At the auction that whalehead stranger might have bid on Moss's old tractor. What for then? What for, if the man could go and die on you? Moss Greene had left the table before the feast was over. Back in his own kitchen, Buck could break a plate and scatter food, trampling the mess into the kitchen floor. Jamming ooze in the wooden cracks, stamping again and again, spilling the gravy and pounding the roast. Stick your neck out—what did Moss Greene care now?

Drew held the windchimes before Buck's eyes. He noticed the buttercup curve of her throat, soft as sifted flour, and her fingers delicately holding the mother-of-pearl scales. Lomax was left to sit in the truck bed, to figure things out for himself. Drew ignored her brother too, and snatched the windchimes from Buck's sight. She edged past him on the porch. Fingers twitching, he almost reached for the cleft of her buttocks, deep and infinite.

The back porch of the Walker farmhouse had four posts that kept the roof propped up. The posts were painted white, and to the builder's credit and his genial fancy, a decorative molding was tacked under the porch roof's edge. A useless cosmetic construction

—wooden dowels, dozens of tiny columns, six inches apart—was nailed neatly in place to the underside of the porch roof, hanging like the lacy hem of a lady's dress. Buck had painted the damn things more than once and from experience knew that nothing gets whitewash on your face faster than a molding. But now the decorations took on a new light.

Drew stood under the porch roof, near the last post on the corner. She tied the windchimes to the molding and let them swing free, her finger striking the chimes gently once. They tinkled softly in the air, and whitewashed Buck from head to toe . . . he'd painted that dumb molding for just such a purpose. He looked around and saw Tina and Mrs. Moon go into the kitchen. He heard their voices over the windchimes' glassy clamor, but could not hear the words.

"Better than bees." Drew, better than honey, leaned against the porch post; the mother-of-pearl touched her shoulder.

"Bees?"

Drew watched the eye-light discs twist, twirl on their strings, scales chink-chink, tinkling on her shoulder. "Bees are good luck. But chimes are better. The house is blessed."

"What did we do wrong?"

That buttercup closeness spread around his ears. "What might you do?"

Buck was hopelessly lost between bumblebees and windchimes, the curve of Drew's throat, a beckoning promise, a house blessed and the stroking of the infinite swell of her fauna haunches. He couldn't even guess if she remembered. Would she coo deep again, could he ask her?

"I'll take your word for it." Like a blind singer with a hand out, the tokens clinking sightless in the cup.

Lomax had gotten down off the truck and had somehow wandered aimlessly down a cotton row. The buds were still green and had not opened; they would not flower till the first frost came. But already Buck saw the black scars of the boll weevil growing in the healthy bud, rotting it out, making the bulb putrid and soft, unfit for picking. He had seen too many scars to count. His father had seen this too, for now Drake was working harder than ever, irrigating the corn and the wheat, hoping for the bumper crop that could offset a bad yield of cotton. Lomax walking in the cotton row was pointless, idiot's entertainment. Buck had to join his father with the water wagon; he was late already.

He stepped off the porch into the dirt patch by the garden. The air was very still; the sun beating down on the crown of Buck's head made his eyes swim. Drew came to his side and took his hand. His palm was sweaty and Buck heard the windchimes clamor softly, with that glassy tingling. So useless and so clean. No breeze brushed his face, but the windchimes hailed, spellbinding his scalp, their hundred tiny songs a chorus in the sunlight. Buck glanced at the porch expecting to see his sister tapping the chimes, making them cry. But the porch was empty and the chimes had ceased to sing, hanging motionless and quiet from the molding.

"Now maybe you'll see there's good luck even with the bad." Drew's lips grazed his ear, hesitant and soft, like a painter's first stroke on canvas. She led Buck to the cotton row and presently they caught up with Lomax as he wandered, trudging aimless and slow. Lomax inched along, a two-step shuffle, not faster than a belly crawl. The doughhead boy's sleeve brushed against the cotton bulbs, grazing. Buck stopped in his tracks—what idiot's game was this?

Again Buck heard the windchimes jingling jingle jangle—no breeze and his hair was matted to his forehead. The sweat was warm; the porch empty. Drew breathed across his cheek. "Lomax is blessed too."

Buck felt the sun on his head, beating down, making his eyes swim. Lomax was far down the first row now, and as he reached the end of the cotton he turned and trudged back, his sleeves at his sides brushing the green, sickly bulbs.

"You give him water." Drew's honey oozed into his ear. "You never mind anything else and you give him water every time he comes back the row." Buck went for the water. He prayed his father would not miss him, and he knew his father would. Miss him, and find him at this stupid game—waiting to watch Lomax take the water can and slosh his muc-muc while the real work was done in the far-off field.

Drake rode the fickle tractor and pulled the water wagon till noon, the sun nearly drying out his brains. Eddy stood at the back of the hitched water wagon, holding the sprinkler hoses. Ryder pumped. They sprayed the wheat as Drake drove and cursed his son under his breath. At noon they unhitched the water wagon and each man went his own separate way. Drake headed for the house, the shade within, and Sarah's food. He stopped the tractor when he reached the barn.

Buck was down the rows of cotton, holding a water can, and the idiot boy was shuffling through the hanging bulbs. Just fooling in the cotton, damn fool boy. Drake touched his belt. Buck was big, but not that big. Not so big he could get out of a day's work while the two tenants did the work of three and the wheat was drying out. Not that big. Drake never raised his voice; he took his belt off and folded the leather into a strap.

Then he saw the windchimes hanging from the molding of the porch. He looked where the idiot boy was walking and heard the women's gab in the house over the idle motor's rumbling. He straightened out his belt and slung it over his shoulder, ready to kill the tractor and dismount. Then a twinge sneaked across the seam of his tender ribs—the air pinched in his lungs. By all God's right, he ought to have been breathing through broken bones today. And yet he worked and his fields lay watered.

Not those of his neighbor who lay waiting in a wooden box, nor his neighbor's woman who rested in the quiet hollow of her casket.

By all God's rights it might have been his own boy burned in his own bed, but now Buck wandered, safely distracted through the cotton rows with a fool companion while Moss Greene's children lay, their faces covered. Drake shut off the tractor and between his legs the machine sighed as if stretching out in sleep. Its last murmur was the tink-tink as tiny metal parts settled themselves down. Drake smiled, and the breath eased out his nose. He touched the tender stitch along his ribs. Inside, the house was cool and shaded.

Sykes dropped the wet rag into the bucket and stepped back, getting a better view of the Studebaker parked in front of the barbershop. The flies had all but vanished; a lone straggler hovered, waffling in the general vicinity of the windshield, but this fly was the last. Bart Lowell came out of the barbershop door wearing his white smock. He took off his smock and hung it on the door handle. The white smock hanging on a doorknob outside the building took on airs, as if liberated, playing hookey from a chair back or reprieved from strangling on a hatstand. Lowell rolled his sleeves down over his hairy arms.

"Thanks for the bucket."

"You can leave it outside the door." Lowell glanced at the church and then back at Sykes. "Planning to attend the service tomorrow?"

Sykes had not really thought about it. Outsiders were generally welcome, and he had after all been Engine #2 for the Blue Vista Flats Volunteer Bucket Brigade earlier that morning. Moss Greene's funeral didn't seem the type of occasion where one needed an invitation. Sykes was not even slightly religious—not that it mattered. Church, any kind of church, was an awesome numbing shrine. Sykes was the son of an upstate New York boardinghouse owner. He had been inside a church maybe twice in his life. The symbol was awesome, not the reality. God's house of humble self-sacrifice: Sykes figured he could stomach the sermon. He did not care about religion. When he slapped the poopsheet and read the bottom line, Sykes did not particularly care one way or the other.

Sykes' supervisor in the Farm Bureau gave him one piece of advice before he disappeared into the country. "First off, Moses," the supervisor said, "don't call yourself Moses. Call yourself Moe. Makes it sound like you came from anywhere—Chicago, Detroit, Des Moines. Anywhere."

Right, boss. Sykes pushed his hat up over his brow.

"Yeah, Lowell, I suppose I'll be there." He brought the bucket to the barbershop door and sat it on the pavement. "Think Lepke's in the diner?"

"Heck no. He's probably up by the grain elevators."

"Where's that?"

"Same road that goes to Moss Gr—" Lowell stopped, embarrassed. "Route 6. Take a left at the train trestle. We passed it this morning."

"Guess I wasn't watching," Sykes admitted. A slight breeze rustled the leaves at the top of the oak tree. Sykes had heard somewhere that small towns liked their scandal raw, but now that seemed an unfair observation. He wondered if Eve upstairs knew about the fire. In any case, he was not going to need the Sheriff's introduction. After all, Eve was a neighbor. Borrow a cup of sugar? What for? Never mind, Sugar. One loose woman. One Sheriff. One barber. One Preacher. That's all any town really needs. Sykes looked up to the second story of the rooming house. Eve's window was open. The soft breeze was making the white curtains in her window dance slowly on the sill.

"On the lunch hour?" Sykes wondered out loud.

Lowell grinned and drew up to Sykes, whispering as if no one was supposed to hear. "I shouldn't think so." He looked up at Eve's window, wishing his eyes could pry over the sill. "She's not going anywhere. Got all the time in the world."

Lowell moved away from Sykes. "She's my wife's sister." He smoothed back his hair, as if that explained everything. Sykes left the curb and got into the car.

"By all means," Sykes said, out the passenger window. "That's a marvelous arrangement." He started the car, backed it up, and headed for Route 6 by the side of the church. He glanced in the rear mirror. Lowell was still standing on the pavement, but he was not grinning anymore. Sykes waved.

Route 6 was rutted, but not that badly. The Studebaker moved through a wind wall of trees, down into a dip, up over a knoll and Sykes saw the black-tar water tower and Lepke's grain elevator on the far side of Yellow River. He drove over the access road attached to the trestle and stopped the car on the north side of the tracks. Weeds grew along the edge of the gravel beds and near the piles of stones of which the railbeds were made. Lepke's grain elevator was three lofty silver towers and a large square wooden shed, more like half a barn, where the produce was weighed and, if necessary, bagged. Few of the farmers had their own grain elevators, so when the time came to sell, people came from all over and turned the produce over to Lepke. They kept only what was needed for feed or private use. The rest lay in the railroad way-station, waiting to be dumped onto railroad cars for the distributors and the mill men at the capital who bought the produce at the far end.

The C&C Railroad way-station amounted to no more than three sets of tracks running east-west. One set of tracks was for trains passing through without stopping. The other two branched off the main line east of the station. One was for flatbed and rail repair: a freight car could be rolled off the main line, torn apart and refitted. The other ran beside the coal tender, the water tower and the grain elevators. Two wooden green-painted shacks were built near the Bulls' bunkhouse where the Bulls stored their tools, driving irons for the spikes, spare switch parts, storm lanterns, flags and lantern signals in the shacks. Small piles of rock gravel bed were scattered around the houses. Spare rails and stacks of rail ties lay side by side, covered with tarpaulins, ready for use; some of the rails were exposed and the metal rusted. Tar was oozing from the ties' wooden cracks heated in the sun.

The water tower was built on stilts with a mammoth metal spout, hinged so the spout could be lowered over the engine. The coal tender was as big as a house and was built on rail ties slightly higher than the engine's own tender. The coal bin used a door and chute so the coal could be scuttled into the engine's tender. Spots of tar clung to the ground, and as Sykes crossed over the three sets of rails he noticed that a pool of water had collected on the gravel under the water tower. A rusty pipe snaked up the side of the tower and Sykes tried to trace it back to the source. The pipe roughly followed the tracks down to the river. He wondered if a pumphouse was built somewhere on the riverbank that he had failed to notice.

Lepke's counting house leaned against the elevators. A window cut into the side of the building was directly adjacent to the cavernous doors, which could slide open wide enough to let in a team of horses and a rig, all piled high. A ledge was nailed to the building wall under the windowsill, where farmers could rest their elbows while Lepke filled out his ledger and completed the transaction. Lepke was sitting under the window, leaning back in an old chair. Sykes could not see his face. The restaurateur/grain merchant was holding a newspaper, the *Sioux City Star*, and from ten yards, Sykes could read the headline on the full-page spread:

RED GANG BUSTED

Farmers' Union Denies Ties

Suddenly Sykes was very glad he worked for the Government Bureau and not the union organizers. The union was not having such a good time of it.

Over the window a slate board was hung. Down one side the goods were listed.

Corn
Oats
Wheat
Cotton
Sorghum

The goods list was painted right on the slate; across the board prices could be chalked. The slate was chalk-dusted, rubbed out—no prices listed. Lepke did not take his nose out of the *Sioux City Star* even as Sykes approached, his footsteps slapping the ground.

When he reached the building, Sykes paused for a moment expecting Lepke to drop the rag sheet. He didn't. Sykes cleared his throat. Lepke rustled the paper.

"You haven't posted your prices."

Lepke dropped the paper.

"What?"

"I said, you haven't posted your prices."

Lepke stared at Sykes for a moment and then folded the paper, his concentration broken. Pointless to read. As he folded the paper for the third fold, the black ink smeared onto his hands and across the page.

"Why should I post prices? It won't matter till a day before the train comes through. And it won't matter until people dump their goods. Anyway, it'll be light hauls for the next month."

"People want to know."

Lepke sat forward in his chair and it came away from the wall, landing on the two front legs. His face was thrown into shadow. "So far, you're the only one who wants to know."

"Well, it's early in the season."

Lepke rocked back again in his chair. "You got a point." He dug in his pocket and fished out a piece of chalk. He got off the chair, stood on it and scribbled a price on the slate: WHEAT . . . . . . $2.50–b. Lepke was joking; even in the best of times no produce went for more than 20¢ a bushel.

"Think you'll get that price from the middleman?" Sykes asked.

"Between you and me," Lepke rubbed his nose, "I'll be lucky to get *any* price from the middleman." He sat back in his chair.

"Why tell me that?"

"Because you know it already."

Sykes stroked his chin. "Some people think the Index is going up."

"Yeah." Lepke understood the way of the world. "Some farmers smell like shit, too."

Sykes turned from the elevator building and started walking. "Let me know when you're going to post a price."

"Why?" Lepke called.

Sykes took a moment to answer; then he called over his shoulder, "I'll make sure they don't smother you in shit."

Sykes thought he heard a laugh, but maybe Lepke only grunted, and he kept walking back over the tracks toward his car. Sykes was out of sight of Lepke's chair when he noticed the two railroad men sitting on the hood of the Studebaker.

One was large with a big bald head and a gross belly that stretched his shirt. Sykes saw that the domed fella was making a dent in the hood of the car where he sat; the shocks were compressed and the front tire bulged. Baldy carried a nightstick.

The other Bull was skinny, wiry, red-haired and fast. The butt of a revolver curved across his waist. A face-kicker. Fall down in the dirt, the guy would kick you in the head. He might be a thousand kinds of evil, but he'd still love his mother. Or the memory of her. The type only a mother could love. While he kicked you in the teeth. Yeah, the thin one probably loved his mother.

Sykes stopped about four feet from the Studebaker. He stopped just close enough for the Bulls to think he was not afraid, but far enough for a leaping head start, if he needed to run. No sense losing his teeth to a couple of railroad geeks. The car keys were in his pocket; the new model did not have a starter button. The wiry man might catch him if he ran, but forget the fat one. The Sheriff would hear all about it, then send someone out to collect the Studebaker. Sheriff Tate might get all righteous, that I-told-you-about-the-railroad-boys stuff. Right, Sheriff. What were you saying about the *only* whore in town? The skinny guy's revolver butt pressed against the man's waistband, creasing it. Can't outrun a bullet. Maybe roll over and play dead. No, that's the perfect invitation for a face-kicker. Maybe if he knew I loved my mother too...

"You got business with us?" Baldy asked.

Forget it, can't reason with the monkeys. The big fella rolled the nightstick up his thighs under the palms of his hands.

"No." Keep calm, keep calm. "No business with you."

The skinny one screwed up his face like a prune. He wanted to smack something. All he needed was an excuse. "Anything on these tracks is our business."

Baldy rolled the nightstick back down his thighs. "Nice car you got there, Mister Adjuster."

"Glad you like it." Sykes, cool as ice, hiked up his pants. "Come into town tonight. I'll buy you a milkshake and take you for a ride."

The thin bugger slid off the hood of the car, his feet touching the ground softly; he favored one foot. Sykes did not move. Any drifter would take a step back. That was fatal—take a step back, show you're afraid, the creep would definitely strike. The widget's breath smelled like rotten food sitting in a cat's basket. "Next time you come around here, Sharpy, you best have good reason."

Baldy slid off the car hood; the car body sprang back, easing up and down on the shocks. His eyes glistened, the crows' feet curved chipper and cheery, but his mouth fell. "You listen to Meriwether, Mister Adjuster. Be a shame if the government lost a fine man such as yourself over some little misunderstanding."

Meriwether jerked his hand across his belt, his palm brushing the revolver. Then the skinny shit eased off, hands still at his sides. He backed away, almost smirking. The big bald man strode toward the bunkhouse. Meriwether followed. Sykes got into the Studebaker and started her up. His hands trembled as he put the key in the ignition. Meriwether might have hit him, whether he took a step back or not.

Preacher Simon's house was right off the square in Blue Vista Flats. From the second-story window he could see his church steeple and the face of the clock in the tower. Preacher pulled the lacy curtains back from the open window and sat on the edge of his double bed, elbows on the sill. The town was quiet. The late afternoon sun beat down on the houses, warm and glowing. The roofs' shingles looked lonely and naked, as though even the sun realized its waning power, lingering, showing less and less excitement at shining on. From the parlor downstairs, Preacher heard the soft voices of women talking, the clink of china teacups (a wedding gift from his mother, late mother, God preserve), and cutting through the fray of conversation good Marybelle's voice: "Now, now, now, now . . . don't—but if you must . . . "

Preacher had to admit, his wife's voice struck with a piercing quality, a brass bell ringing, a signal that the woman was born to speak. The Temperance Women's League listened, and the Blue Vista Flats Chapter of Moral Obligation listened, and the White Oak Society listened. The battle of beer was lost, but the fight went on. Lie not. Drink not. Lust not. Sisters of the Faith, do not succumb to the lesser instincts. Tell the truth. Lie with no man save your husband, and then only if he demands it. Sisters of the Faith, be true to the faith. The only faith.

Preacher heard a slight sigh, like a willow weeping; it came from the square, as if the sun had finally given up its fight to preserve the day. Soon the sun would retire beyond a bleak horizon, surrendering its blistering domain to the cold fruitless moon. But ultimately vanquished, the night would dissolve as the sun returned to seize the earth once more. From the parlor the voices rose and fell—now a high one, now a deep soft one, now a chicken's squawk, now a tisk-tisk. They were talking about the fire at Moss Greene's farm. Downstairs the chicken squawked, "What a shame . . . and where was *he* when it happened?"

And then Marybelle's voice: "Oh, it all goes to show. You can't ever tell . . . really, it's not our place to judge."

To judge. Damn the judges. Only one Judge existed, and He saw all. The banker couldn't stop Him. The Sheriff couldn't stop Him. The barber couldn't split His hairs. Lepke couldn't bag Him at the grain elevators. The farmers couldn't grow Him. And Moss Greene owed. This much was clear. His neighbors sought to stack the deck. This much was clear. And now the government sends in an Adjuster. A bank robbery and then the government sends in a busy bureaucrat to count the take. "Plow up a third, burn a third, drive the prices up." This had all been said before. The AAA and the government had no business in Blue Vista Flats. Blue Vista was set on the face of God long before them and would remain there long after Adjuster Sykes went on to California with his, "Plow up a third, drive up the prices."

Total proceeds from the auction . . . $3.50. Moss Greene ought've known better. He ought to have taken his medicine like a good brother, not let the sin of his neighbors drench him in a greedy stain. Render unto Caesar . . . pay the bank and go with goodness. Mercy was not the bank's to give, nor for the men of Blue Vista their opportunity to rob the bank. They should be tending to their fate, not plowing up their future, changing the laws and leaving the debts to men unpaid. You let one debt go, and then you let another, and then another, and soon it matters little what you owe, or to whom you owe it. Bad practice. Let Yohanna Johns and the other uprights think what they wished. Moss Greene was a farmer and his land would yield or not yield as God wished. Rightcousness would bring forth flower.

Henry and his rabble down Baskum's way took God's judgment from the Divine Hand. Likewise Walker's tenants had no business coercing the fate of a farmer rendered helpless by the All. The Divine Eye cast a spell upon the land—tamper with that spell, sing taboo incantation, and the icy touch would blow from the Beast's nostrils: slowly at first—here a touch, there a touch, a broken window in the church, canned meats gone rotten on their shelves, a withered daisy, a lone dog snarling on the U.S. Route, all for no good reason, except that the Beast had risen, long planted deep in the roots of the square's oak, now harrowed, now sprung forth, warming the soil beneath the town with its rancid stench.

And yet, only one soul, himself, might sense the Beast at first. The church window could be mended. The canned meats thrown out. The withered daisy could be plucked and thrown away. The lone dog would trot past Baskum's place and disappear over the horizon. But deep under the square, the Beast breathed in the soil; the dust would blow over from Iowa and each family would wail, wondering ever so vainly where they had tarried by the side of the road. Righteousness was not for sale. And it could not be given back, once lost, by running a penny auction or "plowing up a third." Preacher smelled the Beast, and as the sunlight waned, the rooftops glowed, and he could see each particle of mortar in each chimney, and he could see each flake of paint peeling from the house walls, and he knew the Divine Eye had seen this too.

He let the lace curtains drop and stood up. As he smoothed out the wrinkles on the bedspread, a breeze from the open window touched the small of his back and ruffled the tiny hairs along his spine. The hairs hackled, tickling, as the bedspread smoothed out like cream, snow-white. The parlor downstairs had quieted down some, but still the voices drifted up to the top of the stairs, and they got stronger when Preacher closed the bedroom door behind him.

The stairway's banister was gleaming smooth; oiled when first carved, now the wood glowed with the palm-polished luster of endless descents.

At the bottom of the stairs an arch opened onto a parlor; one woman sat, her gracious rear quarters pressed into the cushions on his velvet couch. Only her neck and head were visible. Beyond the edge of the arch, out of view, a pair of legs was crossed, the body hidden. Across from the couch, with her back to the window, his wife, Marybelle, was posed in a Morris chair. Her print dress was tucked tightly around her knees. By the arm of the chair a wooden crib on rocking boards, red-stained pinewood, was gently swaying back and forth. With one light hand, Marybelle touched the edge of the crib.

Marybelle glanced up at him as the woman beyond the edge of the archway said, "Bart wouldn't go to the auction—said there wasn't anything to see. He was wrong, but then I didn't go either." The woman paused. Claire Lowell. She started up again. "I'll tell you though," her voice went low, very confidential. "He couldn't have stopped me, if I'd wanted to go." The woman at the edge of the couch, near Claire Lowell, nodded her head, the round bun at the nape of her neck bobbing. Marybelle, her hand on the edge of the crib, rocked it slow and even. She glanced again at Preacher, standing in the darkness at the foot of the stairs. The lady with the bun whipped her head around. June Tate, the Sheriff's wife. She was a sturdy creature with a slightly pinched face and long years in service to a man in County service had drawn the spring blood from her brow. The lines across her pale forehead wrinkled before she smiled.

"Why Preacher! Why are you standing out there in the hall?"

Preacher entered the parlor and went to where his wife was sitting; he put his hand on the crib and took over the rocking. The child lay in clean crumpled white sheet strips, cut from old worn bedding. She was a beautiful girl, one of those rosy-cheeked things, and plump; lips pink and a face moistened with the child's open eyes. A cherub, but not with the slightly aged and knowing face or the dove wings that were painted on the murals. No, this was no painter's prey, no composition drawn from the artist's mind. She breathed. She cried. She gurgled. She smiled. And she cooed when your face was in her ear. When you touched her she reached for your hand, grasping two fingers with her fat palm, warm and slightly moist. She opened her soft toothless smile, and a thread of saliva stretched between her gums; the spit band broke and Preacher wiped the wetness from the child's bottom lip with a soft handkerchief.

June Tate coughed. Preacher looked up from the baby. "Pardon this intrusion—I'll retire if privacy is desired."

Marybelle looked up at him. "Not at all—"

June Tate protested, chiming in, "Oh no, Preacher—"

"Did our noise disturb you?" Claire Lowell asked.

Marybelle piped up, "Claire tells me Bart will be along soon. And there, you see, you'll have a man to talk to . . ."

Preacher was watching Claire Lowell. Sitting in the chair, the barber's wife crossed her legs and recrossed them. Her voice was low again, as if she told a secret. "We hardly ever get a chance to see you."

He could see the lace fringe of her slip when her legs recrossed. Claire parted her lips in a soft smile; the brown mole that clung to her upper lip looked heated, swelling. Preacher thought he saw some fragile spark, a fragment of splintered glass in the white wetness of her eyes, a reflection of window light perhaps, or the innocent glint of a sleep crumb left unbrushed from a teary lid. Preacher could look at her knees and the eye glint all together, and the more he looked the less innocent the glint appeared. The wetness flashed at him, unhurried, obvious. He sucked it down like a lungful of air.

"*Heya! Heya!*" Bart Lowell came in through the front door. The wetness in Claire Lowell's eye vanished.

"Hello all." Bart puffed himself up. "Well, Preacher, what new treasures have you collected?"

Tea time. A habit Marybelle Simon picked up after reading all about it in a magazine. Gentility. Grace. The maintenance of standards. The right standards.

Preacher Simon hated tea. Detested cream and sugar; lemons were way above what he thought prudent to pay for out of the congregation's stipend. Soda pop was more to his liking. Orange Nehi, to be exact, but Marybelle would not let him drink it from the bottle. She served the pop in a teacup, instead, with the saucer.

Nothing was harder than attempting to drink a fizzy Orange Nehi out of a teacup. But Preacher tried. Were Marybelle to bake her lemon cake, Preacher would authorize the lemon purchase, but lemons squeezed in tea, dribbled on the tablecloth, or squirted in your eyes . . . not bearable.

"Could I have some lemon?" Claire Lowell asked.

"Right, Marybelle," Bart added. "How about some lemon?"

Marybelle smiled slightly, frowned, and glanced to the parlor where Preacher was pulling a book from the shelf. This was the new treasure, ordered from the Seminary clearinghouse in Baltimore.

Marybelle cupped her hand to her mouth and whispered, "He only lets me use it for the lemon cake."

"And what else?" Claire asked. The glint in the corner of her eye, that wet glass shard, appeared. June Tate giggled. Marybelle shook her head. Nothing else. Lemon cake was served at Christmas. Once a year. Claire did not pursue the lemon issue and Marybelle had nothing on her mind. Claire looked at her dumpy husband, and then at the bowed but rigid Preacher standing in the parlor, leafing through his book. Strange man that devil-dodger: a wealth of sacred facts, cut in black cloth—the man seemed sharp around the edges, sharp enough to split a hair. Blade drawn, he could slice your hand. Claire was not a fool; she had heard her Bart more than once come slinking down the hall, opening the door softly, thinking she did not know the whos, whys, and wherefores. She never mentioned this, or held it up for him to see; after all, Eve *was* her sister, and if Eve could take the time off Bart's hands better than his wife, well . . . no use spoiling a good diversion. Keep him peaceable and occupied. Preacher turned the page of the book; the crisp page, dry and honest, fell into place. Preacher's time would come. Amen, Preacher. Just you wait.

Claire helped Marybelle clear away the tea things. Preacher was showing Bart his new book, and Bart was nodding in appreciation. He hardly ever read. Magazines were one thing. Books were another. Marybelle was chattering a blue streak. "I always wash up right after meals. I always do. They say it's better that way. Mr. Simon likes a clean house. And so I keep it clean. He's happy that way. Mr. Simon says God smiles on a clean house. Do you believe God smiles on a clean house? I do. Mr. Simon does. Do you?"

Preacher Simon closed his new book with a firm snap. The teacup trembled in Claire's hand. Leaving the cup and saucer on the kitchen counter, Claire touched the mole on her upper lip; the mole felt warm and tender.

Simple rubbed his dry palm over his dome; he watched the work train pass over the trestle and keep going west. The work train was checking track. It had also dropped off the mail. Simple clutched the letter in his hand.

C&C RAILROAD
Wilkes-Barre, Pennsylvania

Office of the President

A. K. Semple
Foreman
Way-Station
Blue Vista Flats

Dear Mr. Semple:

In accordance with the 1903 Lending and Loan Act, two weeks' prior notice must be given on any foreclosure action.

You are hereby authorized to give such formal notice by written document (this document) to Drake Walker & company on the intention by the C&C Railroad to foreclose on the Walker farm mortgage and the adjacent tenant land mortgages.

Reason for foreclosure action: $210.24 delayed or unpaid since due: August 1st, 1933.

Please cable collect acknowledgement of receipt of this document.

Sincerely,

Doyle C. Dumbarton

Doyle C. Dumbarton
President

DCD:bl
cc: Parker Watts

C&C
"Coast to Coast"

Simple kneaded the rolls of skin at the back of his neck; his mousy eyes were two full jiggers. Doyle C. Dumbarton had not spelled his name right—that much he could tell. But you could hardly fault the man for that. He walked toward the bunkhouse. Meriwether was leaning against the bunkhouse door jamb.

"Meriwether." Simple always loved getting mail. "You gotta reed me a letter."

Late in the afternoon Lomax was on his last row. Back toward the farmhouse Drake Walker's tenants walked single file down the access road to gather in the yard outside the house. Buck saw his father come outside and stand for a moment, talking. By their movements, hand-wringing, pointing, finger-wagging, each tenant was putting in his own two cents. His father listened. Then Drake leaned forward; this meant he was adding his own opinions. Lomax finished the last row and Buck handed him the water can. Lomax grabbed for it, drank blindly—finally Buck took the can away.

"Enough for today?" Buck's shirt was drenched, salty. Lomax said nothing; he turned and shuffled toward the farmhouse. Buck followed by his side and did not bother to talk. The sun, now low, glanced across the fields, striking his cheek and Buck's skin twinged —pores open under the heat. The sweat gathered under his arms and ran in thin trickles down the sides of his body. When Buck and Lomax reached the farmhouse, the tenants stopped talking. His father, Ryder and Eddy watched them approach. Lomax angled off toward the back porch and Buck stopped a couple of feet from the group.

Drake nodded in the direction of the pickup. "Bucky, take my men where they want to go." Eddy was the first to move. Ryder followed, and then Buck. The two men paused before climbing into the truck. Eddy was looking down the road, shading his eyes against the sun. A car was coming from town—the engine growled, clouding the air. "That's Simple's."

Buck did not understand. "What's he want here?"

The car roared down the road, not slowing. It screamed past the house, shooting a hundred yards beyond, spewing a wave of dust. Meriwether was sitting in the passenger seat and both men were laughing. Simple hit the brakes; the tires smoked. Turning a tight circle in the road, the tires shrieked. Drake had come up onto the U.S. Route now; Buck stood on the other side of the house, watching. Simple gunned the car and burnt rubber came from the vehicle. The car shot past the house again, nearing fifty, heading toward town. A rock thrown from the car flew past his father, crashing through their farmhouse window. The women inside yelled. Sarah burst out the front door, holding the rock. "This nearly—!"

Drake had his gun, a shotgun. Buck had not even seen him get it from the house. The long metal gun appeared on Drake's shoulder, steady and still, like an empty flagpole bolted to the side of a building. The car was fifty yards and going. Finger creased in the trigger guard, Drake's shoulder jolted with the recoil, spitting the hollow *chuck-chuck*. The metal birdseed screamed and the car kept going.

The rear window cracked, glinting in the sun. The car swerved, but Simple held the road. The car rocked back and forth but kept on, a little slower, disappearing over a hill.

Mrs. Moon followed Sarah out on the porch. Then Drew. Then Tina. The women stood in the shade of the porch roof, like brave prowheads carved to the flagship bowsprits. Mrs. Moon, wise and wary, held her hand close to her body, moving her dry lips, muttering lower than Buck could hear.

Tina, the scaredy-cat, stayed close to the front door, dreadfully curious, but all skittered up. She flared her nose and pop-eyed all the grown-ups, looking for an explanation. Drew hung back; she smoothed the dress around her thighs, and her legs stood out for a short moment before melting behind the loose folds.

Sarah held her chest erect, like a boxer flexing in the ring. She took each breath slow and full, as though daring the Bulls to come back and try it again. Sarah was still holding the rock and she weighed it in her hand. A scrap of paper was wrapped around the stone; the paper was filthy and tied with string. Drake was on the porch; he took the rock from Sarah and pulled the string off. The paper was torn, cut by the window glass. Drake smoothed it out on the porch boards, keeping it from tearing further. He read the paper and then reread it. He said nothing but passed the scrap around the circle, so each could read in turn.

Ryder read the paper, pulling on his hawk's nose. "What the—?"

Eddy was next; he read it quickly and his round Mex face sagged. Eddy's boots made the wooden floorboards sigh. "You did make the payment, didn't you, Drake?"

"On the twenty-fifth."

"What's this?" Ryder's eyepatch shifted over the socket.

For a moment Drake was silent. Then he asked gently, "What would you have me do now?"

Ryder said nothing; he took a ragged handkerchief from his back pocket and blew his nose.

"The bank's closed for today." Drake was not the sort to let his men dangle, uncertain and wary. "I'll see Parker Watts tomorrow."

Drake left his tenants standing on the porch and went into the house. Ryder watched his bossman go and scratched his head. "Well, let's get to it. Bucky, you drive."

Tina, Drew and Mrs. Moon were still standing on the porch. Buck was watching them in his rearview mirror as the pickup started down the road.

Ryder sat next to him in the cab. "Go straight through town to Baskum's place—but don't turn down the road."

Eddy stretched out in the truckbed. Ryder lit a cigarette, took a puff, and passed it to Buck. Buck pinched the scag between his fingers without taking his eyes off the road.

They passed through town and kept on the U.S. Route. Another two miles slipped by and they came up on Baskum's farm. The telephone wires slung down the dirt road, disappearing into the grove of trees. "Keep on the Route for another quarter mile." Ryder was looking out the window.

A quarter mile on, Buck pulled off the road and parked on the slanting embankment, far enough off the road so the truck would not be sideswiped but not so far down the grade that they would have to push the pickup onto the macadam. Ryder was out of the cab. "You coming?"

Buck got out of the cab and followed the two men, already on the move. He had passed through this stretch only a couple of times. They were on the edge of Bone County. Where J. J. Baskum's fields ended, a forest rose up, deep and impenetrable. Ryder led them through a footpath cut on the border of Baskum's fields. Strictly speaking, they were not on Baskum's land till they got to Yellow River, but if Baskum spotted them, he might not see it that way. Buck guessed Eddy kept his still nearby, but never asked for fear of being rude. Corn liquor should be talked about politely.

They followed the footpath for about three quarters of a mile, and when they reached the line of trees at Yellow River, the men broke through, jumped down on the bank and splashed into the shallow water. Buck followed, last. This was the dangerous part; Ryder, still in the lead, used his one sharp eye to guide them back up the river, their boots soaking through as they walked against the light current. They splashed along the shallow river, kicking up spray and making a lot of noise. Not talking.

Ryder kept to the ankle-deep parts, where the sand and the silt piled up. He led the line around the bigger rocks and boulders where the water went deep, knee-deep. Where you could break your leg if you stepped the wrong way. But Ryder felt safer treading on Baskum's border, not on his turf. Buck let the river flow under his feet. It was Henry's place they were heading for. Backtracking up the river, in the water's dip and eddy, right in the flow where yesterday the dead man floated like a log face down. Passing that way in the night, on the edge of Baskum's land, past Henry's sleeping shacks, clearing the snags and the snarls, with only the owl to mark its passage.

And Buck still heard the Bulls' laughter, long evaporated. Yet here in the river, despite their warning he treaded again, and treaded lightly. Back in the river despite their laughter, where the fishing was lousy and the nightcrawlers slept in their cool dark holes. Meriwether with his sod-knife close at hand, ready to cut him down to size.

There! Meriwether! Where the sun was sending shafts of light through the trees, the Bull's slick body passed from one tree to the next, cutting off the sunlight.

Buck turned his neck to get a better look.

No Meriwether. No body passing silent by the water's edge.

There! The long dangerous arm, the bristle of hair. But when Buck stared off in the trees, and looked again, the sunlight shafts came through like easy weather and there was no one close at hand. No one stalking them as they moved against the current. Just his own spooks and the Bull would take his time, if he ever got the chance . . . and now more souls lost before another dawn. The newest dead offering, burnt in a hot fire, cinders in Moss Greene's sleep.

They could see Baskum's tenant shacks now on the river's edge. Buck slapped a mosquito on his face. Two seconds later he did it again. The bugs must have been murder on Henry and his people. Maybe that was why their kids always looked so inky and scarred.

Smoke drifted across the river, and the smell of a cook-fire came with it. From the nearest shack a black tin stovepipe poked through a hole cut in the roof. From the shabby chimney smoke rose, floating into the air, sucking toward the cool moistness of the water. Ryder was the first up on the bank, and from around the shack a scratchy mongrel stuck his muzzle, sniffing. The mongrel looked like it wanted to bark but suddenly changed its mind and ducked out of view. A woman came out of the shack and she stopped, facing Ryder. The dog was behind her; it sat, sticking its nose in the air, waiting.

"He ain't here." The woman left it at that. No explanations.

Buck splashed up the bank. Eddy caught him by the elbow, his Mex eyes stone gray and his lips moving. "You gonna hear this. But you ain't gonna remember nothing. You got that, Bucky?" Eddy was saying he drove good, good enough to haul his daddy's men around, but that was all.

Ryder thrust his hands in his pockets. His one good eye never fell from the woman. "But he told you?"

"Yes." She had been told. Moss Greene was dead. A fire's smoke travels far. The dog took the opportunity to scratch its ear. "He knew you were coming. Wait up, he'll be here soon." The mutt stood, stretched its front paws forward, and stuck its butt in the air, tail pointing to the sky. Flexing its pads, the dog scratched marks in the soft earth. The mutt circled the woman slowly and then sat down again, in the same spot.

"He won't bother you—"

The dog yawned.

Ryder looked back down the river. "He don't."

Buck saw Henry first; his brother followed. Henry was walking in from Baskum's fields, toward the river. He did not have his shotgun and looked strangely loose-limbed without the weapon. Henry's hands flapped when he walked. Henry's brother spotted a chicken clucking its way across the clearing. As the chicken passed his foot, the crushed little man stooped over, smooth as silk, and grabbed the bird by its neck. He walked with the biddy, his hand around its scrawny neck, back to the coop.

A swarm of a thousand gnats, whirling in a moving cloud, passed into the shafts of sunlight off the river; the gnats disappeared and reappeared, swirling into the trees on the far bank. Baskum had given Henry and his brother the worst spot to live. They should have been mad by midsummer, simmering under the insects and the river heat.

Ryder's coal eye was flat, no sparkle. Henry was waiting, ready for anything. Henry's brother returned from the coop. Buck had seen his son at the auction, sitting in the rig, the useless leg curled into a frozen paralyzed lap . . . the boy had to be somewhere nearby. But the father wanted some say in all this, and he tilted the wormy straw boater back on his head. Suddenly the crushed little man looked almost debonair.

"Your boss Walker sent you, but did he tell you what to say?"

Ryder smiled, his lips drawn back against gray teeth. A slight sparkle danced in the one eye. "C'mon fella, you know we do everything democratic. One man, one vote."

He looked at the sky, jutting his jaw. "Sheriff Tate's gonna let Preacher bury those bodies and then he's gonna sniff around the jailhouse walls; he'll make out a long report and then he's gonna lose the file . . . " Ryder's voice dropped, trailing off into the shafts of sunlight and the swirling gnats.

The crushed little man kept on. "What about the Bulls?"

Buck knew damn well about the Bulls. They sat up there by the railroad tracks and they could beat a man to death in the early dawn and they could throw him in the river. They could burn down a house and never get caught. That's what they could do.

Now Henry and his father's men were settling their business.

But they were settling it for Moss Greene and not for Buck, his back to the Bulls' laughter and a dead man who floated face down. No way around it: that Meriwether sidled up to him, the red dawnlight in his bristly hair . . . no way around the lousy fishing or the nightcrawlers that inched in all directions.

Two firm hands dropped on each shoulder.

"Steady, Bucky." Eddy stood at his side. The skin was sharp and sunburnt over the tenant's cheeks, and his scalp pale through the crew-cut. "You looked about ready to bolt."

"I'm okay, Eddy."

Eddy's mouth curled and he squeezed Buck's shoulder. "We'll see . . . we'll see."

Suddenly Buck saw all the chips piled high at these gamblers' elbows. They were gonna bushwack the Bulls and leave them bleeding. Henry backed off a little; he tipped the felt fedora at an angle and rubbed the soft brim. "You can tell Drake I'm with him. After the funeral. Let's give Simple a chance to think we've settled down."

Sarah Walker's voice was slightly tired. "Thank you, Lord, this food before us will take us through tomorrow's work. And thank you, Lord, for bringing these people into our household, for letting them share with us your goodness." Sarah, at the end of the table, unclasped her hands and looked up.

"Amen." Tina alone.

"Amen." The rest.

Except for Drake who said, "Umph." Drake never thought he would question the passing moments of his own life, but Moss Greene lay ready to bury and now Drake stared into the shadow across his napkin and a new prayer murmured, unspoken, a dirge for Moss's family while his own ate well . . . *eat for me my flesh today, tomorrow cast the spell away. Look for me at the ringing bell, and wish me luck as I fly across the river, far from life's last hell* . . . Drake pulled the napkin up his lap and the shadow vanished from its white fold.

The table was too small for all seven of them. Drew and Lomax had taken over the counter by the basin. Buck sat only a foot from her at the table, but as he looked over his plate the gulf seemed wide and Drew's attention was to feeding Lomax.

Sarah had killed a chicken earlier that afternoon, plucked it clean, and gutted the bird's innards. She roasted it with butter and salt and some parsley from the garden and stuffed it with stale bread. Potatoes were roasted too, and soaked up the drippings in the bottom of the pan. Dried peas were soaked for a day and now steamed away in a separate bowl. Drew, her hands smooth and strong, had not taken a plate for herself yet, but she had taken a plate for Lomax who could not feed himself. He could chew and swallow if spoon-fed. Lomax seemed bored at first with the food. He took a spoonful of peas, gurgled them in his throat and then spit them out. They bounced on the plate Drew was holding and rolled to the floor. Drew got up in a huff and took the plate to the table. "Have it your way. See if you're hungry later."

Lomax cared nothing about the threat. He was agitated. The idiot's eyes jelled to focus and he stared at the wall, as if something was there, or something beyond. He was as chafed and rattled as that time in the car. Now Buck saw his lips part but the muc-muc was not for his father falling from the tractor; this time the muc-muc was for something else.

"He's usually hungry." Mrs. Moon let him have his way. She did not force her son to eat, but she noticed his eyes and kept close to herself.

Buck picked up a chicken leg from his plate and jawboned it clean right down to the gristle. The day's hunger had him, a hunger that Lomax's muc-muc would not stifle. There could be a thousand reasons for the idiot's bad digestion.

"Lomax worked hard today. Sometimes I'm not hungry at all after I work all day. Sometimes I just feel like sleeping. Sometimes—" He caught a glance from his father and shut his trap. His father was funny that way. If Drake felt like talking, they would all talk. If he didn't—nobody would. But Mrs. Moon could not have known the family rule.

She looked at Drake. "My boy played in the fields today."

Just a statement. Drake looked up from his plate, his face empty as the sky. Mrs. Moon could have smiled, but she did not.

She tore a shred of chicken with some of the skin from the piece on her plate and laid it on the side. "He'll eat that."

"The skin's my favorite too," Buck said. No glance from his father this time.

Tina did the dishes. Her turn. Sarah started the coffeepot. Buck squirmed in his seat and looked at Drew. Finally the words came from his father's low voice. "You may be excused from the table."

Buck was standing in a flash, not sure which way to go or how to get Drew along, alone.

His foot still pained him, where he plucked the barb driven into his skin. The sole felt swollen, but it did not look red or rankling. Simple said he was prissy, just a scratch. But when he lay down, the flesh throbbed, and when he walked it pounded as if the foot had a heart of its own. He could not rest his weight because a pointed thorn, invisible, stabbed to the bone. The fields rose up around him and he smelled the food smoke from the Walker farmhouse. He was close enough to smell the roasted chicken, close enough to hear the murmur of voices, the scraping of chairs. Meriwether fished for the sodcutter in his pocket and opened the knife; he ran his thumb along the blade. The night fell around his ears. The little Walker bitch. She was the scrub catch, but a peach all the same. She would be just the soupbone to garnish his stew. A tasty concoction, cooked up right to choke in Drake Walker's craw. "No slipups." Simple was cautious, but Meriwether knew what he was doing.

"I'll bring her back in one piece. Alive."

The door of the Walker farmhouse opened and Meriwether bellied down in the field. Not Tina. The guttersnipe son was standing on the porch. Go away, boy, you'll get cut from the guzzle to the Jack. Watch out, sonny.

Buck stood on the porch and heard the back door slam behind him; he did not dare turn around for fear that Drew might be watching. He stepped off the porch and headed toward the barn. He kept walking slow. She could catch up, or she could see where he was going.

"Not so fast."

Her. Night rained a thick dark current through her voice.

"What's your hurry?" Again that question of *tell me, tell me!* He turned to face her and the question stood before her thighs; out of all, out of them all . . . whom do you love?

Better than you love me?

"No hurry." Cool, yes, but the question stood before her waist and she took his hand. The sky, now almost night, was colored eagle-scream blue, that dying hue of twilight where even the crop in the fields stops growing and the grass is very still; the sky becomes a ceiling and the earth becomes a floor, and you can reach with both hands to measure in between.

Inside the barn was dark, and through the cracks in the clapboard the twilight burned fading blue slivers that fell on nothing. Cracks in the clapboard, no rays of light. Drew slid the barn door shut and it groaned on its rails. The latch caught with a bang, firm and final. A claw scratched way up in the eaves. Then a flutter, a swoop and a bat dived across the clapboard-blue slivers, a black shadow against the soft edges of light. The bat landed on a beam, scratched its talons; a slight shuffle of its soft wings, and it hung, as if stuffed.

He took her hand and led her to the hayloft ladder.

"I can't see."

He put her finger through a beltloop at the back of his pants and once on the rungs of the ladder, she needed no help. Buck crawled onto the loft platform on his hands and knees. He spread his hands out in front like a snow angel. Nothing. He crawled forward. He spread his hands out again, searching. The meat of his forearm touched the chill prong of a pitchfork, right through his shirt.

"What's holding you up?"

"Nothing now." He grabbed the pitchfork below the prongs and turned it away. Standing up, he edged to the wall of the barn and pushed the pitchfork into the soft wooden floor. "Come on up."

The light between the warped slats faded; it was impossible now to tell where the wood spread in gaps, since all but the large holes were black. Hay dust danced into his nose; only some of the hay was bound, the rest was deep. He lay down in it and she followed as if she had known all along. Curling up against him, her thigh spread his legs. Lovelock oddly flat, where her thighs met her crotch, a fleshy ridge like the mound on the heel of your thumb— he wanted to touch it with his hands, but her legs were wrapped so tight. And she moved a little, rolling herself over the muscle in his thigh. Her mouth was wet, a dark tongue clean against his teeth. She was flattened and he throbbed. She rolled on his thigh and her nose grease softened with slight sweat.

Mrs. Moon left Lomax sitting at the counter, a half plate of the table's leftovers beside his elbow. The boy still had not touched a scrap. Tina watched Mrs. Moon go out the back door and vanish into the darkness. Tina finished the last two greasy dishes and bolted out too, lickety-split, slamming the back door as she left. She stood out on the porch and listened to the night wrapped too tight for comfort. Was Buck in the barn? The fields? Tina heard a rustle. The fields. Bucky with his hands full . . . she could sneak up on him.
And her.

He saw the scabby little bitch. Meriwether rustled stalks on the ground. And she looked deep into the field. She started walking toward him. That's right, my dear: let's see what's making all the noise. Odd sounds on an odd night. Come, come, don't be shy . . . it's not in your nature. Forgetting his foot, he crouched, nearly groveled. She was peering, the curious puss. Closer . . .

Tina followed the sound into the fields. As she approached it, the rustling pulled away, and she followed the noise, nose sniffing the way.

"Buck?" A cramp, dull and unfamiliar, blossomed in her gut. Not a gas cramp . . . different, deeper inside; heat sprinkled the back of her neck. The watery ache swelled and rolled. The spasm in her gut gripped, then eased . . . then gripped.

"Buck?"

No answer. More rustlings. The goon rose up, slithering on two feet. No face, but the glint of a blade . . . a stalker, man-walker spook. He came limping slightly, one hand outstretched. The cramp churned in her belly. She spun, running, tripping. He rose above her, breathing foul—his head dark against the night. The dull ache edged in deeper, gripping.

A rush of air, a swooping and Tina turned to look. The bogey danced with his hands to his head; an owl snagged in his hair, clawing his scalp, wings beating like a feathered crown. The talons slashed deep, quick punctures in and out. He whirled thrashing, flailing; he used the blade. Missed, the owl lifted off, arched and slashed the hand that held the knife. The sodcutter fell to the ground. Tina scrabbled on the dirt and the cramp flowed to nothing. She looked no more and ran. Ran as her throat pounded, couldn't scream, ran white around the eyes. And fell, sagging against the safe porch. The field was quiet. She heard no rustle—a scraping, moving fast away. No flutter of wings. No owl. No hollow eyes, blank and round. Her hands shook and she pressed them between her knees.

"Why child, you look frayed and wits tattered." Mrs. Moon stood some way out in the darkness. The woman was slightly mussed and from the house's lantern glimmer Tina saw that Mrs. Moon's dress was torn under her arm, her skin white against the frayed edge. Tina went to Mrs. Moon and she held her arms open for the little girl, the warm wave of great relief. Tina touched the white skin showing through the tear in Mrs. Moon's dress, and Tina's hands stopped shaking. She looked up at Mrs. Moon, into eyes that seemed to know what was right and what was wrong and what lay in between. "Thanks . . . " Tina murmured, so low she knew she never made a sound.

Sarah came out on the porch. "We got coffee. Tina, fetch some chairs. We can sit out here." She carried a lantern which she hung from a hook on a porch post.

"And Tina, find out what your brother's up to."

Drew ran her hand up Buck's leg. In mercy's name, he throbbed. She took his hand. Pressing her swell against his palm, she kissed him again. She laid her forehead against his jaw and breathed. He could hear his heart in his chest, a runaway pump. She straddled his thigh, moving, back and forth and back and forth, and—

"Ma says there's coffee." Tina. The girl's voice was down below the loft. The barn door had opened without a groan.

Buck heard Drew sigh. She unsaddled him and put her face to his thighs. Jack strapping, he shivered. She bit him gently through the pants cloth and he shuddered.

"Later . . ."

Rollem, rollem, roll dem bones and praise de Lawd. Bones in the sky. Bones don't lie. Bones in the graveyard, eight miles high. Rollem, rollem, roll dem bones and praise de Lawd.

What was that song?

> Mammy's little babies love shortnin', shortnin'
> Mammy's little babies love shortnin' bread.
> Mammy's little babies sleepin' in bed.
> One was sick.
> And de other was dead.
> In come de doctor
> And de doctor he said:
> "Feed dem babies shortnin' bread!"
> Put on the kettle.
> Put on the led.
> Feed dem babies shortnin' bread.

Preacher Simon had watched Ollie Cottle bring the little coffins into the church on his shoulders. He had watched Hanson help his Negro with the big boxes. They used a couple of saw horses to lay the caskets out. And when it came time to place the bodies in their pine beds, Preacher lent a hand. Hanson had said he'd be damned if he'd keep the bodies in his meat cooler. So the bodies had remained in the church, lying on the pews as if asleep. Hanson looked and looked, but discovered, alas, that he was fresh out of formaldehyde. So they took their chances that the flesh would not ripen. And they took their chances on the flies. And the maggots. And the ants.

Oddly, the bodies did not bloat. No flies buzzed, looking for a handout. Preacher wondered at this, but figured that like hickory-curing, the fire's smoke may have preserved the flesh. Yet the bodies were not burned and their clothes were neither charred nor scorched. Preacher had taken Moss Greene's armpit in one hand; the armpit, unscathed by fire, was still dead meat. Hanson took him under the other arm and Cottle took the feet. They lugged him from the pew to his coffin and rolled him in. They rolled him in face down and had to turn him over. Then they went back for Liza. She was lighter and as Cottle stooped over to grab her ankles, Hanson noticed her thighs exposed and Cottle's face inches from the skin of her calves.

"Hold it."

Cottle backed away. Hanson smoothed the dead woman's skirt down over her knees and took her ankles.

"Cottle, you get the arms."

Hanson hated the thought of the dark skin touching the white woman's legs. Terribly indecent; maybe the woman would know as much in heaven. And disapprove. The children were easier. Cottle lifted the boy. Preacher took the girl. When each was laid in place, Preacher lowered the coffin lids and Hanson gingerly hooked Moss Greene's index finger around the wire that ran the length of the coffin top; the bell clapper trembled when they put the lid down. Then the bell went motionless as the finger within the coffin hung on the wire, dead as a doornail.

"There's a shovel out back." Hanson liked giving orders.

Cottle did not ask what for. He left the church and went around back of the church to where the town's small graveyard lay quiet and asleep, where the gravestones were teetering, and the wooden crosses staggered to and fro. On an empty plot the cocoa man began to dig the dark graves. Hanson left Preacher alone in the church and went looking for the Sheriff to see about payment for the funeral expenses.

Preacher sat in a pew and looked at the four coffins. The two little ones seemed hardly worth noticing; toys, a dwarf's version of the real parade, not real children, not real coffins. Fake pieces in a fake dollhouse. Not like Moss Greene's big coffin with the special bell. No mistaking that. No sirree. That big one with the big brass bell. Hell's bell. Preacher wiped his forehead. The church air was mousy and used. The little ones were like a lost pair of shoes, a dull razor, a comb with no teeth, an empty chair. One look at the little coffins and you would not think about the children—you'd say how *small.*

Preacher got up from the pew and, head bowed, walked down the aisle to the open church door.

"No simple words for a simple service, Preacher?"

Halfway down the aisle, Preacher looked up. Claire Lowell paused in the church doorway, lit a cigarette and the match flared, the sulfur's glow glancing off her cheekbones, glistening in her eye's wet shard. In the heat of the night her sleeves were rolled up and two buttons lay open at her throat. The blue tobacco smoke clouded Preacher's head and he smelled the weed burning up his nostrils. He moved to within a foot of the door. "No. No words tonight."

Claire smiled; the mole on her lip curved ripe and ready in the cigarette's glow. She leaned, her back to the door frame, stretching her shoulders, the shift moving along her arms. She had light hair on her arms and softly, with the cigarette held in two fingers, she ran her hand from elbow to shoulder. Her neck muscle strained as she hugged herself.

"Doesn't Bart wonder where you are?"

Claire did not look at him. "I don't care about that . . . " She felt Preacher looking at her and she dragged on the cigarette, letting the smoke flow from her nose. "And neither, Preacher . . . " she said softly, "do you."

Preacher stood erect. "Now just a minute . . . "

Claire faced him, came close and looked him in the eye. She dropped the hand from her shoulder. "I saw you looking under my dress today."

Preacher flinched from her fleshy taunt, his hand waffling at his throat. Then logic got the better of him—he recoiled, bristling: "Now you just hold on!"

Claire brought her hand smoothly between his legs. She cupped his Jack through the cloth and held him so he could not back away. Preacher froze and his hackles flattened. His eyes were open wide and she felt his sex stir.

Claire let go and went trippety-trip down the church steps, heading for the barbershop. She looked over her shoulder and Preacher caught the glint again, the wet crystal shard in her eyes. "See you, Preacher . . ."

Ollie Cottle hung a lantern on a wooden cross. Digging four graves was gonna take him half the night. Then what? Coupla hours sleep. Wake up. Church, services, last rites. Then you fill up the holes. He held the shovel's handle, stepped on the blade and broke the ground. The first shovelful pried loose easily; Cottle turned the dirt over and started the first pile. Tattered clouds slipped across the moon and a gust of wind like a long sigh urged the clouds faster. They raced across the moon and the white face seemed to turn like the spinning millstone of a knife-grinder's wheel, the clouds licking it faster and faster. The clouds drove across the sky and the moon became a faceless blur, but pale light still filtered down and Cottle hoped the moon's setting would not see him still bent to the ground.

Parker Watts sat in his teller's cage; he snapped on the green-shaded lamp. Opening the teller's cash drawer he took out the gold coin. Turning the money over in his hand, he felt its smoothness and smelled its gold perfection. The coin weighed heavy in his palm, seared the skin—better than a thousand whores, a thousand banks, a thousand penny auctions. With money you could buy love, barter for respect until your price was met; you could punish the innocent with the guilty. You could fix a horse race, buy a politician, marry a countess. You were always witty and bright. Men quivered when you appeared with a loyal stocky henchman at your side, the goon's hands big as hamhocks; you would never lift a finger. You would never have to. Your word was consecrated, your lowest mumblings the law, your honor never questioned. Your handshake the most coveted boon, never refused. You were always right.

You could join the club, drink sodas with nine-year-old girls, in some countries you could marry them at twelve and divorce them at sixteen. Then choose again, spoil her, despoil her and reach for another plum. Men of great learning would sit at your feet. They would write about you, examine your every move, what you ate, what you wore. Every murmur, joke or declaration would cause an avalanche of discussion, dialogue and criticism. There was no end to obsession; it was bound and drawn, time stretched unending . . . hold that twelve-year-old close on a leash so she fawns when you approach and whimpers when you leave.

Parker Watts rubbed the gold coin between his thumb and forefinger. The warmth in it faded and the coin grew very cold, like iced metal, chilling the flesh. He placed it in his palm and there it chilled even more, his palm turning blue and red. He dropped the coin back on the desk's blotter and watched its gold gleam under the green-shaded lamp.

J. J. Baskum took a deep breath and tiptoed down the hall to the kitchen, hardly creaking the floorboards. The kitchen was empty. Without a sound Baskum opened the kitchen cupboard and found the bottle of Seagram's whiskey he'd bought from Hanson in celebration of the Volstead Act modification. Baskum had already taken a nip or two from the bottle and now he checked the level to see if Jo had sneaked some on the sly. The whiskey level was the same. If she had sneaked some, she might have brought the level back up with funneled water. One would not necessarily be able to tell. At least for a while.

Baskum poured himself a drink, bottomed it quick and then poured himself another. The alcohol was warm and he loosened up a bit. He rolled his sleeves to the elbows. He kicked off his shoes. He unknotted his tie and slung it over a chair like a snake hanging from a jungle tree. He slipped his wristwatch off his wrist and tossed it on the table. Finally, he undid the button on his trouser waistband and unbuttoned three buttons on his fly. He relaxed, downed his second shot and poured a third. He sat down at the kitchen table, leaned back in the chair and planted his feet on the table.

From upstairs he heard a cough. "J. J.? Is that you?" The love of his life. Jo.

Again. "J. J.? Are you down there?"

Heh. Heh. What the hell did she think?

"J. J.! Why don't you answer me?"

Okay, you old war horse—if it's J. J. you want—it's J. J. you'll get. Baskum got up from the table, downed his third whiskey, got another glass, grabbed the bottle by the neck, and headed up the stairs to his wife and his bedroom. He climbed the stairs two at a time, but quietly, using the strength in his stout legs. He paused at the open bedroom door. She was lying in bed. The foot of the bed faced the door, but Josie's face was out of range. He could see her feet under the covers, huge trunk thighs, and the depression in the sheets at her crotch. Then the round belly, that was all. "J. J.! I know you're down there! I'm *talking* to you!"

"And so you shall, my dear." Baskum rolled into the room around the door frame, the bottle swinging in his fist.

"Bless me!" Jo cried. "I thought you were—"

"Indeed."

Jo looked at her husband, without his shoes, without his wristwatch, without his tie and with his pants unbuttoned. Baskum's thin hair which he normally combed back now hung over his forehead. When he walked the gold tooth flashed. Jo's eyes narrowed. Her broad pancake face grew tight and the deep crease at her bosom trembled when she breathed.

"J. J., you've been drinking."

"Ah, you've noticed then. Just a nip my dear. Something to while away the pleasant hours of the evening. A libation—quite healthy if taken in moderation. Did you ever know a man who didn't drink? Perhaps some little Miss Molly, but did you ever know a *real* man who didn't drink?"

"J. J., you've been drinking. How much?"

Baskum held up three fingers. He went over to the bed and sat on the edge. Jo noticed the second glass. "Would you care to join me?"

"Oh, I just couldn't."

"You could."

She put a fluttering hand to her throat.

"Oh, how could I?"

"Easy." Baskum poured his wife a drink and held out the glass. "You do it when I'm not around."

Jo took the glass in her warm hand. "Well, maybe just one."

Baskum poured himself another and watched Jo take a dainty sip. He edged closer to her on the bed. She took another dainty sip. Then she screwed up her courage and downed the rest in a hefty gulp. She was an old pro from way back. Baskum freshened up her glass. The second one she took without an argument. She was getting loose and she tugged the bodice of her nightgown to no visible effect. Her bosom heaved and the skin turned scarlet under her throat. "J. J., open the window." Baskum did not stir. She downed the second and the redness at her throat deepened. Baskum still had a fingerful of whiskey at the bottom of his glass. He swirled the brown liquor round the glass and neatly tipped the contents; it splashed down his wife's cleavage.

"J. J.!" Her breasts shook as the whiskey seeped down the soft strong crease and into her nightgown, staining the cloth.

"Sorry." Baskum tossed the empty glass away and it rolled on the rug. "I'll get it." He plunged his face between her wondrous breasts, burrowing after the running booze. The glass in Jo's hand slipped to the bed and lay still.

"Ooh, Jaay Jaaay . . ."

June Tate let the bath water trickle down her arms. The Sheriff was sitting out on their porch, and June could hear his rocking chair sigh on its wooden rails. Their house was off the square, but still within sight of the great oak's topmost branches. The bath water ran in streams, steaming in silk wisps. She patted the water, sending little splashes over the rim of the tub. She soaped under her arms, she soaped her face, she dunked her head and soaped her thighs. She started on her knees when the soap bar slipped between her fingers and skittered along the bathroom floor. The soap bar spun slowly around and then came to rest. She stared at it idly, not wanting to leave the warm bath. A drop of sweat formed at the base of her neck and ran down her back into the water.

"Taay-yaate." June splashed in the tub.

Out on the porch the rocker stilled; she heard Tate get up and the rocker spring without his weight. She heard the heavy climbing through the house and then he stopped outside the door. "Yes?"

"Come in here, Tate."

Slowly the door opened. Tate stood in the hall, averting his eyes.

"The soap, Tate."

"What about the soap?"

June caught his eye and smiled. "It's on the floor, honey. Bring it here."

Tate saw the soap bar on the floor and picked it up; the soap popped from between his fingers and sailed back into the tub with a splash. A tiny wave rippled across the surface of the tub and sloshed over the rim. June looked down into the water and touched the back of her neck where another sweat droplet ran down her back. "Why Tate honey, I just can't find it . . . "

She caught the next sweat droplet as it ran from her neck and she brought it to her mouth on the tip of her finger. "Why don't you roll up your sleeves and have a look-see . . . "

Tate took off his shirt.

Outside on the porch Tate's rocking chair creaked gently back and forth, painted with the moon's glitter, swaying slowly on its wooden rails.

Claire Lowell sat in her husband's barber chair with her legs crossed. The barbershop was dark and for a while she sat there in the dark. She felt the leather razor strap dangling from a hook on the chair's arm; the strap was smooth burnished leather, creamy to the touch. On one wall Bart kept the shaving cups, and the badger brushes to lather up his clientele. About three dozen cups were set in place on a big wall rack. The polished wooden wall rack was cut into cubbyholes: four levels, ten cubbies to a level. One lather cup and badger brush to a cubby. Each brush and cup belonged to a particular customer. Bart would only use Lepke's brush and cup on Lepke—nobody else used it. Almost every nook was filled in the rack; several cups on the bottom belonged to no one. These were used for temporary clientele—the Adjuster Sykes, for one.

Claire swiveled slowly around in the barber chair, seeing herself in the mirror, then the back door, the cup rack, the front door. She got off the moving chair, went to the front door and locked it. Then she pulled down the shade. The back door was never locked, but she locked it anyway. She found a straight razor in a drawer under the mirror. Holding the leather strap taut and stiff, she slapped the razor back and forth, sharpening the edge. She put the razor down on the ledge under the mirror and went to the cup rack. Baskum . . . Hanson . . . Lepke . . . Lowell . . . Johns . . . Meriwether . . . Simple . . . Simon.

Simon.

She took down Preacher's mug and brush and ran some warm water in the sink. The water steamed and she wetted Preacher's badger brush. She swirled the brush in the lather cup, and the soap billowed into a good head. She put the foaming cup on the ledge. Claire hiked her dress up around her waist and stood with one leg bent, foot planted on the seat of the barber chair. She felt the hair growing on her calves, bristling, rasping against her fingertips. But the skin was smooth underneath. He should have that skin . . .

With the badger brush she lathered up her calf and part way up the thigh. She took long smooth strokes with the razor, and the hair came away from her shins, floating off in a sea of foam, tasting the blade's sweet tongue. She flicked the foam off the razor's edge, letting it splatter in the sink. Then she went back and finished the first leg. The second leg was even easier and in seven or eight strokes a dripping mound of hair stubble foam floated in the barber's sink. She took a damp towel, soaked it with witch hazel, and spread the heavy astringent over her skin, right up to her thighs. Her skin prickled, felt clean and moist. She dropped her skirt so it fell sweeping below her knees, and then she shrugged off her shoulder straps, so the dress top hung at her waist. Four strokes under each armpit. More witch hazel. Back up went the top.

She cleaned the sink, folded the razor and put it away. She cleaned Preacher's badger brush and put his property back on the rack. She unlocked the front door and raised up the shade. She heard the doorknob on the back door rattle. She got up in Bart's barber chair and looked at herself in the mirror. Bart grumbled behind the back door. Then he unlocked it.

"What you doing here, sitting in the dark?"

Claire straightened her hair. "What does it look like I'm doing?"

"Well I don't know." Bart came up behind his wife and massaged her shoulder. He came close to her ear. "Why don't you and me go on upstairs . . . "

Claire whirled the chair so she faced him. He danced away from the hard metal footrest, out of range. Her tongue darted and she licked the mole over her lip. "You're an enterprising man . . . I'm sure you can find some entertainment."

"Now what the hell does that mean?"

Claire leaned back in the barber chair. She hit the handle and let the rusted hinge go back all the way. She stared at the ceiling. She saw Preacher's hard angles, his cutting edge in the wooden ceiling planks. "You're on your own tonight, fella. Make the best of it."

No denying it. Preacher walked Jack-stiff all the way back to his house. He prayed for the Lowell woman's soul. He cursed her husband for letting her run amok. He chided the town for producing a craven "hoor." He pledged fidelity to Marybelle and damned temptation. He repeated the Lord's Prayer. And he walked all the way home with a hard-on.

When he reached home Marybelle was in the kitchen, and she noticed nothing out of the ordinary. She helped him off with his coat and hung it up. She sat him down at the kitchen table. She popped the cap on an Orange Nehi. She even slipped each suspender off each of his shoulders. She fussed over his hair, pried open his clenched hands to examine his fingernails, and wondered about the bags under his eyes. While peering at those sorry bags, she suddenly exclaimed, "Do you know, Simon, that early yesterday morning . . . or was it day before yesterday . . . or? Anyway, early one morning I saw our own Sheriff Tate leaving Bart Lowell's rooming house before six a.m.!"

Preacher sat up straight in his chair and let Marybelle's fingers fall from under his eyes. "What were you doing out of the house that early?"

"Early?! Why the baby gets me up early. You know that. And of all things . . . " Marybelle paused.

"Why do you suppose a single girl like Eve would live in a rooming house full of men?"

Preacher said nothing.

"You don't suppose she . . . ?" Marybelle whirled a finger in the air. "Oh, you don't suppose, she's familiar with . . . Oh certainly she couldn't really—with all of them." Marybelle found a chair and sat quietly at the kitchen table for a moment. Then it dawned on her. "Why!" She was gasping like a fish.

"Why, that's debauchery! At the very least! Debauchery!" she said again. "Why certainly it can't run in the family. Certainly Claire Lowell doesn't suspect. Simon, do you think Claire suspects? And what about *June Tate?*"

Preacher, dumb as a brass spittoon, said nothing. He swallowed and wiped his lips.

"Simon?"

He brought the Nehi to his mouth and took a sip. The fizzy soda went down the wrong tube and Preacher coughed it up through his nose. He caught the discharge on his sleeve. Marybelle's back was turned and she never noticed.

"Simon, we have to save June and Tate's marriage. The holy bond is at stake." Marybelle had decided; her mind was made up. "There's nothing else to do. No. I'm wrong. *We're* not going to save it. *I'm* going to save it. A man can't do that sort of thing. Women are special creatures. Eve must be handled gently. No wounds opened up that can be sowed with salt. This, Simon, we shan't allow."

Again, Preacher said nothing. The Orange Nehi trembled in his hands; he started to take a sip but stopped himself and put the bottle down. He placed each hand palm flat. Marybelle came around to his side of the table and stood by him, stroking his neck. She didn't feel him shudder or cringe under her touch. She stroked his neck and didn't notice the muscles stiffen in his shoulders.

"Why don't you come to bed, Simon—you look all petered out."

Preacher knocked the Orange Nehi over on the table. The juice ran in a puddle, staining the tablecloth.

Upstairs in Bart Lowell's rooming house, Adjuster Sykes lay down on the bed and stared at the electric light bulb hanging from the ceiling by a wire. He left his shoes and pants on, and his shoe heels made creases in the blankets, ripples in a sea of wool at the far end of the bed. He kept his window open, and the tattered curtains at the window frame tugged sluggish at their sashes. The night air breathed an eager whiff into the stale faded room.

Same air the town Looney Tunes breathed . . . same exact air. Sykes held up one hand . . . steady as a rock. Funny, all the squalid business at Moss Greene's farm had not hit him yet—as if the strange town air had no effect, never poisoned his lungs, nor ran the circle in his veins. Tomorrow's funeral was another matter. The air over the graves might be damp and foggy. But at least that small-town air was far from the grit of Washington and the New York soot. Not like the Washington Farm Bureau Office which reeked from the fetid smell of small-time bureaucrats with big-time ambitions. No, the air seemed cleaner out here—the air that Johns or Lepke or Baskum breathed, nice and clean, good air for the Loonies in a Looney Tune town.

An unopened bottle of Seagram's whiskey stood on the rickety dresser, watching itself in the dresser's cracked mirror. Ice was too much to hope for. Seagram's was the only brand Hanson stocked in his store. "Just the essentials," Hanson claimed. "Just the essentials."

Seagram's. Essential shit.

All the great booze in the world open to the public, ready to flow, by popular demand, and what did Hanson stock?

Seagram's.

Shit.

That man had a thing or two he better learn about drinking. Canadian Piss-Water. Chicago Sewer Slop. Peoria Pus. But Seagram's, as it was generally known, was the only game in town.

Sykes got off the bed and went to the dresser; his shoes clicked neatly on the floorboards. He snatched the glass by the washbasin in the corner. The tumbler was gray with dust. For some odd reason his room had a faucet that worked; Sykes did not imagine the other rooms could claim such a luxury. When he twisted the handle over the tap, the pipes squealed and the spigot dribbled brown juice, then cleared. He cleaned the glass as best he could.

He took the Seagram's fifth by the neck and unscrewed the

cap, cracking the seal. Only sound in the world like it—cracking the seal on a brand-new bottle of liquor. Same sound the world over: a fresh snap of the paper sticker tearing in a sweet crease around the bottom of the cap. Warm and delicious. Like ham and eggs on Sunday. That crisp paper seal breaking as a new bottle gave grace to an otherwise disgusting habit.

Disgusting? Well, maybe that was a little strong. The habit wasn't half as bad as the brand itself. Sykes poured himself a double shot and could almost see the cloying aroma reflected in the cracked dresser mirror. He gulped half down and thought of Johnnie Walker Black. Didn't help. Seagram's was Seagram's and Johnnie Walker Black was, well . . . heaven. In the parking lot of Paradise, to say the least. Downing the rest on raw nerves alone, he braced his chest to the inevitable burning. The hot flash never came. You could tell something about yourself when the liquor did not jolt you any more.

Alcoholic?

Maybe.

Disgusting?

Child-molesting was worse. Two shots down and Sykes' vision crystallized at the edges. Normal at the beginning. Two more shots and the water would fall over the rim of the horizon, as it did when the world was flat. He'd get fuzzy at the edges. But the first two shots were always the best. The third heightened clarity for a moment. The fourth shot destroyed it.

He heard the stairs creak down the hall. Then the door across the way opened and closed. 10:30 p.m. Lights out, boys and girls. Ladies' matinee? Hell no, Jack. Adult entertainment. One show only. And now, ladies and gentlemen, Blue Vista Flats and the Bone County Women's Auxiliary are proud to present for your amusement and distraction . . .

Sykes grabbed the bottle and glass, and went across the hall. He knocked on Eve's door.

"Yeah?" The woman's voice was bored, as if nothing unexpected might ever knock on her bedroom door.

Sykes put the bottle and glass on the floorboards and tucked in his undershirt. He cleared his throat. "The Agricultural Adjustment Administration would like to buy you a drink."

Eve did not answer immediately. Then she said, "It's about time. The door's open."

Sykes picked up the bottle and went into Eve's room. She was sitting on her bed, fully clothed. A stand-up ashtray was next to the bed, like they had in movie theater lobbies. The ashtray had yesterday's cigarette butts strewn inside the metal basin and a new smoke burning on the rim.

"No ice?" Eve asked.

"The Farm Bureau has had to make sacrifices."

"Sure," Eve said. "There's a glass on the dresser." Why waste time? A dresser much like the one in his room stood against one wall. Sykes put his own glass on it, and poured Eve a double shot. Then he poured one for himself. She plucked her cigarette out of the ashtray before taking the glass. He stood next to her as she lounged on the bed. Like a fool he shifted his weight from foot to foot, looking for a place to sit. There wasn't any. So he stood by the side of the bed like Jack and the Beanstalk. Like the Beanstalk.

"Cheers." She swallowed half and shook her head twice, helping the stuff slide down her throat without so much as a shudder. She took a deep drag from her cigarette, using the smoke as a chaser.

"Hanson really ought to stock some classy juice. You can get tired of his gumbo pretty quick." She exhaled through her nostrils and the plumes of smoke shot down, spraying her lap; sucking the cigarette again, she filled her lungs with smoke before clearing them from the first drag. Sykes stood by the bed, not sure what to do. So he went for his third shot and gulped it down. This time it burned and he coughed. A breeze tugged at the pink curtains of her window and the door swung open as if pulled by a string. Bart Lowell was crouched on his knees in the hall, listening in at the keyhole.

"Get an earful, Bart?" Eve took a drag from her cigarette. Bart, caught in the act, danced up, brushing himself off.

"Thought I smelled smoke," Bart tried to explain.

"Where there's smoke there's fire," Eve remarked offhandedly. "Now go sniff under your wife's door. Get lost."

"Right." Bart acted as if he had been thinking the very same thing himself. He backed down the hall, his footsteps receding.

Eve turned her head from the open door and then looked up at Sykes.

"Why don't you sit down, handsome?"

"Don't see a chair."

A wan smile slipped across Eve's lips; she balanced the cigarette on the edge of the ashtray. "There isn't one."

Sykes did not know what to do.

"Go close the door." Eve touched her thigh. Bart was just gonna have to play with himself tonight. "And make sure it latches." She patted the space next to her on the bed. "Then come sit down."

Sykes latched the door, went back to the bed, sat down, and swung his feet—

"Take off your shoes dammit! I only do the wash once a week."

He swung his feet back to the floor and unlaced his shoes. She gulped down the rest of her double shot and chased it with a drag. She held the glass, looking at the ceiling bulb; the light glared, sparkling the few drops left.

"While you're up"—she tipped the glass back and forth—"would you mind?"

He did not mind. He could see very clearly now; getting her another shot, he filled his own glass with another and eased himself back down on the bed in his stocking feet. She was smoking again and the Seagram's seemed to drain from her glass very fast.

"Another."

He got her another. She stubbed out her old cigarette and lit a new one.

"You going to be here long?"

He wasn't sure what she meant. "Till harvest."

"You're going to try and get the farmers to plow up a third, aren't you?"

Those bushy blond eyebrows came together across his brow; she wondered if he ever combed them. He said nothing.

She glanced at him out of the corner of her eye and shrugged. "They won't do it." She paused. "And nobody can make them do it."

His turn to shrug. She did not like it. "Is Mr. Roosenfeld going to feed them? Who's gonna feed them?"

"Didn't think you cared."

She squinted through her glass. "It ain't necessarily so." She got off the bed and reached up to the bulb hanging from the ceiling. She switched it off and her cigarette glowed in the ashtray. Sykes' eyes adjusted to the dark and he noticed her unbutton several buttons on her blouse.

"Is this going to cost?"

She went to the window and the breeze stirred into the room; her neck was moist and the air cooled the skin. "If it costs you, handsome, it'll be at the taxpayer's expense. Besides," he could not see her smile, "you haven't been invited yet."

Sykes took a swallow from his glass. She came back to the bed and sat down on its edge with her back to him. He got up and put his empty glass next to the bottle of Seagram's on the dresser. He passed her on his way back to the corner of the bed —she hooked her finger in his suspenders and drew him close. He stood in front of her and she sat on the bed, her back stiff and straight.

"See what damage the hooch has done. See if we can salvage you." She reached for his waistband and the buttons of his fly.

"Does this mean I'm invited?"

"This means, Mister Adjuster, that you better plow up more than a third." She reached into his fly and pushed his shorts up his thigh. He was soft in the palm of her hand. "Tisk. Tisk. Bad damage."

It always started that way. Most men wanted a mouth. And they made their women go for it first. Their women accepted. A mouth was more convenient. No one made you swallow. But most men could not get it from their wives—no matter how much they pleaded. And most men pleaded.

She felt him stir . . . poor Mister Adjuster, booze and bureaucrats conspire to geld the sorry devils. Sykes . . . what the hell kind of name is that for a man? Sounds Swedish. Well Mister Adjuster, let's see what the big-city life does for you here. You came a long way out—this might just be the medicine you need. She felt him swell in her cheek. Maybe you won't be so bad after all. There's one thing you ought to know, Mister Adjuster: if the government hasn't already got you by the balls, a real woman will.

Sarah lay down beside Drake and a single cricket chirped, lonely in the Walkers' fields. He lay on his back with his shirt off, the paste bandages that wrapped his chest now dried stiff and brittle, his ribs sore. He was breathing; Sarah could see his collarbone straining beneath his flesh, and his flat stomach receding, receding.

The flesh moved at the edge of his cast. He was not asleep, she could tell. Was he thinking? That she couldn't tell. Did he love her?
That she had to trust.
Hogwash.
Trust was something rich people could afford. Working people did not trust—they were trusted. Oh so-and-so is a good man, yeah, and she's a good wife, too —and damn, they can get the job done. Whose job? Your job? Your family's job? Somebody else's job? So what was left after sweating and the grunting and maybe it felt good and maybe it didn't? Do you wonder if he's gonna run after another woman? Sometimes you can see a stranger in the street, his hatbrim breaking across his eyes, a lean no-name, and he smells you out, gently, in your direction. And if you decided to do it, you wouldn't ask his name. You wouldn't want to know. No names. No trust. Don't need any.
But ask a man his name and it all starts there.
"Drake, goddammit—do you love me?"
Drake breathed deeper, but kept quiet.
What the hell is he gonna say? Yes dear. No dear. What was that again, dear? If he ever went for another woman, Sarah would chop it off. Try that on for size, dear. She stuck her hands between his legs and got a good grip. She felt him move the tiniest bit. She put her lips to his ear. "I asked you a question, Drake."
Still with a firm grip below the bell clapper, she tickled him. "Remember, what's yours . . . is mine."

Sykes looked down at Eve's body below him. She was faking her heat. This much was clear. Who cared? Not Sykes. He liked her hamming sex show anyway. She had not bothered to take off her dress, and she wore nothing underneath. Her blouse was open and spread loose like an untethered sail flapping in the breeze. He could see her heaving dimly in the darkness. Skirt hiked, firm thighs waiting, she guided him along with a strong practiced hand. Breathing erratic—short gulps—this much was real. But under parry and thrust, he tried to make it work. He failed. The Seagram's was none too obliging; he went numb. He did not wilt, but he wasn't popping.
Delilah never bent over for Samson's curly locks. He knew it. And she knew it. And she hammed it up anyway.

Eve stared at the ceiling for a moment; Sykes' body weight was a little more than expected, but now upon her the weight seemed natural. He wore his undershirt and his socks. That's all. His coarse woolen sock scratched her ankle. Then itched. Even as he broke the gate, she knew he'd never make the clubhouse turn without some help. Poor devil, the Government crammed the bit between his teeth. The Seagram's too.

She was full up. Better now than never—after all, they *were* neighbors. She reached under her thigh and, with fingers used to strengthen sad old tired men, she held him in her lock and made him bloom, ripe for the plucking. The time had come, the true show to make. She whipped her head from side to side, as if enthralled; her breath came in sharp gasps, she squawked, she groaned, she drooled, she clutched in oblivion. She gripped and squeezed, and felt him lose control. He was done for, and he did what she wanted all along. He could not resist. Her act was good: it made him slave to the adroit contractions of her cat. As his heart pounded and he shook his head from side to side, Eve breathed regular. She was reaching for her cigarettes before he rolled off.

When Sarah made the advance, Drake never threw away the chance.

"If what's mine is yours"—Drake held his tender ribs—"treat it well." He wanted to take the tape from his body, shred it and forget it.

"So don't deliver the merchandise in damaged condition." She climbed on top of him, careful not to rest any weight on his chest lest his ribs bruise or grate. "Slowly." She was strong. "I'll take you slowly."

The air was motionless in the night, the fields steady and aloof. Drew and Buck could not return to the barn, now occupied by Lomax and Mrs. Moon. Drew rose up, as though taller than he; her olive skin molten, she took him by the hand and led him swiftly.

And he followed, caught headlong in her woman's scent, ready at her footsteps.

Tina, crouched on the porch, watched them go. This exclusion seemed unfair. Still, these stealthy spooners' serenade in privacy might bare an opportunity for Tina's sweet hungry eyes. She saw them walk north along the access road and waited for their tramping to fade against the night. Silence came once more; Tina moved, then halted.

She moved again walking hard, down the road, pursuing, wishing her footfalls closer and closer to the ground. She saw Drew and Buck walking up ahead and she slowed. They stopped and Tina dropped to her knees. They wandered off the road into the soft alfalfa. And Tina crept closer.

They had lain in the green alfalfa; the rustling of the broad sword leaves blossomed in the darkness, far from the stars, out of earshot as the moon, an outlaw, hung cross-legged in the east. A forbidden watcher, watching the forbidden toil, watched the innocents walking the boards of their secret theater. The crickets sang in chorus, then a lonely solo, a duet and on. Tina crawled on hands and knees, barely breathing, closer. The gripping watery cramp returned, jumbling her gut; the sprinkling sweat was back at her neck. Then suddenly, as sudden as a locust blown out of the copper sky, crashing against her forehead, Tina saw them in the field. Drew was on her back, and the pale blushing skin of her legs shiny bright in the darkness catching the starlight shone ghostly gossamer to Tina's fleeting eyes. Almost hips rocking at Buck's gentle stuff, Drew made a sound, a cooing, and a whisper low and far away. Drew ran her fingers through his hair, to the neck and across his scalp again. She helped, cajoling, forced his manhood to the swordpoint yielding. Tina breathed near the dirt as that woman took herself a boy in her woman's strength, took him for long moments in that field, and made him melt away.

In her own bed, safe in solitude, lonely between the sheets, Tina felt her flesh and touched herself. She drew her knees up as she had seen in the field, but not as much. Staring at the rough wood ceiling Tina could almost hear Buck and Drew in the darkness, love in the night, the cooing, the gurgle, the hushed strangling whisper.

Between her knees she parted and swelled. She knew no names, nor the names of the parts, nor the roles of the parts in the whole. She found a sullen dangerous mouth, speechless, angry. She wet two fingers with the slippery saliva from her tongue and drove her sugar hand on and on, sliding. She stared at the rough wood ceiling with her eyes closed. Her back was arched and she listened for the sounds of the night, the gurgles and the moans. The alfalfa field was hers to choose. Decisions of the time and simple motes of men.

Lomax left the barn and ambled to the U.S. Route to stand at its edge. The telephone wires stretched against the night, glinting dark lines against a black sky. He stood looking at the wires and presently the silent owl landed. The bird hopped from one sharp claw to the other, balancing on the telephone pole crossbar. It clamped talons to the wood, puffed its feathers fat with air and blinked. Lomax stared silent, his harelip muc-muc drooling when he breathed. The wild moon of summer rode the sky, its silver brilliance passing. The moon turned blood red, as it pulled on the ebb and tide of men's water, the red shadow of decay: for long moments in the dead of night, the moon bled in the sky and Bone County caught in a web of gosling dream was none the wiser.

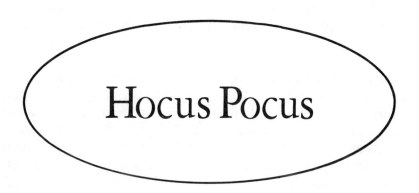

Hocus Pocus

HERE IS THE CHURCH, AND HERE IS THE STEEPLE;
OPEN THE DOOR AND HERE ARE THE PEOPLE.

At dawn Tina woke, like a sharp edge, and she saw how the day could break too suddenly, and her notch in the day might go unnoticed. Caught unaware, snared snug in her bed, how could she convince the others that, indeed, something was strange today? She had wet the bed like an infant, all control lost; but when she touched the spot, her hand came up warm, stained red. Her thighs were sticky and she tasted blood on her fingertips. Not like her mother, years bored by her body's nagging flood, who moped a bit when her time came—this was Tina's time, and like most rousing jolts, her eyes were at the stained mercy of her first release.

Already a blue tint splashed the sky, and she looked through the open window. The shiny blackbirds, usually so prompt, usually strutting out for breakfast, were oddly silent. Sunlight. The taut fertile dawn. Without reproaching her body's sly spur, Tina made her bed. She slowly smoothed out the wrinkles left from her body's impression, and before throwing the coverlet, she bent over the sleepy sheets and kissed the stain of her bloody flow.

The good neighbors came from all over Bone County. For the most part they came to pay farewell and honorable witness, clearing the parting chit to a man most had all but ignored not three days before. Moss Greene's trouble was like many another's. His dirge too, like many another's. As in life, his wife lay silent by his side. In death, his children rested hidden in their coffins. The solemn carnival began with the shuffle of boots rasping against wooden floorboards. Preacher's church was crammed to the doors, the air steady in the morning's light. Sunday's Best was buttoned right to the Adam's apple. Shoes were polished to reflection; vests were brushed; hair combed and oiled; dainty faces scrubbed, lacquered, rouged and powdered; bodies perfumed with lavender, primped and pampered: all in all rightly done for Preacher's final service, his sultan's speech and broad hand smoothing the furrowed brow. A deathsong sweetly sung could bier no better audience.

Yohanna Johns with his three nitwit sons tramped in. A crease of immortal severity cut across the bonebag's lips. He said nothing, pointed to a pew and his brood fell on their bottoms, collapsing to the wood. In grunting whispers the boys spoke among themselves, looking around with surly glances, finding not much to their liking and less to draw their moth-candle minds. With his dry open hand Johns slapped the back of Elroy's head; the boys sat still in their seats, afraid to breathe.

Josie, J. J. Baskum's wife, took up two seats, her ponderous buttocks pressed into a girdle of monumental restraint. Baskum snuggled in beside her, plucked the plump hand from his wife's lap and folded her flesh over his own. Josie was not crying yet, but no doubt she would gush forth in the final moments and Baskum was at the ready: a bright yellow handkerchief flew like a flag from his breast pocket. Baskum had even laundered his white tie.

June Tate, her hair bun wrapped tighter than a jaybird's ass, pulled the Sheriff right down the aisle to the front pew and nearly pushed him onto the bench slats. June did not want to miss a word. Sheriff Tate resigned himself to this, praying Preacher would not drag the service out.

Parker Watts sat in the back, ramrod straight, staring dead ahead, his eyes steady as stones and twice as blank. He fiddled with his tie clip, rebuttoned his collar, jiggled his tie and pressed the knot so it stood at attention.

Claire and Bart Lowell came down the aisle arm in arm; though no one knew, her clean-shaven legs were silk to touch, and the hollows under her arms smooth and fragrant as a child's. She walked lighter than on air, letting Bart lead her close to where Preacher would speak. Bart sat first and then she, dropping her wrist on Bart's thigh, waiting for him to take it. The good barber made no such gesture, and so Claire spread her fingers along his leg, her nails creasing the fabric of his pants. *Just you wait, Preacher . . . just you wait.*

As if by an earlier arrangement Eve came in with the Adjuster Sykes; the government man was uncertain and so he let Eve go before him. She walked, her carriage high and proud, letting the world see her with an abandoned man, letting the Adjuster man see her in the world, not giving a damn for whispers or sniggering. God could throw her out of His own house, but no one else. Sykes slipped into the pew beside her, stuck a pinky in his ear and wrung it around. Then he examined the ear wax. Eve glowered and Sykes plunged the fisted pinky into his trouser pocket, forgetting to wipe it off. His eyes were puffy.

Henry and his brother arrived from Baskum's spread in the black gloom of clattering horse-drawn wagons. Henry, lean as a willow sapling, held the arm of his terrified wife; with his free hand he swept the fedora from his brow and the broken felt hat dangled from his fingers. Behind Henry, the crushed little man came down from his wagon and mounted the church steps. The little man's lame son sat on the rig till Henry turned and, with his brother, held the boy by the arms and let the withered leg hang useless by its shredded tendons, pigeon toe scraping the steps, ankle bent out. They sat the boy by the door and the crushed man fanned his child's head with his wormy straw boater.

Like two hedgehogs looking for trouble, Lepke and Hanson appeared at the church door. Lepke had dropped his grease-stained apron and seemed naked without it; he did not know what to do with his hands. Lepke was a cook in Sunday clothes and never one for church on the Lord's Day. A watch fob stretched across his middle, gold encircling the dirty bird. This fob was a trinket stolen from an unknown stranger's corpse, pinched seconds after the stranger fell in a St. Louis movie theater lobby, struck in the head with a bursting blood vessel. The call went up —*was there a doctor in the house?* Lepke said *I am,* give him air, back off, loosen his tie, take off the chain—no one questions a doctor—I'm very sorry, there's nothing I can do. Let me call the ambulance. Lepke slipped toward the pay phones and lit out the front door. He hated funerals.

Hanson hung back, shiftless. He brought a burning cigarette into the church and then thought better of it. He jittered outside again and crushed the butt on the steps, scraping it over the side onto the ground. The Goods Store man, standing all goody-two-shoes at the church door—Hanson came to the funeral, because everyone else did. And besides, those were *his* coffins lying in state. Sheriff Tate and Watts had not settled on the payment, but Hanson was not going to raise the issue till the caskets were safely lowered into the earth. Once the bodies were interred, Hanson's charity and the transaction would be as final as they could ever get. Then, by God—pay up!

Drake Walker's green pickup circled the oak tree and parked in front of Lepke's Diner. The truck bed was squeezed pretty tight: Buck, the two tenants, and the Moons. They squatted, sat, or kneeled in the trailer, pressed up against the metal walls. Drake, Tina and Sarah sat in the cab. Buck jumped out first, then the tenants and finally Mrs. Moon and Lomax were helped out of the back. Drake led the way to the church, Sarah with Tina, Drew with Buck. Eddy and Ryder walked together. Mrs. Moon and Lomax trailed behind. They reached the church steps just as Preacher Simon started closing the doors. Preacher looked at Drake as he mounted the steps and Preacher's hand fell from the door and it swung free. He backed away and let Drake usher in his people. Drake stayed with Preacher until his crew was seated, and he helped shut the church doors, stifling the air within. Drake stood with his back to the closed door and Preacher tarried for a moment. "Don't see you so often, Drake—you don't come as regular as you used to."

For a moment Drake said nothing; he looked over the heads in the crowded church and heard Preacher's soft high breathing at his side. One by one a head would turn as some nosy so-and-so peeked over his shoulder to see what had become of Preacher.

They would see him standing in the back and then quick whip their heads front so as not to be caught staring. Flies hovered over the four caskets. "Get on with it, Preacher."

Outside in the square the low rumble of an auto engine died in a gurgle and a purr when Meriwether cut the motor. He parked in front of Bart Lowell's Barber Shop and sat with his forearm resting on the rolled-down window. The scratches and cuts from that damn bird were healing, the scabs now thickened and drying. The owl had clawed the top of his head, and where the talon broke the scalp the hair was matted in a clot of blood. Simple had offered to shave off the spot, but Meriwether hated the idea of walking around with a square bald patch of pink skin eyeing the sky where he could not even look at it in a mirror. Sooner or later the blood would flake away and you could never tell the difference. Inside the church behind the shut door, the organ piped a tune and a hymn was struck. The hosanna struggled through the church's wooden walls, testing the building's own quiet strength.

Preacher placed his hands on the rough wooden pulpit and without his even asking "Shhsh," the murmurs died away. Preacher pursed his lips; palms down, he tapped one index finger three times, as though setting his metronome to the proper beat. He nodded his head as if listening to the spoken word. He began in a normal leaden voice and his first words carried into the church air, hanging dismal and dangerous over the heads of his congregation.

"When I first took my studies at the Seminary, I heard it said that you can petition the Lord with prayer." Again he tapped his finger three times.

" . . . petition the Lord with prayer . . . " The incessant flies darted over the caskets and one rude insect landed on Moss Greene's heaven bell. The bell did not tremble. " . . . petition the Lord with prayer . . . " Preacher shook his head from side to side and his eyes rolled in their sockets; he shrugged, amazed at the stupidity of the whole business. As though honest people should know better, as though the truths were self-evident, as though you had to be deaf, dumb and blind never to realize the simple alternatives. Preacher wagged his head.

"You can . . . *not,*" he shouted, "petition the Lord with prayer."

"*You cannot!*" Preacher hurled even louder, *"petition the Lord with prayer."* Winced and jolted, the front pew trembled and withered.

Preacher calmed down and tried to reason with the dullards. "You can work hard from day to day. Yes, you can do that. You can be righteous. Oh, yes you can. I'll even grant that a good man can be lazy. He can raise a hand against his children. He can covet another man's wife. Your wife can covet another husband. You can forgive. She can forgive you. Your children may sin against you, and in your heart of hearts you may even find it in God's mercy to forgive them. *But you cannot . . . you cannot . . . petition the Lord with prayer.*"

Josie Baskum broke down with a low "Whooo . . . " and J. J. flourished his yellow handkerchief as his wife buried her head in the hollow of his neck. Baskum never took his eyes off the pulpit, and with the first swipe of the tear rag, missed his wife's eyes altogether, brushing the cloth against her ear.

June Tate in the front pew began to tremble, her knees dimpling with the strain. The Sheriff put his arm around her shoulders. Preacher saw Tate do this and leaned down over the edge of the pulpit.

"Don't comfort that woman," Preacher hissed at Tate. The Sheriff's face broke out red and sweaty.

"The Divine Eyes have witnessed the pain in her temple of righteousness. Don't interfere." Sheriff Tate dropped his arm from around June's shoulder and wiped his forehead with his sleeve.

Preacher looked out over the crowd. "Hot enough for you?" He smiled a little. "That's what the Devil's gonna ask you when you hit the molten bottom—he's gonna say, 'Hot enough for you?' "

Claire Lowell and Bart were staring straight up to the pulpit. Claire's hand gripped Bart's thigh and he wriggled in his seat; Claire's eyes were glassy, and that glint, that shard of broken crystal, glistened wet and ready. Her tongue darted between her lips and she licked the mole on her upper lip.

"What is this petition business?" Preacher asked. "Petition is . . . *can I have this, God? . . . and can I have that, God? . . . and if I* do such-and-such, *will you do this for me, God?"* He stopped, dropped his hands from the pulpit edge, and took a step back. He twisted his trunk from side to side as though limbering up for calisthenics, and he loomed again at the edge, hands planted on the wood.

"Righteousness is not a poker chip. You can slave all day in the field and you can pray and you can be sure the Divine Eye has seen your toil, but if you are not righteous, the Divine Eye will see this too and your fertile labor shall be in vain. The flower will wither in the field, your hay will rot even on the driest days . . . you'll say, *'But God, I toiled so hard!'* . . . and let me tell you friends, this will make precious little difference if you have not been righteous."

Preacher rubbed his hands together. "So what is this *righteousness?*

"This divinity is first knowing the face of the Beast and when its ugly face has turned upon you. This divinity is knowing the touch of the Beast, and when its vandal's hand has rested on your shoulder. Know the Beast when your hay goes moldy in the driest weather. That ain't chance. It ain't fate. This is a signal.

"So when your farm goes broke, and the insurance man comes around, and when the bank starts calling in its loans, *this,* my friends, is a *signal."*

Preacher unclasped his hands and leaned forward over the pulpit. "The bank doesn't know of your righteousness and doesn't care. The insurance companies live in Hartford, Connecticut, and *they* don't know about your righteousness. *So who does?"*

Claire Lowell steadied her grip on Bart's leg and whispered, "The Lord, Preacher."

He heard Claire's soft voice. "That's right. That's absolutely right. The Lord *knows.* The Divine Eyes *see.* The banks don't see. The law can't see. Justice is blind, Innocence is forgotten, Guilt is mislaid, and the ever-loving insurance companies live in Hartford, Connecticut—*so they can't see."*

Preacher took a deep breath. He counted three beats of his heart, and tapped his index finger in rhythm. A stillness in the church rolled, curling like a great wave from behind the pulpit, crashing upon the bodies nailed to the pews.

"So." Soft and easy. "So."

He let the word hang in the air and the great wave washed back and forth over the heads of the assembled.

"So, when the world sets you on the balance, and scales teeter tipping gently against you, your neighbors will feel sorry . . . they'll say, 'Oh look what's happening to that poor soul, what a shame . . .' and they'll say, 'Let's give him a helping hand,' and you know something—they'll think they're being righteous Christians and so they are, and they'll think this is what they're *supposed* to do. And so it is . . .

"But!"

The crowd leaned forward.

"But . . ."

Their bottoms strained on the wooden seats.

"But, my friends, what these upright Christians have failed to notice will cost them dearly. They have trespassed on the privilege of the Divine Hand. Divinity decides . . .

"Divinity decides if a man is worthy of being rich. Divinity decides when a man shall be punished, and Divinity decides how long a man shall suffer—whether he shall suffer one day . . . or one month . . . or a hundred months . . . or a *hundred years.* And Divinity decides when a man has suffered enough. And when a man has suffered enough, Divinity will rescue him . . . not his neighbors, not his wife, not his children . . . Divinity decides and Divinity will restore him. *Divinity decides* the time and the place."

Preacher stopped again and wiped his forehead with the back of his sleeve. "Let Divinity decide, and you shall not trespass on the privilege of the Lord."

He dropped his hands from the rough wood ledge and turned from the assembled folk. Marybelle, at the side of the altar, struck the first chord from the hand-pump organ and the note cut straight back to the last pew and pulled the seething tide over the heads of the people. The water ebbed away as though pulled by Preacher's own gravity, the swell falling over his shoulders behind the pulpit from where the wave had risen. Preacher had done his best. They had all heard the words he had thought to say, but not the ones he had left unspoken, nor those he kept for his own salvation. Words whispered in his bitter loneliness, words of greater fear than any that came before . . . that the name of the Beast can never be said . . . that Divinity hides behind a veil of chance . . . that God's message is hidden in the puddle of his brains, warped by Preacher's own poor sight . . . that sometimes the best endeavors fail to parlay a blind bargain, like coward gamblers folding their cards at the slightest bluff. And Preacher waited, hoping for a sign to bend his reason, the vision of her coming shrouded in white, lips parted and strong wings folded down upon her back. He staggered down the street of desire, knowing—worst of all—that angels came as the messengers of God, but that they never stopped the Roman slaughter of the Innocents nor kept Pharaoh's wizards from turning staffs into serpents to tempt the eyes of Aaron. That God's message would serve God alone . . . that Moss Greene was dead, and was staying dead for good.

Claire Lowell dropped her hand from Bart's leg and pressed her thighs together; the crystal shard in her eye would not vanish on command. A familiar hymn took form slowly and from where he stood with his back turned to the crowd, Preacher Simon heard Claire Lowell's voice clearly through the chorus, and the crystal wetness ran damp and ready down between his shoulder blades. He could tell Claire was staring at him now.

June Tate sagged against the Sheriff; her husband was damned if he would take his arm away. Preacher's turned back had nothing to do with it. Preacher made no mention of the four bodies, but there would be time enough for that after the caskets had been lowered and before the handfuls of dirt were thrown willy-nilly into the grave. Sheriff Tate felt a tight bulge in his pants pocket. The blue woolen watchcap.

Elroy Johns and his two brothers were driven to distraction, bored into oblivion; they had taken about as much of Preacher's wind as they could stand. For that matter, they had swallowed too much hot air, sung a little too loudly and were now eager to get to the good part—dropping the stiffs in the hole. Elroy looked at his father, sitting stiffly in the pew. Then he looked at the coffins lying in state.

"Paw?"

Yohanna Johns' Adam's apple bobbed in his throat.

"Paw? How come they don't keep the lids off? Why don't they keep the lids off so we can see their faces? Paw? We can't see their faces."

Johns' turkey neck twisted and he grabbed his son's cheek between his thumb and forefinger. Johns squeezed and Elroy's lips popped out like a guppy.

"They don't keep the lids off so the flies don't land on the dead folks' noses. That's why they don't keep the lids off."

Josie Baskum had herself under control now. J. J. Baskum's yellow handkerchief was soggy and when Josie gave it back, Baskum wrung the rag out. But floods of tears drown little; Baskum only managed to squeeze one tiny drop of salty water from his yellow rag. The single tear fell from the handkerchief and spotted the crotch of his pants. He glanced around, but even Josie had not noticed. As the crowd began to leave the church, Josie got up to leave. Baskum rested a heavy hand on her arm. "Not so fast . . . "

He wanted the spot to dry: no pee stains while standing at the gravesite.

Parker Watts, a man of few words but of mighty aspirations, stopped Sykes as he walked down the aisle with Eve. Sykes looked down at Watts' hand gripping his sleeve and let a few more hurried people edge around him. Watts was evidently agitated and his erect tie knot jiggled when he spoke.

"You don't suppose they forgot about the pallbearers, do you?"

Some aspiration. The damn fool forecloses on the guy's loan and then wonders whether he'll be picked as a pallbearer. "No, I don't think they forgot about it, Mr. Watts." Sykes did not know for sure, but he sure as hell did not care.

Eve pulled on Sykes' other sleeve and, tethered, Sykes let himself be led toward the doors. Eve whistled a low two-note in his ear. "That Mister Watts oughta try one of those bone boxes on for size some day."

The woman was right.

"He's just the type that wants a perfect fit." Eve winked when she caught his eye.

Lepke and Hanson, standing just outside the church door, watched the crowd descend the steps and gather around.

"Fine speech." Lepke fingered his gold watch fob.

"Indeed," Hanson agreed. "Fine sermon."

Hanson had heard Preacher say something about "divine hands"; this only prompted Hanson to look at his own hands, the dirt crusting under the fingernails.

Lepke remembered something about "insurance companies in Hartford, Connecticut"—but to Lepke, never well traveled in Connecticut or elsewhere, it seemed a damned useless place to keep an insurance company.

A crowd gathered at the base of the church steps. The doors propped open made a dark cavern like a toothless mouth, and the pallbearers, deathwatch coolies, carried the coffins on their shoulders, pinewood ships, ready to litter the last wharf. The children's caskets came first, borne by Yohanna Johns and his three boys. They came slowly down the steps, careful not to tip the boxes too far. Henry, Drake, Buck and Sheriff Tate carried Liza Greene's box. Ryder and Eddy, Lepke and Hanson, took Moss Greene's. The men carrying the children's caskets stopped when they reached the ground and waited for the two other coffins.

Mrs. Moon stood off at the edge of the crowd, near Hanson's Goods, and looked across the square at Meriwether sitting in his car. Meriwether, smoking a cigarette, saw her too; he flicked the butt out the car window and he spat a green phlegm gob over his arm and out of the car. The spittle didn't quite clear the sill and ran down the car door.

Without command, the blackbirds in the great oak sent up a chorus shrilling, dancing on the branches, kicking up such a ruckus that the oak leaves trembled. A few heads in the crowd turned to look at the tree. Most did not. The blackbirds clattered and then lit off—a hundred birds at once beat their wings lifting into the air, sounding tiny drums on a summer's day. The small black cloud of feathers formed in the air, swooped in a circle around the tree and dived over the church roof, flying for the air, free on the open fields.

The clock in the church steeple struck noon, a long low chime. The clock struck again. *Dong* . . . and Meriwether sat up straight in the car seat. For him the crowd had melted, and Mrs. Moon stood alone in the shade of the empty oak. A breeze ruffled her gray hair, and the eyes that touched him ran strong fingers over his scalp.

Dong . . .

A tiny bead of sweat hung from Meriwether's chin.

Dong . . .

The scabs from the owl's talons itched on his arms, a wormy itch, and he cracked the scabs, scratching them open.

DONG . . .

The scab on his scalp swelled ready to burst, the skin peeling. He clawed the matted hunk of blood-dried hair, tore it out, and stared at the moist clump, damp in his fever fist.

DONG . . .

The sole of his foot throbbed, the canker needle twisting, a briar thorn caught, hooking his flesh.

DONG . . .

The smell of gasoline ran in his nostrils, plugging up his ears.

DONG . . .

His hands were black with charcoal and he wiped them on his pants.

DONG . . .

He looked in the car's rearview mirror and saw Moss Greene sitting stone silent, watching, in the back seat.

DONG . . .

He whipped his head. The car was empty.

DONG . . .

The Moon woman was at the car door. Her face filled the window. She reached into the car, down between his legs—Meriwether saw the nails on her fingers, reaching . . .

The car engine died and Mrs. Moon dropped the car keys in his lap.

"You were gunning the pedal." The razor tongue. "That's bad for the motor."

The clock struck for the twelfth time. Preacher stood on the church steps, between the two large caskets with the bells. They were ready to descend. The clock hands stopped moving, stuck on high noon. The clock struck once more, *Do-*, but a gear somewhere in the works caught and jammed, breaking a spring, curling a cable, stripping a wheel . . . the hands began to fall. As if stripped and loose, with a broken part deep in a brass heart, each hand fell away from twelve noon, slipping past the Roman numbers. The minute hand went counterclockwise, retracing the last half hour; the short hand fell past I, II, III, IV, V, the two hands met again at VI, little brother kissing big brother. They hung at VI. The clock was finished.

Most of the assembled jostled together waiting for the pallbearers to descend the steps. Meriwether rubbed his face and blood from his cracked scabs smeared on his lips. Mrs. Moon was gone now, standing in the shade of the green oak. Preacher stared up at the steeple and saw how the clock had broken down. He dropped his eyes to see who else had seen it too.

Sykes and Eve were looking hard at him, bitter disbelief tugging at the corners of their mouths. That Buck Walker boy, and his little sister too . . . they saw it for they were looking in the faces round their shoulders, looking to see who else. Sheriff Tate gave Preacher the evil eye as if to say, "Jesus, fella, your damn clock picked a fine time to kick over dead."

The rest of the crowd was waiting for the pallbearers and Preacher stamped his foot.

"Enough!"

Preacher shook his fist, threatening the dawdlers and the crowd itself for pausing at the church doors. "Enough! We came here for last rites. Let's get on with it!"

Preacher bounded down the church steps and the pallbearers followed. The crowd fell in behind the caskets, around the side of the church, out back where the graves were neatly dug and ready. The death bells on the large coffin lids gleamed brassy: metal silence in the sunlight. The boxes swayed on strong shoulders, in a private battle of ceremony over gravity. The graveyard beyond the church was small and cramped; wooden crosses mostly served for monuments. Death was quick, burial quicker and a stock of marble tombstones was the last item needed in Hanson's Goods for supply to a town that wanted sustenance in life more than fashion in death. If a cross teetered and wasted away, make another. If such endeavors were not worth the effort, the dead would lie just as quiet under dry parched grass as under an eternal flame.

Ollie Cottle leaned against his shovel. The dry earth was packed in four neat heaps; two little ones, two larger ones. The

adult graves might be termed the deep six, but not the children's
—the deep three perhaps, never six. Never deep. Wooden two-by-
fours were laid over the open pits; the caskets were lowered slowly
onto the slats and they rested temporarily at ground level. Ropes
were curled in sailors' coils by the graveside ready to be unfurled
for the final descent. Preacher took his place at the gravehead. He
carried no book. The assembled gathered around, not jostling, not
craning, not weeping, somber, yet barely morose. A white picket
fence enclosed the graveyard; Preacher kept it freshly painted, his
maintenance for the dear deceased.

Beyond the picket fence, Sheriff Tate saw the dog sitting in the
tall grass. Moss Greene's black hound rested on its muscled
haunches, not even panting in the heat. The dog's skull was
cracked, a wound closed and healed, a seam holding the brains in
place. The dog sat, staring straight ahead.

Preacher cleared his throat. The coffins waited.

"I do not bury thee . . . Gabriel buries thee.

"I did not love thee . . . Gabriel loves thee.

"When thou toiled . . . Gabriel toiled with thee.

"When thou rose in anger . . . so did Gabriel.

"When thou showed mercy . . . Gabriel's gift was freely
given."

Again Preacher repeated, "I do not bury thee . . . Gabriel
buries thee."

Preacher moved his lips. He let the archangel bury the dead,
washing the deed from the crowd's own past, dissolving their com-
plicity and ensuring their silence. Lips sealed, the cold stroke was
pushed aside: Gabriel buries you . . . not I. Pain vanished from
Preacher's sleight of hand, like his own church's magic, robbed
from the altar by the Beast's unspoken warning. He moved his lips
and soothed the crowd, with the only balm their God allowed.

Tina saw it first—only Tina, for the others, heads bowed,
looked soul-struck at their mournful feet. Moss Greene's coffin bell
trembled. Preacher, preoccupied with the sound of his own voice,
saw it not. Tina's hungry eyes engulfed the tremulous bell; she
tugged her mother's sleeve.

"He's alive . . . "

"Sshh . . . "

"He's alive!"

"Sshh . . . "

The coffin bell trembled, and more—it rang. Pealing, *gang-gong*.

Gang-gong!

Tina danced on her toes. *"He's alive! He's alive!"*

No more mournful feet, no toe-tapping, no more hollow throaty coughs, no more preoccupation with the resonance of a thin-lipped voice. Sarah held Tina, straining by the shoulders, the young girl's eyes ripping the air.

GANG-GONG!

Drake Walker moved first, grabbing the shovel plunged in the dirt, wedging the blade under the coffin lid.

GANG-GONG!

Sheriff Tate came alongside and helped him pry.

GANG-GONG!

They threw their weight together and Ryder came around, jamming his fingers under the lid, pulling at the nails.

GANG-GONG!

"Harder." They strained and the nails inched up.

"Give him air."

Henry, too, jammed his fingers under the lid and the nails were pried, twisted, out of the wood; the heavy lid fell in the hole.

GANG-

Moss Greene lay face up in the casket. His face had withered in the fire's heat, pinched and wrinkled as a prune, but blacker than a prune; his hair was singed, a great white blister the size of a silver dollar puffed above his eye. His hands were charred, bones burned, the fingers tapered with the blaze, the nails peeled off and melted. His cheekbones had broken through the flaking flesh and a wormy maggot waved its ugly head. Before a tear could well, the blister over the dead eye cracked. The pus dripped and ran. Drake heard a low moan.

In their hurry Yohanna Johns and Hanson lent a hand; Lepke too. The other coffin lids were pried open as the first was just uncovered. Now all could see the little bodies burned and Liza's head charred to a faceless ashen lump. Drake dashed down from coffin to coffin, checking the dead. He grabbed a lock of hair over his own forehead and yanked on it. The bell had rung but Moss Greene had lied and still lay dead. Drake knelt by Moss's casket. The breath came hot down his throat. Again someone moaned behind him.

A little brown chimney swift poked its eager beak around Moss Greene's shoulder and looked up out of the casket past Drake and at the sky. The swallow caught inside the coffin seemed to wonder not at the bell, but at the fresh air, the commotion, and the brightness of the day. The bird chirped once, and then flew up, darting over the cemetery ground, sailing past the points of the white picket fence.

Look for me at the ringing bell . . . No one moved; the moaning stopped. Nothing left now. Drake ran his hand across the smooth pine edge of the casket. The bitter sickly smell of the body rose up into his face, the deep putrefaction of a lost corpse and the sewage of its flesh.

"Cover him up."

No one rushed to nail the lids back on. Sarah's shaking hands squeezed Tina's shoulders, hurting. Tina saw her father glaring at the faces pressed around the graves. He had risen and seemed to tower now, the muscles in his chest and arms moving as he breathed. *"Cover him up!"*

The coffin lid was fetched out of the hole. Someone found a hammer and started tacking the nails down. Drake watched over as strong arms uncoiled the rope and lowered the coffins into the ground. The fistfuls of God's earth came next, dropped by slow hands, the muffled thud of ground cascading, the smooth step of people passing—they threw their dirt and left. One by one, each threw a handful; not one man's eyes met another's. They hurried off, back to the living and away from the dead.

Adjuster Sykes stepped to the gravesite, the dirt heavy in his hand. Tate was standing at his elbow; the Adjuster looked down along Tate's stubby legs and his boot toes, nearly at the grave's edge. He heard the Sheriff's deep breath at his side. "Swell coffins, Tate."

"They ain't mine." Tate's voice was soft in Sykes' ear. "Hanson dug 'em up from the back of his store—" Tate stopped suddenly and wiped his mouth with the back of his hand. "I mean . . . "

"Forget it." Sykes looked the Sheriff in the eye. The lawman's sober daylight face of duty was set hard like a plaster cast. Bells or no bells, burns or no burns, birds or no birds, Sykes saw the facts on the Sheriff's bulldog face: Moss Greene in the ground and the dirt coming down. Sykes dropped his handful of earth and stepped away from the hole.

Eve took his hand as he came down toward the picket fence and they left the cemetery together. She was pale but steady on her feet, and she walked up close to him, her curves brushing up along his side, as if by touching she could wrap herself in the living warmth of his body and the blood stone of his soul. Sykes let her walk against him, liking their paired bodies and liking her. "I could use a drink."

"To hell with a drink." She turned to face him and put her arms around his neck. She kissed him right there under the great oak, right in the square, and she did not care. Sykes liked this too and held both hands on her strong waist. That Looney Tune County air ran through him like a fresh dawn breeze. Better than the dirty air back east. Better than anything he'd breathed before.

"I could still use a drink."

Sheriff Tate was the last man at the burial plot, but he threw no dirt. He took the blue woolen watchcap from his pocket, folded it over in his hands and threw it into Moss Greene's grave. Ollie Cottle, leaning on his shovel, saw the Sheriff and moved to stop him —too late. The hat fell into the pit.

"My hat."

"What?"

"Dat's my hat. I ain't goin' in to get it."

Tate drew up to Cottle and laid a hand on the Negro's shoulder. "You saying that's your hat . . . ?"

"Dat's what Ah sayin'—what'd you tho' it in the hole fo'?"

They were alone at the gravesite, and Sheriff Tate leaned his weight a little heavier on the Negro's shoulder and squeezed the flesh in his hand. Tate was not so dumb as to go and think Ollie Cottle was some match-happy nigger bent on burning good folks outta house and home. Murder, too? Tate looked Cottle straight in the eye and the black man looked him back, his doe's eye-whites yellow with age. Tate knew Hanson's man a long time and those fire-happy bastards better think it all out again if they figured Tate was gonna lynch up this nigger on the basis of a lousy hat. Lucky thing the others didn't see. "Ollie, you remember when you lost the hat?"

"Yeah, I remember."

"You ain't gonna forget are you?"

"No, Tate, I ain't gonna forget."

"You gonna stay around town, right?"

Cottle's eyes narrowed and his forehead wrinkled in a frown. "Tate, where'm I gonna go to? That there Model A gotta be fixed. How about it?"

Tate left Cottle to fill in the graves. "That's fine with me."

Parker Watts sat behind his teller's cage and fingered the edge of the green-shaded lamp. The glass was smooth, the shade rim partially sanded so it still had texture. Then he noticed his wristwatch. The big hand and the little hand had fallen to the six. He took his watch off his wrist and put the timepiece to his ear. The movement was dead. He shook the watch and heard nothing.

Watts eased off the stool and walked past the wooden, thigh-slapping swing doors to the bank's front window. He slipped the wristwatch off his wrist and fingered the stem, ready to wind it. At the window the roller shades snapped round and round. Watts stared up at the church's steeple. The tip of one finger touched the tight metal in his wristwatch's winding stem; up above the great oak the steeple clock's hands hung at six, the minute hand overlapping the little hour hand, motionless in the stillborn day. Watts pressed his thumb over the smooth glass of his wristwatch's crystal face. He fingered the metal winding stem and rolled it between his thumb and forefinger, hearing the spring tighten in the watchcase like the midday creak of heavy coffins on men's shoulders.

Watts held the wristwatch to his ear. No cogs turned, no spring unwound. The piece was silent. Through the crystal face the watch's hands hung at six, the minute hand overlapping the little hour hand, motionless as the day trudged on without their keeping time.

The bank door opened. Watts thrust the watch into his trouser pocket. Drake Walker, his wife, Sarah, his two tenant goons and his boy, Buck, were coming in. Watts smiled briefly—gotta make the customers think they're welcome. Drake led the way. He carried a rock in one hand, with paper folded around it, tied with a string. He dropped the rock on the teller ledge, scratching the polished wood.

"That's this?" Watts jittered, his smile gone.
"Read it, Parker. We gonna have a little chat."

"Don't you ever say nothing, Lomax?" Tina put her face up to his.

Lomax said nothing.

"Where's your momma? Where's your sister?"

In broad daylight the square had emptied out. Tina heard no clatter from the diner. Hanson's Goods sagged on its foundation. A car hummed, idling by the curb. Tiny drops of sweat formed under Tina's arms; they gathered dripping down her sides. It seemed stupid to keep the car running in the heat, burning up the gas. Maybe the motor didn't mind. Some cars were like that. As if the driver suddenly cared, he cut the motor and the engine went dead. Through the car's rear window Tina saw the driver run his hand over his head. The man's hair stood on end, ruffled and matted; he picked at his scalp as though looking for nits. Then he scratched his arms, idly searching for an itch. Tina left Lomax standing in front of the bank and walked toward the car. Lomax turned his head and watched her go, his lips parting and gums glistening in a silent muc-muc.

"Well, I just don't understand." Parker Watts held the foreclosure notice in his hand. "You paid up on time, I'll admit that, Drake. But this here says you didn't."

Parker Watts began to check off the possible reasons: "Could be your check bounced, but then I'd be the first to know it. Can't be that.

"Could be a clerical error in the railroad finance office. Difficult to trace.

"Could be the railroad finance office got you mixed up with another Drake Walker—you know of any other Drake Walker?

"Could be that my payment credit against the loan didn't go through from here, but I wire it, keep a receipt, and file it."

Sarah Walker leaned up against the teller's cage. "Check your file, Parker. Show us the receipt."

Adjuster Sykes came into the bank, shutting the door quietly behind him. A sweet whiff of Eve's bottle came off his fingers. He figured his breath was worse. He had done away with his tie, his shirt flared open at the neck and his back was sprinkled with sweat stain. Thoroughly miserable in the heat, Sykes ran his fingers through his blond hair, and a cowlick shot up at a crazy angle, swaying like a bandleader's baton. He saw Drake Walter's people gathered round Watts' teller's cage. Sykes said nothing and only Buck turned to look at him. The Adjuster edged back against a side wall and leaned, standing like a stork with one leg up. Parker Watts, with the crowd pressed around the bars of his teller's cage, never saw Sykes come in; the banker slipped off his stool and headed for the files in the back.

The car idling at the curb was hot to the touch. Tina saw Meriwether sitting in the driver's seat. He was not looking at her; he seemed not to realize she was even near the car. One by one the blackbirds returned to the large oak tree. They dived out of the fireball sun, black lightning in the dayshine, swirling around the branches, landing in a two-step. They strutted in the leaves—no soul save the Devil dressed in a dinner jacket was quick enough to knock a preening blackbird off a tree branch. Tina watched them, her hand against the back fender in the driver's blind spot, the metal warm; sure enough, the Bull sitting up front could not care less.

Standing in front of the bank, Lomax pressed his shoulders to the brick building wall, scraping his bony blades against the mortar; his eyes ran in clear pools, focused. He stared at Tina standing by the car and moved his cloven lips. At his sides his hands twitched by the wrists as if tugged by little strings. His lips came together in a muc-muc and the saliva drooled out the corners of his mouth. He opened his lips to make a sound, to gurgle, to groan, but only a big silent saliva bubble with a violet streak welled from his mouth. The drool bubble trembled, then burst in silence and dribbled down his chin.

Parker Watts sat jackstrap straight, barely able to suppress the rising tide of his satisfaction; he pronounced the verdict as delicately as he could. "The receipt's missing. I have no record of payment."

Ryder squeezed his face to the bars of the teller's cage; the black patch was creased into the socket but Ryder squinted with his good eye. "You're a liar."

Parker Watts stood back with the filing cabinets, afraid to move closer. Drake's tenant looked mighty cutthroat with the black eyepatch jammed up to the bars, his nose poking through the space. "Now, now, Mr. Ryder . . . let's not jump to conclusions."

Eddy plucked a burnt-down Lucky from his lips and ground the cigarette butt on the bank floor, a thin wisp of smoke snaking from his nostrils. He blew the smoke clear of his nose and balled his fingers to a fist so his knuckles stood out like large rivets. "Maybe we should come back there and help you look."

"I don't think that would be a good idea. In the first place it's against bank policy to—" Watts caught sight of Adjuster Sykes leaning against the wall. The banker took a breath, somewhat relieved now in the presence of another civilized gentleman. Watts waved his arm over the heads of Walker's people. "There! You see! Ask the Adjuster!"

They turned from Watts and saw Sykes leaning against the wall. "Isn't that right, Mister Adjuster?" Watts moved closer to his teller's cage. "No receipt? No record? No payment? No luck."

Sykes had cooled off a little and some of the color had come back into his cheeks. Still, sweat glistened in the hollow of his throat, and with a smooth hand, Sykes wiped it off.

"No kidding." Sykes pressed his lips together and pouted; his eyebrows arched and meshed. "Mr. Watts, these people here think you're a liar. And I think you're chickenshit."

Watts seemed to wither behind the teller's bars. The Adjuster's low voice kept on. "Chances are that you're a little of both."

Tina stood behind the car and watched a blackbird in the great oak hop and fly from a high branch to a low one, flexing its wings as it sluiced through the air. She still had her hand on the warm back fender; she chanced to glance at the bank. Lomax, whose eyes always wobbled like egg yolks in a cup, was staring staring straight at her, his eyes dark as walnuts. Glistening spit had run down his chin. His body was flattened against the bank wall as though nailed, and he sagged, his knees weak. He moved his lips; they were bright red and parted in a gash.

Tina would have run to him, but the car started. Dark exhaust shot from the tailpipe and the engine shook the fender; Tina snatched her palm away and jumped. Then a gunny sack blotted out the sky so fast, Tina lost a shoe. She felt it slip from her foot, and her stocking brushed the sidewalk. The stiff back car seat scraped her shoulder and a heavy hand clamped against her mouth. Like the fun part in a game, her heart welled in her chest and she wanted to pee.

The car door slammed and she felt the car move. Then like a heavy belch blowing up her throat, Tina knew this was not Ryder or Eddy playing a joke, that Bucky wasn't driving and that Meriwether sat up front. A rough hand rolled her onto the floor and kept her pinned; she smelled the gas fumes. The car jolted along the rutted road, her head bumping against the back seat. A thin ugly voice whispered in her ear, "Now you know us . . . and we know you. Be still, doan make no trouble and before you knows it, your daddy'll come and get you."

"Jesus, Daddy! Jesus, Daddy! Jesus! Lomax, shout! *Lomax!*" She was shouting and a stiff hand fell back across her mouth. Tina's eyes welled, and her bladder, double-gutted, was cramped in between her legs.

Parker Watts had gained back a little confidence. "Surely, Drake, you've kept a deposit slip. I make one out for you each time you pay an installment. Pity you forgot to bring it with you."

"We didn't." Sarah advanced to the cage and passed the yellow paper under the grill.

"I see." Parker didn't act a bit disappointed. "The deposit slip. Very good." He examined the paper for a moment. Then he shook his head, the cool professional. "Very bad. Now you see, you've dated it here up top, but the bank's date stamp didn't take—you can just make out the impression, but you can't read it. Very bad."

Sarah still said nothing; she looked at Sykes leaning up against the wall. Sykes caught her glance and he hiked up his trousers.

"It's better than nothing, Mr. Watts. Go back to your file. Start at the first date to the loan. Count out the installments, one by one. I think you'll find that you're one short. As you said, the bank's receipt is missing. You'll then stamp three empty deposit slips with your bank's date stamp, and then you'll give them to me. I'll forward your three blank slips and Walker's faded impression receipt to the Treasury Department—all four will then be examined. The Treasury Department will verify whether all four were stamped by the same date machine. As Government witness in lieu of a Treasury Department Field Regulator, I will stand in and help you go over the Walker installment record. Fair enough?"

Parker Watts was not about to argue. "I think we can see our way clear now. But this procedure will certainly take more than two weeks. The foreclosure action doesn't allow for mixups of this kind . . . I'm afraid—"

"Mr. Watts, the foreclosure action is, in any event, against the directives of the National Recovery Administration, the WPA, the TVA, the AAA, the Farm Bureau, the Banking Act of 1933—in short, Mr. Watts, the opinion of the United States Government is that the Blue Vista Flats First National Bank *ought* to be a tad more cooperative."

Parker Watts couldn't help jiggling his tie. "The Blue Vista Bank will do its part for the National Recovery."

Everyone looked at Sykes. "I'll make a call to the Farm Bureau —the foreclosure action won't go through."

Walker's tenants, grouped like a pair of kings in a poker hand, were ogling Sykes the way children look at a magic show. Drake Walker had gained his reprieve and seemed satisfied, relaxed, Sykes grew ten feet tall.

Sarah had stopped watching the proceedings; her face was drawn tight, the corners of her mouth edging down. She had gone to the bank's window and was looking out into the square.

"Drake, honey." Sarah pressed her face to the glass. "Drake, didn't you tell Tina to wait in the truck?"

Buck watched his parents and their tenants spill through the doors of the bank like horses breaking a corral gate. The sunlit square was warm and quiet as before, the stillness settled and relaxed in the hushed leaves of the great oak. Lomax was leaning in the sun against the bank wall, knees buckling. Everyone ignored the idiot boy. Neither Buck's father nor his mother caught the dull focus in Lomax's eye or the saliva drop clinging to the cloven lip. The older folks fanned out into the square, all looking for Tina, for any trace.

Mrs. Moon and Drew came from behind the great oak. They said nothing, but Mrs. Moon walked swiftly from the tree to Lomax's side and seemed to catch him just before he sagged completely to the ground.

Buck noticed the little brown shoe lying sole up on the curb near the barbershop at the same time Sarah did. His mother ran and got the shoe, bringing it back for Drake to see. Sarah turned the shoe over in her hands. "Drake."

A shadow passed over his father's face, like an evil tide that blackens calm waters. Sarah undid the laces and pulled the brown worn tongue free of the shoetop. "Drake!"

Sheriff Tate stepped out of his office, and saw the small crowd in front of the bank. In the cool shade of his office, leaning way back in his spring chair, he had been staring at the ceiling and thinking about Ollie Cottle's hat. The slam of the bank door and the voices on the pavement roused him from his musing and now he saw Drake's people grouped together like an angry mob. Sarah Walker set on him before he took three steps.

"Sheriff, the Bulls stole my baby and you gotta bring her back!" She waved the shoe under Sheriff Tate's nose and one of the laces swiped the side of his jaw. Tate winced, flinching as Sarah waved the shoe again.

"Now hold on here." The Sheriff held up both hands; Buck could tell no woman pushed the Sheriff around. Not Tate's wife—and certainly not somebody else's wife. Not *any* woman. The little pieces rattled together and Buck began to understand. He could see Tate knew the score just as well as anybody, that Tina got snatched and the Bulls did it. That they'd hold her till his father wised up, no more fool penny auctions, no more trouble, no more payments on their land. The quicker the better and no questions asked. But the law had first crack, in its own way and in its own time. Tate hiked up his pants; he spat on the ground and rolled his eyes round and round. Then he stuck his thumb in the gun holster and jacked his gunbelt up.

"Now Sarah, you know how kids are . . . they run around and they wander off . . . "

Sarah had no stomach for Tate's hooey—when she wanted something, she wanted it now. "What the hell I gotta prove? I gotta take a picture of them doin' it while you sleeping in your office? That what it takes?"

Tate stared at Sarah with steady stone eyes; Buck figured the Sheriff looked awfully calm for somebody who had just been hollered at by his mother. Sarah's tone brought water into Buck's thighs even when the shouting blew over someone else. But Tate took things easy and said his piece. "Sarah, anybody who goes and grabs your baby runs the risk of facing you and Drake Walker mad as hell and that's damn stupid."

Buck held his breath to see what his father would do. Drake showed no anger. He was bigger than Tate. For the first time that day Buck saw the body drifting in the river, face down and floating like a log with the current. He heard the Bulls' morning laughter chasing him down the railroad tracks and he knew his father was hearing their laughter too. Drake looked the Sheriff up and down once, slowly. His voice was low and silken. "Does the law want to get involved?"

Sheriff Tate gently took Tina's shoe from Sarah's hands and held it in his own two. "The law already *is* involved."

Tate watched Drake's winter stone eyes harden and set. A slight electric jolt twinged in the Sheriff's neck. No way to bluff around the fact any longer. His own law had close reached its farthest point and now Drake Walker's law was taking over. The hard man's justice was coming around and Tate looked at the farmer's eyes and saw the verge of a rampant force, God's swift rain of fire that flattened the world as it stormed along.

Drake turned from Tate and walked toward the pickup truck. Now there was a dull current in his voice, like cool flowing ice. "You're the sheriff . . . " He paused.

"Sheriff."

Drake drove them back to the Eastern Range. No one said much. And Buck felt like each person's face was peering into his own . . . except Drew's. She seemed lost upon herself now. They dismounted from the truck and, standing by the farmhouse back porch, Buck was looking at his father's tenants.

Ryder had his Zippo out; the wheel sparked and he lit another Lucky Strike. Eddy stood a little ways off, staring up into the cotton row. Ryder put the Zippo away. He turned his head from everyone and took off the eyepatch, wiping the sweat from his dead eyesocket on the sleeve of his shirt. Then he put the patch back in place. Eddy squinted into the late afternoon sun and his fat Mex face seemed to glow. The two were with Drake. And Drake was with the two.

"Tonight."

But Sarah wanted action, and she wanted action now. "Drake, you're no better than the Sheriff. You go get my baby, or so help me I'll use your own damn shotgun on you and go get her for myself. You understand?"

"Easy." His father's eyes closed to slits. "I understand Tina don't need a dead mother." Drake came to where his woman stood on the porch and rested one hand on her hip. "We've been planning. No use going up there now. And they'll know we're coming, one way or the other. I want the night on our side to let us get real close."

Drake dropped his hand from Sarah's hip and her demand seemed to fall away with it like rain sloshing off a roof. She would wait. Buck rubbed his nose and wished the waiting over. Drew was sitting on the porch too; in the afternoon glare her skin was honey almond, rich as whipped butter. A wisp of hair flew from her forehead. Mrs. Moon came beside her daughter and touched her shoulder, old sharp fingers tracing a line on a young peach. The mother-of-pearl windchimes hung silent from the porch roof molding.

Tate went up by the way-station. He found Meriwether on top of the water tower, clinging to the access rungs on the tower's curved slat sides. Meriwether was fooling with the pulley that lowered the water spout over an engine's boiler. The Bull had a screwdriver between his teeth and his arm looped around one of the access rungs, letting him use both hands on the pulley. Tate heard the chink-chink of the metal pulley jangling its action. Tate got out of his car and Meriwether glanced down at him, but kept on working.

"Come on down here."

Meriwether heard him, because his hands paused at the pulley. "You see I'm working, Sheriff?"

Tate walked toward the water tower. "Meriwether, I've only got two sides worth knowing about. There's my good side, and there's my bad side. You hear me right?"

Up the water tower, Tate heard Meriwether sigh, like the sound of a heavy boot heel crushing the life out of a frog. The thin Bull stopped fooling with the pulley, and clattered down the rungs to the water tower's stilt legs. He swung like an ape from the crossed stanchions and brace bars till he dropped to the ground.

When Meriwether stood chest-to-chest with Tate, the thin Bull looked in the Sheriff's eye. Tate liked the man even less when he got up close enough to see the Bull's oily pores and close enough to smell the cheap tonic on his clothes, the tonic that came from penny spray-machines in switchyard urinals, sweet and gummy, the smell of strange men.

"I don't suppose you know where Simple is?"

"Why sure, Sheriff." Meriwether was smiling, the gap from his missing tooth dark and rotten.

Tate looked over his shoulder and in the doorway of the bunkhouse Simple leaned like a side of beef. Next to the big man, Daryl, the third Bull nobody saw much, squatted down near the ground, his face set in a scowl like a wrinkled plum.

Meriwether was still smiling. "Well, what can we do for you, Sheriff?"

Meriwether's broken smile was needling Tate in the gut, making him want bad—throw a hard shot right across Meriwether's face and break his nose with the heel of his palm. "Maybe you three jokers wanna come down to the jail, call up your rail supervisor—tell him how I got you pegged?"

"You got us pegged?" Meriwether was all Mister Innocence, and he nodded to himself as if in deep thought. Then he shrugged. "You're the boss."

Tate knew he was not gonna run them in and maybe leave the girl swinging from a tree branch from her ankles and a rope. And Meriwether knew it too. He slouched back on his heels, sure of himself and what he could do. What he wanted and what he could get. Sure that he was free and that Tate couldn't touch him. "Don't worry, Sheriff, I won't come crying to you, late in the night."

Tate walked back to his car, reached down through the driver's window and came up with Tina's brown leather shoe. Tate weighed it in his hand, heavy like a rock. Meriwether looked at it but said nothing.

"Catch." Tate threw the shoe underhand.

Meriwether tried to catch it, but he missed. The shoe slipped through his fingers and thudded hard against his stomach.

"You got it, now?" Tate was already walking back to his car. "Keep it, Meriwether—that'll make a pair."

Sykes and Parker Watts sure enough went through Walker's installment payments. They came up one short. Watts used his dating machine to stamp three blank deposit slips and Sykes left the banker lonely in his money-chamber counting the pennies. Eve was not pleased when Sykes demanded to call Washington, D.C., but she opened up the switchboard in the Sheriff's office and did it anyway. Sheriff Tate came into the jail just as Eve was getting through the D.C. exchange. Tate looked all washed out; his face was sallow and his belly sagged. He glanced at Sykes and Eve but let them be; he slumped into his rolling chair, looking defeated and forlorn. He lifted his feet up onto the desk and put both hands together as if in prayer. He sat that way and stared at them.

Sykes would have said something to the Sheriff—then the D.C. exchange rang through. "You're on."

Sykes' supervisor came on the telephone with a big whoop-dee-do, *"Well, howdy, Sykes, you old . . . "* But immediately, the supervisor's voice began to fade, replaced by a humming, like bees caught on the line.

"Speak up."

Sykes could just barely hear his supervisor laughing. "What a card, what a card . . . you're coming through fine."

"Speak up!" The humming went wild, jazzing Sykes' ear. Eve heard the wire's feedback through her headset. She shrugged; the line was dead. But Eve was not through yet. She rang the switchboard in Saint Louis. No response. She rang the switchboard in Chicago. Nothing. She tried to route the call through Los Angeles. No answer. She tried New Orleans. The Delta City was silent. Eve let the switchboard wires snake back into their holes. Sheriff Tate was mumbling through his folded hands. "That's a hell of a government you work for, Mr. Sykes, that can't get the phones ringing." Sykes pushed the useless telephone across the Sheriff's desk. The folded hands split apart, fingers unlaced, and fell from Tate's mouth.

"I suppose you'll be heading up to Walker's place . . . " The Sheriff leaned back, calm and resigned—not so donkey dumb as to want a little dead farm girl on his hands, next thing have the town crawling with Lefty journalists eager for a scoop. Tate didn't want the girl missing and selling papers for the Sioux City tabloids. He'd rather be handing out ribbons at the State Fair than parking permits to *New York Times* stringers, hot on the trail of some railroad pinko-busters. No thank you.

Maybe he had not gone far enough, up by the tracks. Maybe he should have twisted Meriwether's arm a little tighter. Maybe a million things. And maybe he wouldn't do nothing if the Bulls got themselves in a jam.

Sheriff Tate felt a little better. He breathed deeper letting the air rush in. "Sykes, do me a favor—you tell Walker for me that if those Bulls come crying, moaning or groaning, my guess is—they got only themselves to blame."

Sykes paused at the jailhouse door. "You're the Sheriff."

Tate scowled. "Hey! You think I'm crazy? We got dead bodies that burn up a day late, little birdies jumpin' outta coffins and lotsa lousy phone service. I guess you think this happens all the time around here?"

For a moment Sykes said nothing. He looked at Eve who shrugged and smiled.

Sykes smiled back; then he turned to Tate. "Sheriff, this country's got seven outta ten people outta work. The U.S. Government's got half a million bureaucrats, all think they got the answers for everybody. And in Italy you got Benito Mussolini, thinks he's Messiah, the Son of God."

Sykes leaned up against the door. "Why sweat the small stuff?"

Lepke slammed the diner's screen door behind him and took off his jacket. He hung the jacket on a hook near the toilet. He unbuttoned his vest and unhooked the watch fob, dropping the gold chain in the vest pocket. He draped the vest over the hanging jacket. Then he found his splattered apron and put it on. After the business in the graveyard, Lepke was a little rattled. He touched the hard shiny countertop, the reassuring linoleum. The greasy grill was cool, the fat congealed. Lepke scraped it off into the grill's fat gutter. He tossed the spatula into the sink. The shiny counter, the grill, these things should have been enough, they should have set him back to rights, but no such luck. The goddamn coffin opening, the burned mess of rotten flesh inside, the little birdy jumping out ... Lepke pulled his eyes off the grill grease sitting in the fat gutter. He swallowed. He rubbed his palms against his pants; his thighs itched.

The Emerson radio, in its cathedral wooden cabinet and the brown knit webbing that stretched across the speaker, was a better strongbox than any crazy casket. Lepke twisted the Emerson's knob and the radio tubes in the back began to glow. Lepke was not particular; any program would do, just so long as someone talked, or sang, or made funny noises, making the day go away and the bell clamor with it. The Emerson hummed to life, crackling static. He fiddled with the tuner, searching for a strong signal. The radio spat, crunching ash, audible snow, high whines ripping unseen through the air.

Lepke slapped the Emerson hard with his open hand, and it jumped along the ledge. He steadied himself and turned the volume down so the crackle shrank to a purr. He rested his back against the counter and glanced at the electric Texaco Red Star clock. The second hand whirred lazy and slow around the red star face. The clock's minute hand overlapped the little hour hand. Both hands hung motionless at six.

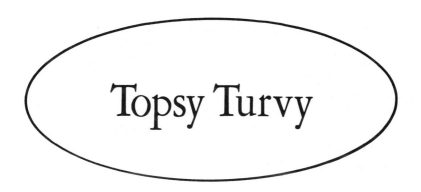

Topsy Turvy

HERE COMES THE CANDLE TO LIGHT YOU TO BED,
AND HERE COMES THE CHOPPER TO CHOP OFF YOUR HEAD.

The afternoon sun hung over Blue Vista Flats heedless of the halted moments. Adjuster Sykes came late in the afternoon to pay a courtesy call on the Walker farm. Drake met the Studebaker, out front of the house on the U.S. Route. Sykes cut the engine and got out of the car. A lock of blond hair hung over Sykes' forehead. He brushed it away.

"The United States Government can't count on Mother Bell's telephones."

Drake nodded. "Bet it's tough for the Government to count on Sheriff Tate's switchboard in a time of crisis."

Sykes raised one eyebrow. He cut the air with his palm, fingers straight like a baseball umpire calling safe. "Now that's not quite fair. Eve did her best."

Then Sykes lowered his head and spoke close to Drake's ear.

"Tate's been up to the way-station . . . " He let this settle in and added, "Tate says they only got themselves to blame."

Drake took a step away from the car and stared back toward town. "That's the damn truth." Then Drake went silent for a moment, the creases in his face furrowed and taut like weathered clothes. "Come around back for a minute, will ya? Got something to show."

Sykes followed Drake round back of the house and found that the tenants had come across the fields from their houses by the tracks and were waiting by the porch. Drake kept walking. He was going toward the cotton rows and the two tenants fell in step behind Sykes. Drake stopped where the cotton rows started up and Sykes found himself staring down the straight columns of bushy green plants. Along the stretch of cotton bushes, the tight green husky bolls were split open just a fraction. On the dark ground dozens upon dozens of dusky worms were scattered, curled like brown-meat maggots . . . stricken and dead. Their putrid heads were drying fast, choking on their own vanishing digestion. The dead boll weevils peppered the earth, row by row, far as the eye could see.

Sykes scratched his chin. He knelt down and picked up one of the dead boll weevils from the ground. "Uh . . . what kind of crop dust you been using?"

Drake looked up at the sun, blinding white in the sky. His two tenants, the one with the pigeon toes, and the one with the eye-patch, were both looking at their boss, knowing his answer before it came. Drake turned to Sykes. "We don't use no dust."

"No dust?"

"No nothing."

Sykes felt a little ill; the sun was very hot and he dropped the larvae back on the ground. He heard the sound of glassy wind-chimes jangling together in the hot air. Sykes' eyes were teary and he squinted through trembling eyelids. That drifter woman's idiot boy was standing on the farmhouse back porch. Next to him was Drake Walker's boy, staring at the group of men gathered at the edge of the cotton rows. The bright whitened sun was glaring through Sykes' wet jittering eyes, but he could see the idiot boy standing there on the back porch, his cloven mouth open and grinning, a saliva smile, half drool and half pink gums; the cloven face was smiling as though filled with happy freedom, the smile of secret delight and of never being wrong.

Sykes wiped the glaring tears from his eyes and looked at the men around him, standing silent and waiting for his opinion.

"Uh . . . yeah . . . no dust. Well, that's the best kind to use."

The tenant with the narrow Mexican eyes snorted and shook his head. "Hey! Hey! You ever seen this before?"

Drake was looking back to his house, to the idiot boy and Buck standing next to him as though paired together like draft horses, hitched to the wagon and ready to go. Drake ran his fingers lightly across his ribs—no pain today at all—and at his feet the dead boll weevils were strewn like blown black cinders, dead and cold and ready to melt at the first hard rain. Drake crushed one with his boot toe. "Easy, Eddy. The Adjuster don't have to be no expert."

Sykes was ready to admit anything. "I'm not."

Drake patted the Adjuster on the shoulder and led him back to the Studebaker on the U.S. Route. Sykes got in the car and caressed the wheel. He said nothing and looked at Drake a moment as if wondering how something so lucky could happen to a man, and then he remembered Drake's little girl. Sykes locked his eyes back on the road and started the car, heading back to town.

At the back porch Drake gathered his men in a semicircle; they dropped the business of the dead boll weevils and got to the business at hand. Ryder held the broken hoe handle. Eddy squatted on the ground, produced a weathered whetsone and ran it down the blade of the short sickle. Mrs. Loomis had returned it, and Eddy was happy to have his old friend back. The stone scraped, rasping against the metal.

"Some folks think this here sickle is a Commie tool." Eddy spat on the whetstone and went back to the blade. "But I says it's just sharp."

Ryder leaned his broken hoe handle with the jagged point against a porch post; now with both hands free he touched the creases under his eyes with his fingertips, smoothing them, wishing them away. He stood on the porch boards and, inches from his face, the Loomis windchimes hung sullen and silent like dead vines.

Drake's twelve-gauge shotgun was on his knee, breech open. Fifteen shells were jumbled in his shirt and pants pockets. He took two shells and loaded the gun, closing the breech. The shells were empty of shot, now loaded with rocksalt. You could blind a man. Close up you could mash his face. Maybe kill him.

Kill.

Cripple.

Murder.

Drake did not care.

Split knuckles and skulls, broken teeth, the nerves seething, voices pleading . . . Drake did not care. He wanted his baby back.

He ran his hand down the tepid metal barrels of the gun; in places the smooth wooden stock was scratched. Drake always oiled the stock, polishing the grain to a high shine, making it silk to the touch, his baby's skin. He felt the stock in his hands and the gun yielded to him like an unspoken promise.

Ryder looked down at his feet, at his boots big on the porch boards. He balled his fist and massaged the ligaments between each ripe knuckle. He dropped his hands and they hung loose at his sides. "Henry and his brother have the word. They'll be coming from the other side of the river."

A sunbreeze rose from beyond the horizon and, curling, brushed the face of Bone County; Drake took the fragile windy rush and swirl, the skin over his forehead tingling gently in the white heat of daylight. The windchimes glistened in the oiled sun, the scales twisting in the wind. Drake's scalp tightened. He heard the windchimes strike, jinga-jinga, the daystar's herald, singing mother-of-pearl. Ryder grabbed the broken hoe handle and backed up against the house wall, stepping away from the chimes' glassy tangle. Then Eddy heard the chimes tink, and felt the dry breeze blow down the landside, sneaking through the tops of trees, hiding in the rutted gullies, creeping through door cracks, dancing along the rooftops. The chimes answered, and the men said nothing. Under the cover of this wanton wind, no one heard the padded spoor of a lonesome angry dog. The dog with the seamed skull sat in the fields, haunches muscled.

Drake checked the safety on his gun and stroked the wooden stock.

Inside the farmhouse Sarah looked at Tina's bed, coverlet smoothed and waiting—waiting for the child to draw it back, slip between the sheets and snuggle in the bed's own safety. The child's berth in harbor sleep, God's soul to take, His to keep; now I lay me down to weep. Sarah pulled back the coverlet and threw it back at the bed's end. She lifted off the top sheet, searching for her child's body impression. The bloodstain, almost brown, dried now in the cotton's fabric. A menstrual thumbprint, and another slash of red where Tina rubbed her hand on the sheet: little girls with dirty hands, never girls again. Sarah touched the stain with her fingers and brought the scent of it to her lips.

She threw back the sheet and the coverlet, tucking them in. The bed would be ready when Tina returned.

Marybelle Simon was burning with the glorious light; it mixed with the very air she breathed. She planned her rescue carefully—Eve must be in her rooming house room and alone. Marybelle prayed no man's clothes would be lying about, smacking of debauchery and aftershave. Women see heart to heart . . . certainly best for everyone that Simon wasn't taking part. A woman must be saved in kind, by her kind; a man's spitballs weren't worth the paper chewed. But imagine! Waking in the morning's light with some huge bulk, snoring indecently, his beard all stubble, his face gray as a mealy-mouthed lecher, lascivious and cruel, prying lips and taking the woman's secret at his pleasure. Imagine, day after day after wanton day, reeling under abandon, dripping with saliva, the rasp of flesh unleashed, heating the breath and curdling a woman's sensitivities.

And the time had come . . . mending the broken shield; a single-bosomed Amazon would throw her weight no less glorious than Marybelle in her brewing righteous heat. But the Preacher's wife was not so imbued with the spirit that she forgot to smooth down the pleats in her dress when she reached the top of the rooming house stairs. Nor was she so distracted that she did not pause and linger, teasing up her tousled hair. She ran a delicate finger over each eyebrow weaving the fine female fiber within itself. Her lips were moist, so she pressed them against her hand's heel; lips dried, she could speak. Wet and the words would slide from sodden lips, oily and forlorn. Knocking on Eve's door, Marybelle bruised her knuckles.

"Come in."

She prayed the whore's room would not reek of men. The disarray of men's discarded garbage made the task more difficult—a challenge, yes, but a goat's chinbeard is the very devil to shave. Marybelle's worst fears came true. Eve lay on her bed in a city girl's half-slip, her stockings rolled to the knee. A shirt was thrown over Eve's shoulders and a cigarette burned idly in the ashtray by her elbow. A bottle of Seagram's, two-thirds empty, stood on her dresser, a dying soldier on parade. A man's blue woolen sock lay draped over the open windowsill, toe outside. The thinning heel was in need of darning. Loose change was scattered across the wooden dressertop and reflected in the mirror: penny copper and shiny nickel, spare coins from the last wallowing carousal.

"Well, Marybelle Simon." Eve pinched the cigarette from her ashtray and stared through the smoke rising around her eyes. "Of all people. What brings you here?"

"Grace." Marybelle's word hung in the air like bad boiled cabbage.

Eve cocked an eyebrow and dragged on the tobacco again. "The offer of grace never did a soul harm . . . I'd offer you a chair in return, but as you can see, I have none. Come sit on the bed."

Eve pursed her lips and smiled; in some other more raucous age she would have been stoned in the square and hung naked from a gibbet. Glad for once that she had no fear, Eve patted her springy quilt and watched Marybelle shudder at the thought of sitting on the bed.

"Come, come . . . close the door and sit here—I don't bite."

Marybelle hesitated, her spirit waning fast, slipping like the steam from a boiling kettle.

"Be a shame to leave now—you've come all this way." Long stairs and fine words were no help now.

"I'll go to my sister's and make you tea. Would you like that?"

Marybelle nodded, jerking her tight jaw. Her throat was swollen, her fire squelched. The bed bounced gently when Eve got up; she paused before the door and turned around. Marybelle faced the window and a breeze brushed the curtains, their hems caressing the sill. Eve touched the woman's shoulders; Marybelle jumped, but let herself be led to the bedside. She sat on the bed, curled up on her knees. The door opened and closed. Eve was gone.

From the bed, Marybelle could see out the window to the

square where the long mean shadows of afternoon were sly and spread along the ground like spilled oil; the daytime sky was still quite light, the bright blue air like a cloudless song, faint and hummed from memory.

Eve returned. She pulled the light string and the room went dark. Marybelle wondered at this, but the breeze again swirled into the small room and pushed her fears aside. "Your eye'll adjust. I hate the walls with the light bulb burning."

"The walls . . . the light bulb . . . oh." Marybelle carefully removed her shoes, leaning over the bedside edge, placing her pumps on the floor, side by side.

"You have the nerve of a real prostitute."

Which woman said that?

Eve said it; Marybelle touched the hem of her dress. Eve let out the slack, no purpose in breaking the line on a solid hook. "The tea is free. So is the talk."

"But you're not. Are you?"

"No. Sometimes." Eve admitted anything. "Not all the time."

"That's even worse."

"You're right . . . I have money troubles."

In Claire and Bart Lowell's room down the hall, the teakettle whistled, a high shriek for those who listened. Marybelle was alone again. Her eyes adjusted to the shade; she could make out the dresser, the mirror, the bottle, even the loose coins strewn on the dressertop. Outside in the square, the leaves rustled in the oak tree; the clock up Preacher's stubby steeple was still broken and mute, chimed no hour and kept no time. If time was kept like women, then men would run down but once a day—but everyone knows, men ease their springs more often than not, and are kept by women regardless of the hour.

Eve's door opened and closed again. The tea leaves brewed; she carried a tray with a teapot and cups, milk and sugar lumps, a little strainer, and two small spoons. She laid the service on the dresser, brushing aside the bottle and coins. In the room's shadow, with her broad back shielding and Marybelle's wayward eyes lost on the window ledge, Eve poured a healthy dollop of whiskey into the woman's cup. She dropped the sugar lumps, stirred the tea and licked the spoon. Much to her surprise the whiskey left only a bare trace. She brought Marybelle her cup.

The china clattered in the saucer; no trembling hands ever

held such a subtle rat—the hooch ready, Marybelle raised the cup to her dry lips.

"It soothes." Eve drank hers too.

One draught leads to another. And another. Eve complied, plying Marybelle once and again with her gentle tea. Innocence is shed in layers and presently Marybelle began to gab.

"I never thought you were an evil woman. Really, I never did. It's just I never *knew*. I've read about it all in books. The Bible too. Simon says I have a voice like a bell. Do you think so? Simon was my first."

Marybelle paused, holding down a frown. "And always will be. He was so gentle the first night. I hardly felt a thing."

Eve turned her head to the window so she would not laugh. Marybelle could not stop herself now. "It must be very strange for you. Are they all alike?"

"No."

"No? Do they hurt you?"

"Not if I can help it. No one's smacked me in a long time. I like to keep it that way."

Marybelle pressed a warm hand to her throat. "For heaven's sake, I hope so. But don't they smell?"

"Everyone smells."

"Why, I don't." Marybelle confessed the obvious. "Or at least I don't think so. Do you smell?"

"Sometimes . . ."

Marybelle shifted on her haunches, stretching the muscles in her thighs. "Now Roxie Johns was an evil woman. Remember? You just knew Yohanna pushed the stone from his chest when she passed away. There was a time there when Roxie was pregnant three years in a row. She was fifty then. Those three babies left their mark on her all right. And she on them. I've heard say, those three boys are a little dim. It comes from those late-life pregnancies, no denying it. But I think the last child took its toll on her. She withered away a year after he was born. Not that Yohanna didn't have a hand in it."

Eve's ears tingled; she rubbed her upper lip. "What precisely do you mean?"

"Well, you *know. You know.*"

"I don't."

"You don't?"

Eve did not reply directly. "More tea?"

Marybelle shook her head. "Well this is how it happened. You know how evil Roxie was. She'd think she saw a spook lurking in the field, she'd roll her eyes and run around the house. Pull Yohanna from his bed and drag him out at night, torches lit, looking for the ha'nt. Roxie has English cousins who'd been born in Jamaica, and she knew all about duppy blood. Duppies, that's the West Indian nigras' ghost. Well Roxie got it in her head that a slain duppy'd followed her white bloodline all the way from the Caribbean plantation house. She was sure he was hiding under the floorboard, sleeping in the closet—and one day, she swore that duppy was walking on the farmhouse roof in the moonlight. She got Yohanna outta bed and pulled him outside in the night. She tried to get Yohanna up on the roof. But he's a God-fearing man and refused. So she went ahead, got a ladder from the barn, a hatchet and a broom."

Marybelle's voice rose to the occasion, its timbre full like a steady oboe under the church organ's six pedal. "She planted the broom handle down in the ground. Planted it right in front of the door—that's so the duppy couldn't get into the house if it fell off the roof. She laid the ladder against the house and holding the hatchet in one hand started up the ladder. Well, she didn't get too far. A ladder rung broke and she fell, bruised herself badly. Cracked a rib. Yohanna Johns put her in bed and gave her a mustard plaster. Don't that beat all? A mustard plaster for a broken rib? Men ain't smart. He got the doctor. But too late. Roxie died the next day, spitting blood."

"All I ever heard was she had a bad fall. Do you think Yohanna Johns killed her?"

Marybelle shrugged. "Whether he used that mustard plaster outta hate or just plain dumbness, I wouldn't guess. Suffice it to say, she died in pain."

Beautiful. Died in pain. Eve rolled her stockings over her knees. She heard Adjuster Sykes' door creak in the hall. And a slim ray of yellow light slipped across the floor under the crack in her door. Good old Mr. Sykes. She figured out a lot about that sometime Government boy. He had a taste for women and revenge, not an uncommon mixture for a bureaucrat.

Marybelle's face was flushed; Eve could nearly see the heat radiating into the darkness of the room. The Preacher's wife was woozy, her high chest weaved back and forth, as she curled up sitting on the bed. Eve glanced at the whiskey bottle on the dresser; the bottle was a dead soldier now, drained and empty. Eve had not touched a drop.

Eve whispered in Marybelle's ear. "Stay here awhile. No hurry. I'll be back."

The door opened and closed. Marybelle was alone once more. She liked the sound of the wind in the branches. The air talked to her now and she listened. She eased tenderly from the bed and found one of Eve's cigarettes. She lit it: the first cigarette she had ever smoked. The tobacco made her head swim, but presently the fogginess drained away and she touched Eve's dresser drawers. One drawer was empty and she closed it. In another, a rolled sock contained money—bills, lots of them. One drawer down, Eve's winter clothes. In the bottom drawer the woman's underwear, pink and lacy—better than what Marybelle expected. She found a silken slip, a bra, three pairs of new stockings—she draped them over her arm and felt their smoothness run radiant against her arm. A whore's underthings. A *whore's*. Marybelle's first cigarette glowed in the ashtray. She felt the lingerie against her hand's smooth flesh and laid the slim clinging garments on the bed. They lay unfilled against the bedspread. Marybelle lifted the brassiere against herself. Eve was close . . . very close to her in size . . .

Eve, sly and lovely in her shirt and city lady's half-slip, opened Sykes' door, careful not to let it squeak. Her dress was slung over one arm, detached, oblivious and limp.

Sykes was bent over in his undershorts, touching his toes. Even the Government has to exercise once in a while.

"Ahem . . ."

Sykes stood up and twisted, facing the door. "You didn't knock."

"You noticed."

"We must be very intimate then. Amazing how one day can change your life."

"Isn't it?" Eve closed the door behind her and leaned against the wood. "I wonder, Mister Adjuster, whether you've ever considered the legal principle of an eye for an eye."

"I've heard of it. Arabs do it mostly."

"Are you still perturbed over the abuse of a Government vehicle . . . by ungracious and flop-flinging hicks?"

Sykes touched his toes again, raised his arms over his head and stretched, twisted his torso and groaned. He dropped his arms to his sides and faced the woman. He found his pants crumpled on the bed and he drew them on. He buttoned a shirt over his chest. Then he put on his glasses. Dissatisfied, he took his glasses off and polished the lenses on his shirttail. "What's the matter Eve—you bored?"

In Lepke's Diner the afternoon's shadows never penetrated; within a shield of greasy plate glass and corrugated metal, the electric lights burned warm and glowing. Bart Lowell had hung up his barber's smock for the day, rinsed out his shaving bowl and locked the shop, retiring to the diner. For lack of anything better to do, he sought out Lepke's company. Bart Lowell was one of the few souls that would. Lepke, as usual, stalked behind the counter; he had long given up trying to work the radio and he now suspected that his Texaco Red Star clock was in cahoots with Preacher's steeple. A deft suspicion which Lepke kept to himself. There was no profit in trying to up the wattage on any old dim bulb that happened by. Bart Lowell—that dim bulb—included.

The barber pushed his coffee cup across the counter and Lepke scowled at it. "The Sheriff'll want his dinner fixed. Run over to the jail and get the order."

Bart Lowell was not taking orders from anybody. "Hey, hey. Slow down. How about another?" He eyed the cup.

Lepke's cat slunk down low under the stools. It leapt on a stool and stepped from one stool to the next and then up on the counter. The cat was rich gray and sleek. A useless animal most of the year, but Lepke kept him anyway. Cats were good company. They did not talk back. Like wisenheimer barbers.

One foot from Bart Lowell's clasped hands and the glowering Lepke, the tom froze for a moment midstride on the counter, one paw up. Ears flicking to the scratch of talons, the iris in the cat's eyes narrowed on Bart Lowell as the prize porker in a butcher's window. The gray ears twitched at faraway hooting in the darkness. He leapt, pouncing on Bart Lowell's hands, snagging skin.

"Damn!"

The cat pranced away, swishing his hips. Bart touched the blood drawn from his knuckle. The scratch tingled; he sucked on the cut. The day's infection ran in his blood.

Lepke pronounced the verdict. "Serves you damn right." But he still had more on his mind. "I said before, the Sheriff'll want his dinner."

Bart was still not in the mood for taking orders. He ignored Lepke and went around the counter. The barber poured the coffee himself. Quick as a wink Lowell was sitting back on his stool, a full cup between his planted elbows. "I heard you the first time."

Never to be outdone, Lepke took a large knife from under the counter and placed it gently point down in Lowell's filled coffee cup. The liquid trembled around the submerged blade. The barber stared at the cup and knife; Bart's knuckle itched and he looked at Lepke who now was smiling.

"Well, then, maybe you didn't hear too good."

In the jailhouse office Sheriff Tate leaned back in his chair and smacked his lips. Bart Lowell waited patiently by the door. After a moment Tate decided.

"Bart, you can tell Lepke, that dough-faced oaf, that I want spaghetti and meatballs . . ."

Lowell nodded his head like a dip dunking for apples; the cat scratch on his knuckle seemed swollen and hot. Tate rambled on with the order and Lowell kept nodding. The Sheriff finished and pulled out his wallet. He counted out a few bills and shook his head.

"Have Lepke put it on the tab."

Lowell headed back across the square, rubbing the swollen scratch on his hand. He tried repeating the Sheriff's instructions: "Tell that dogfaced dope that I want it neat as a rope . . ."

In his stained apron, Lepke reared like a bloody whale behind the counter. He glared at the barber.

"Well?"

Lowell blinked his eyes and tried hard to remember . . . tell the oaf, meatloaf . . . then he spit it out, "Meatloaf. With mashed potatoes and gravy.

"Heavy on the gravy."

"Heavy on the potatoes.
"Broccoli.
"More gravy.
"Rolls. Butter. Two slices of pie.
"Two bottles of Coke.
"And put it on the tab."

Lepke was scribbling furiously. "Yessir." He snapped the pencil point.

"On the tab?"

Lepke leaned over the counter. "Hey Bart, the Sheriff ain't got a tab."

Lowell shrugged. "Not my fault."

Lepke rubbed his hands on his apron. "Well, forget it. He ain't eating till he pays. Maybe you heard wrong."

The cat scratch tingled. "Naw, not so t'night."

The cut had stopped bleeding; the damage was done.

Under a naked yellow electric bulb, Hanson sat at the flatboard counter of his Goods Store and closed his ledger books. He capped his fountain pen. On a separate slip of paper the expenses of the Greenes' funeral were listed and tallied.

Two Coffins with Bells	37.14
Two Children's Coffins	14.42
Gravedigging Labor	2.00
	53.56

Hanson figured he could hold on to Cottle's labor pay for at least a month from the day Hanson himself was reimbursed. He stuffed the scrap of paper in his pocket. He got up from the flatboard counter and walked out on the Goods Store porch, letting the screen door slam. The leaves rustled in the oak, but the Goods Store man ignored their trembling and stepped off the porch, heading for the garage. Up the concrete ramp and once inside near the wobble-wheeled dolly, he smelled the oil fumes, the spots of dirty acid spills and the wafer edges of old rusted fenders. A light tin bead chain touched his face and Hanson jerked back; he wound it round his fingers and tugged. The overhead bulb snapped on. That business Sheriff Tate was wondering on before . . . wondering where the Moon woman got those coins? The Model A sat quietly on its springs; the engine hood was off and the guts exposed. A pair of needlenose pliers and a screwdriver lay in the narrow runner under the windshield, an easy distance from the engine. The Moon woman might have more. He had half a mind to tear through the car, top to bottom, with the garage door closed and the helpful beam of a flashlight. Hanson reached for the pull-chain and turned to the wide garage door. He stopped and his hand fell from the light pull-chain.

The yellow electric glow shone through the car's back window and onto the horsehair seat. Tilted slightly askew, but square in a patch of light, was a sailor's clock with a porthole and a latch. There were two recessed studs for winding and the glass in the porthole was cracked. The long skinny minute hand overlapped the little hour hand; they hung at the number six. Hanson rested both arms on the car roof and peered through the open back window at the clock. He fished in his breast pocket and took out a cigarette. He lit it with a match and leaned down on the roof, his cigarette hand slung inside the car's window, the smoke curling in the cab. Hanson shook his head as he stared at the broken clock and he gulped down a drag. "Well . . . whaddya know . . . "

The overhead bulb flared in a blue flash and died. The glow from the cigarette remained. Hanson pulled away from the car and stood up straight. A mosquito lit on his arm; the tiny needler tickled a pore—he slapped the skin, splattering the insect along his palm. But too late, a drop of blood was drawn, and now the mosquito's venom welled to a reddened hive. Out the yawning garage door, Hanson saw across the square that a soft yellow light burned behind the bank's windows. Parker Watts. Hanson left the Model A and his thoughts of more coins back with the clock. He walked toward the bank scratching his arm. The bug bite itched, but he barely noticed; he walked under Preacher's steeple clock and did not glance up. Two pennies and a nickel jangled in his pocket. He wanted another look at the gold coins Watts was keeping behind the bars of his teller's cage. And he wanted that look right now.

Eve got a hatchet from Bart Lowell's barber shop; Bart said he sometimes used the hatchet to split hairs. She also found a ball of twine. They would search for a ladder in Yohanna Johns' barn. He'd be sure to have one. All these things she stowed in Sykes' Studebaker. The twine bounced on the seat and rolled under the accelerator. Sykes opened the driver's door and pried the ball of twine from under the pedal.

"A broom. Gloves." Eve headed back to the barbershop.

Sykes was in the driver's seat. "I got a pair in the trunk."

Claire Lowell, peeking through her inch-opened door, had watched Marybelle come up the rooming house stairs. Most likely her sister Eve had slipped the dizzy dame a few stiff ones, if she could leave Preacher's wife alone in the room. Bart was distracted over at the diner, running hither and yon, bouncing like a dancing doll between Lepke and Tate. She slipped out of the rooming house and headed away from the square. Preacher would be alone at home. Just you wait . . .

Lepke packed up Tate's dinner in a cardboard box. He packed it carefully to keep the gravy from dripping over the plate. He stacked the two slices of pie, blueberry, against the Coke bottles so they would not tip over. He tossed in the rolls and butter, and covered the whole thing with a sheet of wax paper. He made a final check to see whether the gravy ran. Nope. He slid the box across the counter. Bart peeked under the wax paper.

"Bart, you tell the Sheriff he owes me one dollar and fifty cents."

"One dollar, fifty—" Bart repeated. "Yahzoo."

"And you can also tell him that if you don't come back with the cash, he isn't welcome in my establishment any longer."

"Abba-dabba!" Bart nodded his head.

Lepke watched the diner door close behind Lowell. The cat was edgy and full of nerves. The tom paced in circles around the standing fan, squeezing through the tight spaces, hopping on the tables, disappearing, flying a bit of gray tail beyond the counter. Once he even rolled on his back and bared his needle claws. Cats had no sense—they did the dumbest things.

Bart walked across the square, the claw cut on his knuckle burning a tingling fever heat. With both hands occupied, he could not rub the skin while holding Sheriff Tate's dinner in the cardboard box.

"Now what did Lepke say?" The scratch burned. A dollar fifty and back with the cash? Don't smash the cash? Say you're welcome and don't spill the gravy? Be sure the Sheriff owes the establishment a tab? Bart jiggled his fingers, moving the knuckle, creasing the cardboard box, hopelessly confused.

The Sheriff was waiting.

Bart put the cardboard box on Sheriff Tate's desk. "Lepke says, 'Stuff the cash in the mash and you're welcome.'"

"What?"

"Put the cash in the trash and slash the tab." Bart shook his head. This was all wrong. The barber worked his jaw and pressed his tongue against the inside of his cheek, limbering up. Saliva rolled over his tonsils; next time he would try speaking more slowly.

Sheriff Tate ran his hand through his hair. "Never mind. Did he remember the Cokes?"

"You're welcome."

Tate was not amused. "Bart, what's the matter with you?"

Speaking slowly had not worked; Bart shrugged. Sheriff Tate peeked under the wax paper. He slammed his desk with an open palm. *"I said, 'Spaghetti and Meatballs,' not Meatloaf and Mash! I HATE MEATLOAF!"*

Bart rubbed his knuckle and stared at the Sheriff. "So stash the cash."

Bart was back at Lepke's Diner with the cardboard box in his hands, minus the Cokes, the rolls and the pie. Lepke stopped scraping his grill, dropped the spatula and put his hands on the counter.

"Where's my money?"

Bart swallowed hard; he took a deep breath and pressed his tongue to the roof of his mouth before opening his lips. "The Sheriff says, 'Spaghetti you meatball and you can eat the trash!!' " He held his head with both hands. This was hopeless.

"Oh, is that what the Sheriff says. Well, if the Sheriff wants spaghetti, we'll give him spaghetti with a little something on top."

From under the counter Lepke got a hand meat grinder, and bolted it to the counter's edge. He found a meat cleaver and ran his thumb along the blade. He leaned over the counter.

"Here puss . . . here puss, come, come, where have you gone?"

The cat poked its head up from a booth and eyed Lepke. A mouse's tail was clamped firmly between its teeth. The mouse dangled upside down, pawing the air in a delirium shock.

"Why, you've got a mousey," Lepke declared. "I'll spare you this time, but I want that mouse. Here puss . . . Bart, lock the door —I want that mouse."

"Nix watch, hoo-boy!" Lowell peeked through two fingers. *"Bart, lock the door."*

Up in Eve's room Marybelle ran her fingers along her arm; she shivered, all fleshy goosebumps, and the fine hair on her forearms stiffened on end. She unhooked the back of her dress and let it fall around her ankles. She stepped out of the dress and kicked it under the bed. She threw her slip away. And her bra. And her panties. And these too she kicked under the bed. Standing in the darkness the vague outlines of her body reflected almost silver in the dresser mirror. Her navel was a dark spot, shaded. Eve's bra was lacy, with a wire. She used ones with wires, too, though Simon had never seen them. She put her arms through the shoulder straps, and hooked the back. With her two forefingers she pulled the underwires away and juggled herself in the cups. She let the wires come back tight under the crease. The bra fit. A perfect fit.

She pulled Eve's slip off the bed and fingered the hem. The hem was lacy too —a broad band of lace, in flower shapes; the shapes were daisies. Pretty little daisies all in a row. The silk slip was knee-length, the straps adjustable. She drew it over her head and the silk flowed around her thighs. Marybelle left the mirror and lay down on Eve's bed. She found the stockings tucked under her behind and pulled them out from under her buttocks. She gathered one stocking by the double weave around the thigh, and with her fingers pulling and gathering, she held the stocking in two hands with only the toe and heel left unrolled. She put her foot in the toe; the heel slid around her ankle, natural and smooth. Over her calf, around the knee, draw it up, wipe away the creases. Roll it up the thigh and fold over the double down. The silk stocking clung mid-thigh and would not slip.

Lying on her back, Marybelle straightened her leg and lifted it in the air, knee slightly bent. With the palms of her hands, she smoothed out the stocking again from ankle to thigh. The silk clung to her skin. She dropped the leg and started with the other stocking. Gather, toe, heel, ankle, knee, thigh—fold over and double down. Draw and wipe away the creases. Straighten the leg, lift, smooth again. Perfect.

She stared at the ceiling and a light summer's twilight breeze lifted the curtains at the window, washing her body, even under the slip, between her thighs. She stretched, arching her spine. Is this how it's done? Did she even give it a second thought? Was there a second thought to give it? Marybelle rolled on her side and curled a lock of hair in her pinky. Now boys . . . be nice. That's right. Easy does it. Easy!

You better listen when I talk to you . . . or else. She noticed the bottle reflected in the dresser mirror. Off the bed and on her feet, swaying slightly. A tiny puddle of brown sludge darkened the bottom. Anchors Away! Bottle open, tipped, drippity-drop. A puddle ran in a stream, down the bottle neck and splashed on her tongue. Warm and wet and almost sweet, the whiskey smoked in her nostrils, sinuses afire . . . now boys—be nice. She put the bottle back on the dresser, nearly tipping it over. She had lost the cap.

Back on the bed. Cigarette and match. A hollow breeze sucked the curtains over the sill and she saw the tobacco smoke drifting in a lazy blue cloud out the window. Caught in the bank's lights shining on the ground floor, the smoke swirled and vanished.

Hanson stepped into the warm glow of the bank and shut the door. The overhead fans circled slowly with a low drone. Parker Watts sat behind the teller's cage; his tie loosened, his sleeves rolled up; he wore a green eyeshade, which cast a sickly shadow on his face. He was working on a long column of figures. He looked up and the shadow shrank to a pinched hand across his eyes. "Oh, it's you."

"You expecting someone else?"

Watts said nothing. Hanson stepped up to the cage, pulled the slip of paper from his pocket and thrust it under the grill. "That's what the County owes me for those coffins."

Watts took the slip and nodded, glanced at it and then put it in a pigeonhole under the cage. Some papers were strewn across the polished surface of the teller's ledge. Parker Watts was staring at one in particular. He heard Hanson's wheezing breath, and he singled the paper out. "Wired an appraiser I trust in New York City —he couldn't say for sure until he sees the coins . . . but, well, read it yourself." He turned the paper around and slipped it under the grill to Hanson. A telegram. It read:

> NOT SURE STOP MINT FIVE DOL GOLD
> 1866 AT LEAST THIRTY FIVE GRAND
> STOP SERIES D FORTY FIVE STOP MUST
> SEE STOP
>
> L. ELROND

Hanson could barely contain himself, "Forty-five thousand smackers! Is it a Series D—*is it?*"

Watts took the telegram back. "I haven't checked."

"*You haven't checked?* What's stopping you, Parker—we got two of those little babies."

"Okay . . . okay . . . keep your shirt on. Those little 'babies,' as you put it, are right here."

Parker Watts pulled open the teller drawer and looked inside. For a moment, Hanson was not sure what he was seeing. Parker froze, stone still. His face pinched into a question mark, his eyes narrowed. He rustled some bills in the cash drawer; he pulled the bills out and threw them on the teller's ledge. Some bills slipped through the grill and fluttered to the floor at Hanson's feet.

"Parker? Whatsamatter? Parker?"

Parker Watts jumped off his stool, tipping it over onto the floor. He pulled the cash drawer out all the way. A wad of deposit receipts cascaded back over his shoulder, nickels and rolls of dimes scattered on the floor.

"Parker?"

"They were right here! They were right here!" He pounded the wood surface of the teller's ledge.

"Get ahold of yourself, Parker."

Watts' face was flushed; his eyes bulged like eggs sunny-side up. One of his sleeves was unrolled and the French cuff flapped like a torn flag. Watts gripped the side of the teller's ledge to steady himself. "You're right, Hanson. You're right." Watts took a deep breath. "I must have tucked them away. Someplace safe. We'll just relax. I'll remember."

"The vault?"

"The vault!" Watts dashed from the teller's cage. Hanson followed in close pursuit. The swinging partition creaked like a screech owl, but neither man noticed.

Preacher Simon sat alone in the parlor. Marybelle had been gone some time. She had flown out of the house on cords of gossamer, and Preacher was sure that his wife would not return till the battle was won and the debauched woman saved. Marybelle could not have set herself a more arduous, thankless task. Eve would be no easy fish to hook—harder still to reel in—near impossible to filet. The woman was hard bitter meat, hung years in the smokehouse of abandon. No salmon was as pink, no eel as oily. Like the stars of famous stage and infamous screen, the whore could pander to an audience, delight in applause, show grace in defeat: no simple brat, no blithering nymph, no general's wench, no schoolteacher's folly. Marybelle could not have set herself a more intricate endeavor. Yet this gay painting hung for pleasure, his wife's pure hopes, could not diminish Preacher's Beast.

Its breath hung foul near his face; Claire, the barber's wife, had run him through. Quivering, quaking, shivered and shot, Preacher sat in his lonely parlor and rocked his child's cradle as his baby girl snored an infant's sniffle. The sleeping child bore no malice for her father's incongruity. The child loved the coo and warble of her mother's tongue, the hapless stroking of her father's rasping fingers, the nameless love that abounds unmeasured. Some will catch your ear and tell you of the weighty scales that never balance between siblings; Preacher bought no words from them, for he had but one child. And through one child could he number his days. But women, alas, have no such reign—they are offered immortality, but then sag like dark circles under men's eyes. They are pawed and beaten; they are lusted for and lust for prey. They revolve like the five empty chambers in a six-shooter suicide gun.

Preacher's sleeping little flesh opened and closed her hands, stretching her fingers in a secret baby's dream. Restless, she wrestled with her evening doze and lost the struggle; she slept on. The rippling mother-of-pearl chimes echoed across Yellow River and knocked at Preacher's door. Far away it seemed, yet near enough to hear the separate striking silver cymbals of a miniature marching band—out of step, yet marching on. The random glassy tangle shattered Preacher's musings and he stood up, dropping his hand from the rocker, letting the cradle rock on unattended. He walked to the front door hallway and listened. The windchimes' cry faded deep in a soulless twilight; like the last battalion's skirling bagpipe wail, as the men descend to a valley covered in mist, playing, playing—the men march on and heed no coward brigadier bugler's retreat. Preacher saw that the grandfather clock that stood by the stairs had run down. The pendulum was still and the weights, brass pine cones, dangled from their chains. He opened the glass door and tugged on the upper weight; it slid a few notches down but jammed.

Then Preacher noticed the grandfather's face; a broken gear somewhere in the works, caught, sprung, curling a cable, stripping a wheel... the hands on grandfather's face had fallen. As if stripped and loose, a broken part deep in a brass heart, each hand had fallen from twelve noon, vanquishing the Roman numeral day. The two hands met again at VI, little brother kissing big brother, they hung at the six. The clock was finished.

Last rites all said and done, time still waited holding its breath as Preacher mumbled grasping incantations; prayers half truth, part lie—anything to appease the unspoken gibberish of a casket bell and a darting chimney swift. You there, waiting in the coffin ... a little bird told me—yes, fast wings on that last mile. No harm in all this, forgive me; I mean no harm. He backed away from the grandfather clock, backed away from coffin bells that rang, backed away from words wasted and far-off chimes. He found himself in the parlor once more, in the armchair, his hand resting on the baby's rocker. The front door opened and footsteps padded in the hall.

"It's dark in here . . . Preacher, why don't you trim a wick?"

Preacher said nothing. He saw Claire Lowell's body in the parlor doorway. Claire came toward him in the darkened room, she laid her hand upon his and fell in with the rhythm of the cradle. She looked down at him, sitting in his parlor chair. The mole's impression on her upper lip was swollen, drawing on her skin's blood, sapping him, a heated spell. She would make him kiss it.

"The baby." Claire curled a finger around two of his. "Can I help with the baby?"

Drake Walker stood even and solid, as though planted in the ground, rooted deep. He seemed to rise above the fields towering in the air, his shotgun hanging from his forearm, open at the breech. He drew from his shirt pocket two rocksalt shells; he placed the shells in the shotgun's chamber, plugging both barrels. Gun loaded, Drake closed the chamber on its hinge but did not lock it. The gun still hung, bent crooked over his arm, the breech open a crack. The dusk song swirled at Drake's knees, tugging at his pants cuffs, squeezing under the soles of his shoes. Seconds fell to the earth and lay still.

To the north, way across the fields, a grand purple thunderhead loomed like a huge hand outstretched. It pushed the wind before its fingertips and the wind rocked down across the plain, whipping the cornflowers and the dust up from the road. The huge thundercloud rose from the horizon and spilled onto the plate of the sky like a breath of cigarette smoke blown across an empty room. Ryder looked, eyes to the sky, and then slung the hoe handle over his neck; his hands were free for walking.

The tenant farmer followed his bossman north to the rails, splitting the stalks and brambles, ankles pushing the plants aside, head bent in the thunderwind. The ribbon on Ryder's eyepatch was moist where the back of his scalp perspired through the hair. The wind blew a hard gust and he felt the ribbon shift slightly along the back of his head; his scalp grew cool underneath.

His hawk's nose led him in Drake's footsteps; this time up on the tracks, Ryder was coming prepared. When he swung the hoe he would break a thigh or two: no accident involved. Ryder felt the knuckles tighten on his free hand. He made a fist and cracked four knuckles on his thigh, pressing them into the flesh till they loosened up.

Eddy's hands were dangling at his sides. The short sickle, though rusted along the back, was shining on the cutting edge, and sharp as hell. He tucked it in his belt. The blade gnawed at the leather as he strode along, chewing a notch in the grain. He shifted the sickle to a new spot on the belt; no sense slicing his trousers loose to fall around his knees. In Eddy's hands the sickle was shaved ribs and stabbed shoulders, jabbed thighs and fractured bones, a twisted ankle or a damaged spine. A man would see God before salvation. Above Eddy's head the thundercloud spread across the sky like a leaden cover and to the west the setting sun shone orange under the purple cloud and the sick yellow of a mother storm.

In the Walker garden patch dusk pulled up her skirt and wrapped her twilight thighs around the farmhouse. The alfalfa leaned in the fields under the stiff hot wind and under the dark thundercloud domain. The first cricket chirped, nearly smothered in the wind, mournful and alone. It chirped once and then went silent waiting for an answer in the storm as the twilight deepened. The wooden boards on the back porch of the Walker farmhouse sighed as though miserable and mistreated. Buck stewed, his hair plastered in the wind as he leaned against a porch post; the Moon windchimes chattered and jangled like a wild hophead Chinaman. He watched his father and the men go up the access road toward the tracks. "Stay here, boy, we'll be back."

Not even, "Stay here, boy, and take care of your mother," not even, "Stay here, boy, the women need protection."

Just, "Stay here, boy . . . we'll be back."

Nothing could have twisted Buck's guts tighter, nothing wrung them out and shook them off . . . *stay here, boy* . . . nothing since the Bulls' morning laughter, the nightcrawlers inching in all directions, and the body floating in Yellow River, face down.

The men slipped into the clutching wind carrying weapons for good purpose, and Buck, left behind, paced on the back porch under the purple sky, useless and young. The wooden floorboards creaked under the weight of his feet, bound to the house unwanted, to the women oblivious, to a patch of ground far, far away from where his body longed to be.

"They've gone." Drew laid a hand on his shoulder. She was close to his back and she put her arms around his belly and kissed him on the neck. The thunderwind shrieked, casting dust in the garden, and the tiny hairs on his neck rose electric; she bit them, pulling with her teeth, tearing them out. He winced and her lips were at his ear, hot wax spilling over the lobe.

"They've gone . . . but you're the one who'll find her."

Some promise. Some promise falling from lips blown up at dawn under the sun's own scorch. As if to pinch him wide awake, the sick yellow light brightened in the west and the purple cloud pounded overhead. The windchimes trembled from the porch roof molding as the wind slapped them back and forth—they prickled his ears, stars' crystal collision, a nameless tune, dancing like St. Vitus from their bamboo bar. The sound gave no courage, but only wove for him his net of shuddering weakness, the fearful boy staring at Meriwether's red bristling hair, the nightcrawlers safe in their holes and the sodcutter reflecting laughter in a glint along the blade's edge. Buck stared at his own hands, the hands that shamed him, trembling before Meriwether's dangling worm. Maybe his father and his father's men were right with their, "Stay here, boy . . ."

And so he stood. Stood and waited while the battle dust was rising . . .

The thundercloud moved down from the sky where Buck could almost touch it and a spike of lightning snaked across the horizon, standing out full and savage, blue-white and silent. Then the deep rumble of thunder, full like a hammer-fist on the anvil of his face, and then the hail.

Great hail the size of marbles, falling with the wind, clattering on the ground and crops, shaking the porch roof; the white ice fell like Godstones to the ground, sending up puffs of dust and melting as they skittered still. The hail blew on the porch, shattering on the brittle wooden boards; the windchimes rocked in the wind, swaying like a crazy weathervane. A wind gust took them down, and the windchimes fell from the porch roof molding, flung back against the house wall. Buck moved close to Drew and felt her woman's hips. Again the lightning, the paper whitestar heat, and up in the alfalfa field, Buck heard the clatter of galloping hoofs.

A sheet of hail crashed into the barn like heavy gunfire. In the alfalfa field Buck saw the two great dappled mares rise up, their chests straining against their leather bounds. The horses tore across the field, trampling everything under iron-shod hoofs, pulling Moss Greene's clapboard wagon, axles spinning and one wheel off the ground.

High up on the buckboard seat, Moss Greene sat, reins in hand, whip in the air and lashing down. He came across the alfalfa field, shirttails flapping in the wind, wagon wheels trampling the broad sword leaves. Down the access road, the wagon jolted in the ruts. Moss Greene was rocking in the wagon seat, hair plastered to his forehead. He reined around in the clear patch before the porch and the wagon creaked to a stop.

Moss's eyes were deep on Buck, soulless hollow. The hail clattered and bounced off the wooden buckboard. Moss opened his mouth to speak and his teeth flashed white—no voice came but the furious neighing of a beaten horse, flesh stripped bare on its strong shoulders.

Moss Greene closed his mouth and the neighing ceased. He brought the whip down and the wagon surged past the porch and up on the U.S. Route. The bright hail clattered down around the Walker farmhouse and on the hard macadam Buck heard the pounding of the mares' shod hoofs fading in the wind.

Drew's eyes were dark. She stooped and picked up the broken windchimes from where they lay smashed on the porch boards and hung them from the wood porch molding. The hail began to wane, great gaps of air in the ice, falling thin and sparsely, the thunderhead passing over their heads. Drew struck the windchimes by their taut fragile string and they dangled brightly from the bamboo bar—none broken. The hail stopped, and the clear white marbles lay melting in every direction; the tiny pools of water seeped into the earth.

Drew took Buck's hand and led him to the open patch between the garden and the cotton rows, away from the house and the echoes of his fear and his father's hard command. Buck saw no wheel ruts where the clapboard wagon should have left its traces. The ice was melting darkly on the ground, and the alfalfa leaves were bent over in the fields. Buck looked for hoof marks: hoofprints yes, but no wagon tracks cut in the dirt.

Drew stooped to the ground and picked up a broken tree branch in one hand. The branch was stripped of leaves and bark, the same branch Buck had taken from her grasp down by Yellow River when he stalked Tina in the darkness and nearly brained her by mistake.

Drew came close to him, the branch in hand. Had she kept it all along?

"You've worried now for days gone by." Her free palm was gritty and delicate, grain by grain. "Worried about men and the evil in their laughter."

Buck reached out and touched Drew's thigh; she let him rest his hand there, and in the amber of her eyes, his fear jelled, hardening to the dawn's own stone. "That first morning . . . " He had to tell her, even though she maybe even knew; he wanted to admit it, see how it sounded in the twilight air, have her hear him say it.

"That morning . . . a body floated in the river. And I saw an owl in the sky. The body drifted face down, flowing with the current. The Bulls came." The corded muscle of her thigh was hard under his fingers. "I ran."

She placed one hand over his and pulled his palm up her leg to the saddle of her waist; she seemed to smile. "You'll want matches and a candle."

"Why?"

Drew was looking up the access path; his father's men had long disappeared, perhaps now battered by the hail, lost in the gathering twilight. She was staring out into the darkness. "You'll want a short keyhole saw, a sharp one, and a small sack."

"Why?"

She stopped staring at the growing night and turned back to him; the chimes trembled to silence, and the air ran with her scent. Buck breathed deep and wanted his hand on her saddled waist forever, back in the green alfalfa leaves, to be pulled down on her again. The amber curled like boiling caramel in her eyes; her voice rose, tempered and knowing. "That body in the river . . . that dead man floating face down in the water . . . he never left Bone County."

The nightcrawlers inched in all directions, the early-morning laughter ringing down the sodcutter's glinting blade, sweat sprinkled down the back of his neck again. The dead man had not left —not left—and not like Moss Greene braying at a hailstone's coldness, but the dead still floating in the water close by. He had watched the Bulls throw the drifter in the river's current. And then he ran. To what? To drag the stiff from its muddy place and roll it out on the U.S. Route? To hold the body in warm arms and bring it up to the railroad tracks for the Bulls to wonder at? For what?

"There's nothing we can do for that dead man now."

"No . . . " Drew leaned close; the skin of her cheek seemed white in the darkness and her murmurings liquid in the air. "No, but there's something that dead man can do for us."

Sarah trimmed the lamp down low, and the orange light fell full face on Lomax as he sat stone still in the kitchen. Outside, the hailstones' clatter ceased and the air inside the farmhouse freshened as if after a summer rain. The pink gums on Lomax's cloven face glistened, wet with saliva; he refused food but he drank water. Sarah could not stand looking at the idiot with his flat deadly eyes. Eyes that saw what no one else saw. Ears that heard the evil whispers beyond house walls and heaven. A spoon-fed cripple mouth that made no sound, but grunted a garbled sainted tongue.

The kitchen floor creaked and Mrs. Moon pulled a chair from the table and sat down; her hair was frayed, wisps fluttering around her face. She got up from the chair suddenly and went to Lomax and ran her hand across his forehead, brushing the matted hair back behind his ears. He let her do it, serene under his mother's touch. Mrs. Moon left Lomax and went to the kitchen door as though drawn to the night and its darkness: Sarah caught a glimpse of her eyes, the deadly amber, liquid heat; Mrs. Moon stared out into the dark fields and her eyes' heat ran like smoke from their sockets.

Sarah wanted none of this waiting on the men's discretion—their night's adventure. Her palms were moist and damp, and she rubbed them across her belly and the sweat returned. She rubbed them again. The sweat welled in her pores, sprinkling the skin. All manner and circumstance, memory starved and bloated: a child's empty bed in the next room, covers turned down and ready; a child's dress was hanging on a hook, nearby an extra pair of shoes, a comb, bobby pins pinched from beside her mother's bed . . . a bloody menstrual stain, hidden beneath the covers, dried, waiting for the child . . . waiting . . .

"Drake Walker's coming hisself . . . that's all the better."

In the Bulls' workhouse Simple looked around. All were awake. All ready. Meriwether had tied the chippy bitch up. She was gagged—cotton stuffed in her ears. Deaf and dumb. Not that she was smart enough to know anything anyway. Curled up, knees bent, she moved on Meriwether's cot; a smear of crusted blood across her naked thigh. The little gash was in heat. Meriwether sat next to her; he had one shoe off. He peered at the sole of his foot and muttered. Tina had noticed him limp before. His arms were a frightful mess where he'd scratched the scabs. A clot of matted dried bloody hair hung: a small lump, on the back of his head.

Meriwether stopped peering at his foot and looked at Tina's thigh. He touched her thigh with two fingers and she edged away from him on the cot. He touched her thigh again, tracing a line to the knee; she nudged against the wall. His fingers were raspy and cold; she caught his eyes, slits that watered.

"You and me are going off for a while . . . somewhere safe and private." His words drifted through the cotton wadding in her ears. She couldn't get any closer to the wall. He opened his palm and patted her thigh, kneading the flesh. He gripped her leg hard. Don't look at the hand. Don't look. He's not touching. He's not . . . look at something else. Anything. She pressed her shoulder blades against the wall.

One other man was standing in the shadows. He was a blond skinny kid. She thought his name was Daryl. He was a part-time railman—do anything for the job. The two others gave him all the dirty work—greasing, tar heating, all the slop. The kid sported some yellow bristle over his lip and chin, and his hollow dark-rimmed eyes made him a light-skinned raccoon. Daryl thrust his hands into his pockets. He had a problem with his sinuses, for he sniffled every other moment, getting the phlegm balled up in his throat and gathering it on his tongue. Deep in his throat Tina heard the haangue-haangue as he opened the bunkhouse door and hocked a spitball outside with a soft *ptui*.

Daryl stepped away from the door; he was not hungry for any trouble. "Why you do this, Simple? That kid'll put us in jail."

"You afraid asumpin', Daryl?"

"Jail."

Simple rubbed his hands together as if washing them with water. "Railroad near almost pays Tate's salary. An' who says the bitch's going back?"

Daryl would not quit. He simpered and whined. "Tate get paid wit' county taxes—"

"And who pays most taxes? C&C. If Walker come up here, we throw him off." Simple smiled, his eyes peering out from under heavy folds of fleshy brow.

"By all means . . . we throw him off."

Meriwether's voice rolled off the cot. "But you don't want that little slit near this place."

Simple moved to the table where a lantern glowed; the light spilled under his chin. His lips were bright, his fragile eyes black. "What I been saying, Daryl?"

He turned on Meriwether. "Get that damn boot of yours back on and take that little brat, close at hand, but *off* our property. Daryl, you stick by your place here, but not inside, keep a light burning. When Walker shows, make a little trouble for him. I'm gonna see what kind of house he left all unprotected."

Even under Meriwether's cold palm, Tina's thigh was damp, sweating. He pulled on her flesh and her tendons stretched from her knee. Beyond the bunkhouse walls, the night sang out in cricket whistles, full of heart, a drumbeat on a torn drumhead, ragged. Tina pleaded with her skin, prayed for a quick amputation, sawbones chopping her leg off at the knee—anything to keep that Bull's cold hand from wandering on her thigh.

Simple's bald dome was dark and shadowed. "That kid'll float. Tomorrow, in the river."

Tina cringed as Meriwether's hands twitched across her knee. But then he gripped steady and strong. The skin around his fingers' vise was red and white. Anything to pull her leg away—anything but touching now. Drowning was the least of it, he could spread her legs and look for the flow—nobody would see them and nothing to prove. He could take her now or wait. He dropped his hand from her leg and Tina breathed deep and easy.

Meriwether leaned from the cot, struggling with his foot. "Damn Judas boot."

But he spoke to empty bunkhouse walls: Simple was moving off to his own distractions, and Daryl had vanished with his gun out the door, to cover himself in the woods nearby and clothe his white skin in the dark green leaves.

Lepke terrorized the gray mouser till he relinquished his catch. Lepke advanced, metal spatula in hand, striking every surface, with a *spang!* on the counter, *spang!* on the table, *spang!* on the floor. The cat shot into every little nook and cranny, hackles rising, mouse swinging between his teeth, and shot out again.

Lepke tried to reason with the beast. "Now listen, puss, make a decision . . . it's either you or the mouse. If I was you, I'd pass on the mouse . . . either that, or a busted skull. There'll be other mouseys . . . understand my position . . . "

Spang! Bart Lowell winced, peeking through his fingers. "Ix-nay, Lepkiss!"

Spang! The cat dropped the mouse, which lay on its back, feebly pawing the air. Lepke scooped the rodent up; the cat retreated to a corner, hissing, but presently he calmed down and went in search of more prey. The mouse was still pawing an unknown nemesis when Lepke dropped it in the meat grinder and added it to the hamburger of the meatballs. He grabbed the meat grinder's handle and wrung it round and round.

Lowell gurgled in his coffee and nearly slid from his stool in a swooning moment of caffeine jitters. But he gripped the counter with both hands and hung on; when he was steadier he glanced again at Lepke. The chef had put the spaghetti in a large pot of boiling water and had begun rolling the mouse-and-burger mix into little balls. Lepke seemed pleased with himself. "Maybe I should have skinned the sucker."

Actually the cat had pretty well torn all the hair off the mouse anyway. Lepke made sure the bones were pulverized, and he rolled and dropped the meatballs into a hot skillet where they sizzled brown. The smell was not half bad. The spaghetti was done, the meatballs cooked, the sauce bubbling hot—Lepke was ready.

He packed the dishes up in the cardboard box, which was now

a little limp: a bowl for the spaghetti; a bowl for the sauce and meatballs; knives, forks and spoons; a napkin and a plate to eat from.

Sheriff Tate was still waiting, and he scowled, a trifle peeved at the delay. Lepke, with Bart at his heels, swept into the jail, the cardboard box balanced on one arm.

"A thousand pardons . . . you must be starving."

Sheriff Tate had learned early on in life to forgive and forget, live and let live. The cardboard box steamed away, the aroma of spaghetti and meatballs wafting heavy under his nose. "No hard feelings, Lepke—what do I owe you?"

"A dollar."

Tate forked over the bill and Lepke snatched it off the desk.

Bart Lowell turned a little gray. "Sheriff . . . " The cat scratch on Lowell's knuckle itched. He rubbed the faded claw mark and confusion clogged his ears.

"Yes, Bart?"

"The rat and the cat, meatballs he spat."

"What?"

"Meatballs the cat spat from a rat."

Sheriff Tate dished up spaghetti first, then sauce, and then Lepke's delicate wonders.

Lepke eyed the Sheriff's top-hand desk drawer. "I think old Bart needs a drink."

"Not a bad idea. Help yourself." Lowell went for the desk drawer and pulled out the bottle.

Tate twirled the spaghetti around his fork and stabbed a mouseball. Bart didn't take his eyes off the Sheriff; he tipped the bottle to his lips and swigged. Tate bit, chewed, and swallowed. Lepke watched his Adam's apple bob and smiled.

"Well? Your verdict?"

Tate dabbed his lips with the napkin and plunged the fork again. "Delicious, Lepke. Superb."

He was limping badly—no swelling on the foot, but this did not matter. His sole was too tender for any weight; when he stepped down, a sharp needle jammed his ankle, a searing spindle sunk in the bone. He dragged the chippy bitch—bound, gagged and blindfolded—down along the railroad tracks toward Yellow River. She stumbled on the railroad ties, bruising her knees, but he yanked her by the arm and hoisted, her feet skippity-skipping over the gravel bed. Before they left the bunkhouse Meriwether spun her around and around, like pin-the-tail-on-the-donkey, but as they walked Tina brushed against the metal railroad trestle and heard the running water of Yellow River slipping over the riverbed rocks. Tina knew where she was.

They scrabbled down the far bank; Tina never saw the bank's descent. The land dropped to nothing; she fell into the chasm, sliding on her forearm. Her skin was raw and scraped; her arm pounded. Meriwether caught her by the wrist, hoisting her again; he was swearing and he cuffed her head with his open hand.

He carried her across the river and she walked again, north along the riverbank, her ankles tangling in the weeds. They walked about a quarter mile until the banks were overgrown and twigs snapped against her face. They kept going. Tina figured they might be parallel with Moss Greene's old farm. She realized right, for they plunged up the bank and walked on the stiff dirt of Moss's fallow fields. The smell of charcoal and burned rubber close at hand was clue enough. They stopped at the wreck of Moss Greene's gutted farmhouse.

She tried to peek under the blindfold, but Meriwether was watching and cuffed her on the ear again. "Did I tell you to take it off? Did I tell you that?"

She said nothing, not a whimper, not a peep; at least he did not touch her thigh. He made her sit against a burned timber. He uttered oaths against his shoe, the treasonous boot. He paced. Then he stopped dead still and she heard him crouch. He was scanning the fields, letting the sounds drop out of the sky, ear perked, eyes peeled, nerves jim-jamming under a nightcloak. A devil's coy smile . . . nothing moved . . . alone; only the crickets sang in the fields and a *whippoorwill-whippoorwill* . . . kept time to Meriwether's nightwatch. A restless shiftless guardian, with no thought but his own itching scabs, the patter of dull notions. He paced and listened, stopped, knelt down and listened harder.

He lit a cigarette and the tobacco smoke hissing from his nostrils jetted down his chest. He checked his revolver, once, twice; he kept the safety locked. Six shells, six chambers spinning past the hammer, six leaden presents for the unsuspecting. Bind me six times with six lead bullets; wrap me in an outlaw's shroud. Let the stupid hounds yap at the gates and take the fools up to their empty rooms, whiling away a summer's night ignorant in peace. The moon drifted and the night became a whore, pampered, dress down, lips aglow and eager. Meriwether strutted past the tart's sullen eyes: a swagsman caught under the dog-day's darker half, a gallows bird lost on the summer road. He touched the revolver in his belt and his Judas boot pained him less.

The charred remains of Greene's old farm did not frighten him. He sang a tune under his breath about an old snatch in Baton Rouge: she took a knife and cut her John's you-know-what, diddle-dee-dee—

He couldn't pee.

Moss Greene's barn door yawned open and dark—the cows had gotten out and wandered off. Lowing ships hoofing over the land away from Bone County; they would never return. The bitch sat on a charcoal timber, smudging her dress, bony bottom to bone-burned wood. The snit had no idea, no idea at all. Where's your daddy? Forgot all about his bloody little snatch.

A rustle in the field. Down. Eyes keen peeled. Looking . . . no more rustle. Meriwether saw no angry dog waiting patiently on its haunches beyond the edge of the field. But the dog saw him, through a dog's eyes staring from bone-scarred skull. Even a dog's wet nose smelled the ruined man pacing by the ruins of a ruined home. Never thirsty, never panting, never tired, the dog watched patiently . . . dog eyes open . . .

———

They left the coal oil lamp burning on the table in the bunkhouse. The bunkhouse windows glowed; the place looked occupied, and that was the idea. Daryl watched Simple's bald head vanish without a trace; he heard his footsteps fade into the night-talking insects' conversation. Simple moved best alone—no stragglers, no orders needed, no mistakes. Dainty and sprightly, two hundred and ten pounds stepped forward, leading him closer to a friendly housecall on ignatz neighbors, women who did not know bull from a bull's foot. Drake Walker oughtn't of left his pie at home, resting on the windowsill . . . thinks he can chase down what won't stay put. Now that's a fool's hope.

Simple took the long way round, following Yellow River south, climbing up on the U.S. Route on the edge of Blue Vista Flats; then he walked in the middle of the broad macadam. A mile down, the Walker farmhouse was mostly dark back of the road, facing the fields, but Simple saw a single light burning. That's where the pie was keeping cool, way away from the air's evil effects. Must draw the ladies to their wit's end—a careful, calculated terror, something not easily forgotten. Simple began to gather pebbles and rocks as he walked along the road. He filled his pockets with stones. Not too heavy, but big enough to grip and toss. A calling card that would not possibly be mistaken. Take the Walker slut in his heavy hands, hammer it home, a bride-bed serenade, with bluebeard heavy on top. Lost in the sauce—she'd love it. Every woman wants it that way.

Sykes cut the lights and engine in the Studebaker, and it rolled to a stop, the tire treads soft on the road. In the passenger seat Eve was slumped down, one foot planted on the dashboard; the moon slanted through the windshield, and Eve's calf curved wan in the light. Thinking ahead, Sykes turned the engine on again, backed the car up so it faced out the dirt track, a few feet from County Road 6—ready for a quick getaway. Sykes had some trouble with the props on hand—the twine, the hatchet, the broom. Odd trinkets for a prank, but Eve seemed to know what she was doing. No lights burned at Yohanna Johns' place: early to bed, early to rise, makes a man healthy, wealthy, and . . .

Vulnerable too.

"We gotta find a ladder." When Eve did things, she did things right. "He'll have one in the barn. Got a flashlight? Gloves?"

Sykes went around to the back of the car. "The trunk." He found the flashlight and a pair of work gloves; he eased the trunk closed. Sykes still was not so confident. "How can you be sure he'll have a ladder in the barn?"

"Come on . . . there hasn't been a farmer in the history of man that didn't keep a ladder in the barn."

Sykes played follow-the-leader. "Okay, sugar. If you say so."

Eve closed the car door. "I say so."

They walked down the road to Johns' place. Sykes carried the ball of twine and the broom; Eve took the flashlight and the hatchet. Suddenly, she stopped him midstride, with the butt of the flash. Sykes turned and faced her.

She was dead serious. "I think you've got a great personality," her face tilted to his, her lips close. " . . . and you're hung like a horse."

Sykes' control was slipping fast. "About the hatchet and the broom . . . "

"Shut up." They were nearing Johns' house and could talk about horses later. Eve traded the flashlight for the ball of twine; Sykes angled off for the barn, armed with the torch. Lucky the door was open (you can raise the dead trying to open a barn door). He stepped into the hayscent and bumped his face against a wooden beam. Sykes rubbed his sore nose and turned on the flash; the light shaft cut through the murk. Cows lined up in stalls blinked their dilated eyes, stupid as always, ever ready to accept the strange nocturnal eccentricities of humans.

A cow lowed.

"Sshh . . . " Mustn't wake the old geezer.

A ladder led to the hayloft, but unfortunately, that was all it did, since it was nailed, bolted and screwed into the loft floor. Sykes walked the length of the barn, careful not to step in the manure gutter, careful not to smack his head against a low beam. But mostly careful not to make a racket since Adjuster Sykes was violating both County ordinances and Farm Bureau regulations: he was trespassing. His career in the AAA might pass pretty quick if he called his supervisor from inside one of Tate's jail cells, not even able to sit down because twelve-gauge shot had peppered his behind.

No ladder at the far end of the barn but when he looked back at the door, he saw it. The ladder was leaning right next to the door —he had been inches from it when he entered.

Eve was not where he had left her. She was coming round the far side of the house, twine in hand. A porch ran all the way around Johns' house, and Eve took the twine and looped it on each porch post, twice. Then she went on to the next one and she pulled the twine tight before looping it again. The twine became a taut tripwire, four inches from the porch floorboards. Sykes knew what to do. Gloves on, he gathered cow flop. Plenty of it. He picked the wettest he could find. He spread the manure liberally in four-by-four patches several feet from the porch, at the front door and at the back.

Then he leaned the ladder up against the porch roof where Johns could not miss it when he came out the front door. So far so good. They made no sound. Eve tied tight the last loop and knotted it. She backed away from the house and picked up the hatchet where it lay on the ground.

"Not so fast." Sykes was not ready. "Once you use that hatchet, he's gonna wake and we gotta finish this up. Gimme a moment. I just want a last look. Relish it for a moment."

Eve was breathing slow and heavy. "Be my guest, sport. Be my guest."

"Forty-five, forty-six, forty-seven—" Sweat dripped down Parker Watts' face. A crowbar leaned against the wall. Forty-odd safe deposit boxes lay scattered on the floor, their contents tipped and spilled. Gold watches, chains, jewelry, deeds, banknotes, worthless bonds, Grandma's reams of private poetry, love letters, twenty kinds of gold earrings, but no gold five-dollar coins 1866, Series D or otherwise.

Hanson always figured he could take a good practical joke just as well as the next man, but there came a point—and he was quickly reaching his limit.

"Okay Parker . . . you can stop kidding around. You've scared me . . . oh, a good laugh—I admit it. No hard feelings."

"*Shut up, you third-rate grocer!*" Watts turned on Hanson, wind seething from his nostrils, his oiled hair a total mess. "You think this is a joke? Do you? Some joke! Why don't you stop standing around on your flat feet, you dithering dumbbell. *Help me!*"

"Nothing personal, Parker"—Hanson was cool as ice cream—"but don't you think you've carried this far enough?"

That did it. The cap popped off the soda bottle. Watts gnashed his teeth, tore his hair, kicked a safe deposit box across the floor, the insides exploding in a colored burst of little girls' jacks and a pink rubber ball, which bounced gay and innocent, rolling to Hanson's feet. Parker was not through; he grabbed the top drawer of a filing cabinet and yanked it open. Stacks of files and banking documents flew over his shoulder scattering in a hopeless pile.

Hanson shook his head. "What a mess."

Parker Watts stopped dead still, silent; he forgot the filing cabinet and advanced on Hanson, hands outstretched, moving slowly for the store owner's throat.

"Now, Parker . . . hold on—I didn't mean it. I believe you. Parker? Parker?"

Watts kept creeping closer; a fleck of spittle dripped from the corner of his mouth.

"*Parker! I believe you!*"

Tate happily chewed the last mouseball, scooped up the last strand of spaghetti, and licked the plate clean with his tongue. He belched.

"Wonderful, Lepke. Dee-lightful. Even if I did start dessert first."

Lepke had been sharing the bottle with Bart Lowell, and between the two of them, the bottle was half gone. "Glad you liked it, Tate—I consider it one of my best efforts."

"And well you should, Lepke, my good man." Tate extended his hand for the whiskey. "How about a snort? It clears the palace."

"You mean palate." Suddenly Bart Lowell was back on mark.

Tate shrugged. "Whatever."

Bart was eyeing Lepke. Lepke raised his eyebrows as if to say, Go ahead—tell the gobbler—nobody'll stop you. Bart thought better of it and kept his trap shut. He reached for the whiskey bottle in Tate's hand.

"Not so fast, Bart—not so fast. I wanna catch up. You two rats are hiding in the sauce."

Lepke couldn't contain himself. "Three."

"Balls," Bart added.

Tate, suddenly serious and sober, pursed his lips and squinted. "You know, I think you've hit something here." He belched again.

Tate knew exactly what he was going to do. He would let the Bulls play their game another step; he would let Drake Walker keep his anger and the fate that went with it. Tate was gonna stand it out and bide his time—and then he would pick up the pieces later. He tipped the bottle, swallowed, and smacked his lips. His X-ray eyes rose to the ceiling, to the rooming house above and Eve's double-occupancy bed. "Maybe we should just pay a visit . . . "

Tate stared at Bart. "Maybe that sister-in-law of yours might oblige us with a few moments of her concentration."

"Nice idea," Lepke declared.

Bart stroked his chin, considering. "Oh, I don't think she's gotta concentrate all that heavy—I think she sorta knows what to do."

"A fine suggestion." Lepke was raring to go.

Tate, as master of ceremonies, made the motion to adjourn. "Settled then. We split three ways. Since it was my idea, I get to go first."

Bart riled. "But she's *my* sister-in-law."

"*Shame* on you." Lepke frowned. "I go first; it's been the longest since I've had a piece."

"Irrelevant!" Tate was in command; he lunged for the door, making it outside before either one could catch him.

"Gentlemen . . . " Tate called from outside, his voice fading, "I rest my case . . . "

Sheriff Tate bounded up the rooming house stairs two at a time. Lepke followed, huffing and puffing. Bart brought up the rear. At the top of the stairs Tate slowed the pace with a cautionary hand and eased down the hall, quiet as a mouse. Lepke and Bart walked on tiptoe.

"Watch it."

"Hey, don't push . . . you'll get your turn."

"Shut up." Tate was at Eve's door. He knocked softly. "Eve," but no answer came. "Eve? Honey . . . are you in there?" Murmured rustlings beyond the wooden door. Tate looked over his shoulder at the two men breathing down his neck. He knocked again.

Faintly. "Come in."

Tate drew himself to full height, tucked in his shirt, and puffed up his chest. "Hang tough, boys . . . it might be a while—five minutes with me and they're always begging for more."

The door opened, real easy.

Marybelle, stretched out on Eve's bed, heard the man come in and shut the door, final and firm. She heard him stub his toe.

"Shit, it's pitch black in here."

Marybelle said nothing. So this was where it all ended. Somehow she did not mind. No name. No face. All the better. This one smelled of whiskey, spaghetti and meatballs—heavy too. He lay on top like a potato sack and fumbled with himself—fumbled and mumbled, mumbled and fumbled—this old moose couldn't get it right. He rolled this way and that, oblivious that he had missed his mark. Marybelle took pity on the dud—he wouldn't last long, in any case. He ground it down, heave-ho, and groaned.

A whimper and gone . . . simple as that. The moose rolled over and patted his chest—this one thought pretty highly of himself. Not one for the finer points, but alas, Marybelle's stealthy understanding grew: few men were.

Gimme. Gimme.

Gimme that real stuff.

June Tate bolted up in bed. Tate had not returned.

Out late?

Guarding the welfare of the community?

Gallivanting?

She threw off the covers and began searching for her clothes. Gallivanting! No question about it. The dirty dog was toot-tooting his horn. Off with the boys on a night's gay ride.

The silly goose. Gander?

June wondered little on how she knew these things . . . her guts spoke for themselves, sharpened with an owl's talons. Find Tate. Squeeze the diddle till his pits popped out.

Henry stood at J. J. Baskum's front door and watched. The crushed little man in the wormy straw boater did the honors. His trousers fell to his ankles and he squatted over the bottom step of Baskum's doorsteps. A moment of waiting and straining; Henry held his breath. The man's boater tipped to one side and he grunted. Then he breathed a little deeper.

"Henry, gimme a rag."

Henry gave his brother a rag. The little man wiped himself off and pulled up his pants.

Then he stepped back to admire his handiwork.

"Fine texture.

"Nice shape.

"Couldn'a done better."

"Whew!" was all Henry could say.

They were in agreement—laid on Baskum's doorstep, no mother's milk, nosirree. This discovery would keep Baskum occupied for quite a while—amazed that just a few easy minutes of grunting and straining could produce such distraction. They knew Baskum never was a nature lover.

Henry and his brother withdrew to the edge of the copse that sheltered Baskum's house. Henry let his brother go a distance; then he found a rock. A nice rock, not too heavy, not too light. Smaller than a baseball, but bigger than a plum. He took aim and threw—sailing on air, a perfect pitch—*a strike!* The rock shattered Baskum's upstairs bedroom window. A woman shrieked in the darkness, and then a light came on. Henry did not see the rest—he was already dashing down the dirt road, far away from his results. Time to hook up with Drake Walker's people; Henry would never keep them waiting. His brother swaggered up the U.S. Route, the wormy straw boater cocked rakish on his head.

Josie Baskum threw a fit in the only way a huge woman can.

Big. The mountain of flesh quaked, and her trembles rocked the sea of her empty bed. Shattered glass was all over the floor. Even with the light on, the electric light, she could not contain herself.

"J. J.!" Shrieking out of her wits; J. J. was not beside her in bed and, in fact, nowhere in the bedroom.

"J. J.!"

Not a sound.

"J. J. You chickenshit son-of-a-goat, you lame-brained donkey, you coward, Turk. J. J. you little pecker—*where the hell are you?*"

Nix.

Not inconceivable that he would hide under the priest's frock. Josie Baskum looked under the bed.

Empty.

"J. J., you whore's abortion, you weak, sniveling excuse for a farmer, J. J., you peasant, somebody busted my bedroom window."

Drunken silence.

"J. J., you peacock pansy, you ninny, you im-poe-tent suckling, *why don't you answer me?*"

Josie got out of bed, careful not to step on the broken glass; she pulled on her huge housedress and crammed her toes into beaten slippers. Come, come, my little gosling . . . we can't be too far away, can we? Maybe we're hiding our frightened eyes in the closet . . . maybe we're quivering in the pantry . . . maybe we're peeing in our panties. Josie crept out of the bedroom and headed down the stairs.

"Now we can't all be big strong big daddy bears, thumpa-thumpa your crummy chest—*come out, come out wherever you are,* you weak-kneed, pigeon-livered, milksoppy, gritless, sniveling homo."

Baskum was in the kitchen; he had not heard a word. His feet were up on the table, his tie askew, his head tipped back; he was snoring dead away. The better part of a whiskey bottle was worse for wear. It lay tipped over on the table, three quarters empty.

"Why, J. J." Josie inched close. "You've been drinking, you duck's dink." He did not wake. Josie tiptoed around the table, figuring a way to topple his chair. Baskum's sixth sense caught on, and he cocked one eye open.

"Okay, what the hell do you want?"

Josie froze: difficult for a fat woman poised on her tippytoes. She played it straight. "Listen, you limp worm, somebody tossed a rock through my bedroom window, broke the glass and nearly killed me. There might be a gang of men outside this house this very minute, ready to cut our throats and abuse my body—what the hell are you going to do about it?"

Now Baskum had both eyes open, and he swung his feet off the table; the chair tilted back down to the floor, landing on all four legs.

"Absolutely nothing, Josie. Absolutely nothing."

Sheriff Tate closed the door to Eve's room behind him and came out into the hall. Bart Lowell was pacing back and forth. Lepke was slumped up against the wall.

Tate hitched up his pants. "She's an animal. There's no reasoning with the bitch. Lepke, you're gonna come outta there trussed up like a chicken. Good luck, pal."

Lepke said nothing. He took a breath, sucking in his gut and paused for a moment, his hand on the doorknob. "This, my friends, is where we separate the men from the boys."

Marybelle lay on her stomach and did not even bother opening her eyes. A pair of hands hiked up the back of her dress and then patted her fanny.

"Well, well, well." A different voice. "I read about this in a book once."

Lepke took her from behind. Although a master with meat, this cook could play no ratball with a woman. His hands were firm, and she yielded, though mostly out of convenience; she arched her back and helped him along. He grabbed a rope of hair and held it; she did not seem to mind.

He thrust his hand under her jug, and she arched her spine a little more to accommodate. Squeezing too hard, too long, her contractions were minor suctions at best, but Lepke never noticed. He slammed on, a burger-and-biscuits boy; when she felt his rose rupture, his hand was beside her face and quickly as she could, she bit his thumb.

"Ho ho!" Lepke was pleased, rock sure he had found her passion.

Gimme that real stuff.

Drew, a standing animal with silken olive skin stretched tight, led the way. Buck followed her straight across the cotton rows toward Yellow River, edging close in where the U.S. Route spanned the water over an iron bridge with concrete pilings. A light nightbreeze sighed across Buck's skin, blowing the thunderclouds out of Bone County. The hail had melted once it hit the ground, the small water pools seeping into the earth like so much spit. And the ground had taken up the water, sucking it down without a trace.

With each step taken in Drew's animal wake, Buck felt the dawn's brambles catching him around the chest and Meriwether dangling the severed worm. The U.S. Route loomed like a long battlefield earthwork to one side. In front, the riverbank swelled to a lip and then fell to darkness like a soldier's trench. On his right hand the cotton rows moved steadily by, troops in line, ready for the call to the front. The steel and concrete bridge was a mortar bunker; step by step to the river's trench, Buck's hands grew leaden and his heart pounded solemn in his chest. To have that morning's dawn all over again, all over again now: he would have done anything, then, to spare himself this—anything in that dawn's light so as not to close in on the dead man now like some gun-shy hunter, afraid of the prey and afraid of himself. Buck almost reached for Drew's moving haunches, to grab a swatch of her skirt, to drag her back.

Then they reached the riverbank where it sloped to a black shade. Under the bridge's span the dark grew cold and Buck tried to edge in down along the water. He slipped and his foot sank ankle deep in the current. Drew crawled under the span and in the darkness two amber eyes glowed. Feathers moved, the owl shot from under the bridge, over Buck's shoulder as he stood one foot in the water; the owl circled over the bank . . . the wings vanishing in the night. He heard Drew breathing.

"Hey, c'mere."

The smell of wet river grass and pebbles in mud, the perpetual dank air under a bridge. His eyes adjusted that last degree, and he could see her wading knee deep in the water, the river soaking her skirt to the thighs.

Leaning against the concrete piling, the dead man rested. His chest was out of the water, his knees curled underneath him and his head lolled. The dead man's arms moved inches under the water, fingers swollen and wrists limp.

"His foot's caught . . . let's get him out."

Buck felt the water in his knees, dead flesh against his skin, dead hands to his hands. "I can't."

"Do it." Dead lips to his lips.

Buck reached out, pulling on the dead man's elbow. The shirt-cloth tore, and Buck's fingers squeezed dead flesh. The skin was rubbery and fairly cool, an awkward lump as the body rolled toward the bank like a large filled sack loose in the middle. Drew pushed, splashing, and Buck pulled both arms; they dragged him up the bank and laid him on his back in the riveredge grass. Buck gasped for breath and lay on his own back, next to the body. His mouth was very dry with an oily spit that clung to his teeth.

Drew had gathered the things—the keyhole saw, the sack—

and she gently placed the broken branch on the ground. "Don't rest now."

Buck was on his knees and at her side, this time not afraid of a dead man's flesh. In the moonlight he could see. The dead man's pants were torn at the thigh, the skin there blackly purple, bruised and puffy. The hands and arms were scratched where the Bulls had dragged him through the brambles. His face was worse, bad over the eye with an egg lump over the ear where the hair was scraped off and the pale scalp mottled red.

But the carcass was intact, inviolate. No rat or turkey vulture had gnawed on the bones or skulked close by. Drew touched the dead man's hand first, pulling it by two fingers, stiffening the wrist. Buck reached out to help her; he touched the skin and jerked his hand away.

Drew's grip tightened on the dead man's flesh. "Do it."

This time Buck curled his fingers strong around the forearm. He held the keyhole saw in his other hand and pulled it across the skin. The flesh went ragged, tearing—black blood oozed along the jagged blade. The tendons broke, snapping, the veins and arteries catching on the saw's teeth, still elastic, getting in the way. Hacking and sawing, he broke the bone and the hand came free. Drew nearly fell over backward—but the veins and muscle bits stretched, still not severed. Buck bound them all together in his fist and slashed the blade once more. The gut strands snapped, and one wet sliver of muscle whipped under his eye. He brushed it away.

Drew was left with the dead man's severed hand; it waved in front of her face like a magician's spare limb that dazzles the audience while two living hands slip smooth and furious under the cloak. She held it away and her breasts heaved over strained breath. Buck took the hand from her and put it in the sack. That oily saliva formed a chokeball in his throat. He brought it up and blew it into the river. Buck twisted the sack closed. His hands were very steady and he could look at the dead man in the face.

"You satisfied?"

Drew, lithe now and controlled, eyes smoking; she stood up and brushed herself off. "You'll need it . . . you'll see."

Drake led; he led the other two, creeping slowly to the Bulls' bunkhouse. Firm and silent, Drake locked the breech of his shotgun; he walked slowly, hunched down. Off the way-station clearing the woods were silent and no rustle shook the leaves. Drake stopped more than once to listen for breathing in the trees and he looked for the moonlight glistening off a white eye in the brush. He strained for the subtle whisper of a man keeping still, for the silence where the crickets are too frightened to chirp. He heard Ryder's wheezing cigarette breath behind him, the deep in-and-out, the long whistling as air found the tubes and the tubes found the lungs. Then a pause . . . and Ryder sent the air away, sighing out his throat.

From the corners of his eyes Drake could see that Eddy followed. He barely saw him in the dark, only the flickering movement of his steps. Eddy, turning round and round, walking backwards, to the side: he looked out behind, a watchful rear guard.

As Drake moved closer to the bunkhouse, he saw down the tracks, over the trestle that spanned the river. On the far side, two bodies split from the metal spans and stood out full in the moonlight. Henry and his brother.

Drake waved and after a moment the tall one waved back. As they came on, their bodies melted again to the dark steel. And then the bunkhouse shadow was dark and the moon went behind the roof.

"Easy." Drake held his hand out, stopping the men behind him. "Wait here."

Drake crawled slowly, on hands and knees, his belly nearly dragging on the ground. It took long-drawn-out breathing minutes to cover the short yards from the woods to the bunkhouse. He reached the bunkhouse's wooden walls and touched their hard grain. He inched up, fingers lightly against the rough-hewn wood, and touched the dirty windowsill. Forehead first above the glass, and then his eyes. Inside, the bunkhouse was empty, beds unmade, clothes and tools scattered about. No Tina.

Drake stood up, went around to the front and waved his men over. Ryder and Eddy followed him through the front door. The crude oil lamp burned on the table, innocent and bright. The men's shadows slid against the tar-speckled walls, slimy silhouettes. Drake stood guard at the door considering the next move. Follow the tracks? Spread out and double back to town?

Gunfire crackled, slashing the air; the bunkhouse windows flew to jagged blades. "The lamp!"

They snuffed the lamp and Drake crouched by the door frame, peering out into the darkness. The woods on the far side of the tracks were lit up with the moonlight, white and black, the leaves' surface rising like the sculpted face of a cathedral. Nothing else: behind the first layer of leaves was total darkness. Drake had seen no muzzle flash.

Scuffles, whispers; then Ryder took up a position at the opposite door frame, crouched. "We're okay."

Drake looked at the stiff hoe handle gripped in his tenant's fist —what was he gonna do, throw it? A damn useless stick of wood . . . didn't even have a blade.

Muzzle flash, cut in the trees, within the cascade of moonlit leaves; a bullet grazed the door frame, screaming into the bunkhouse. Matchstick slivers prickled Drake's face. "Keep an eye on the other windows . . . holler if they come close." The Bulls were playing tough and a rocksalt shell was not long range. One thing though: the Bulls could not know they had only one gun between the three of them.

And another thing . . . the Bulls were fooled; they had the numbers wrong. Henry and his brother waited nearby, one more shotgun, loaded and ready.

Simple, standing on the U.S. Route, cared nothing about the noise. Rocks make noise, broken glass makes noise. Women's wails, shrieks, moans, prayers—all these make noise—so Simple cared nothing. He was heavy on rocks and he cracked a brassy grin that nearly shamed him. Simple took his first rock and heaved it toward the Walker farmhouse. The stone clattered against the clapboard, chipping the paint and scarring the wood.

The next broke the other front window.

The third sent shingles sliding down the roof.

Simple took a big rock, the size of a grapefruit, and with a lucky shot knocked open the front door. He stood in the middle of the road and howled, slapping his thighs like a dumb ape escaped from the zoo.

"Well, well, ladies, looks to me like your menfolk left you

unattended. Now that ain't polite." Simple slapped his thighs again and searched the edge of the U.S. Route for another rock.

Sarah heard the first thump as the walls shook under the blow. Then window glass showered the floor. Shingles split, falling from the roof. Sarah dropped Tina's bedspread over the sheets. The back door banged open in the kitchen, and the night air breeze swept through the house, tugging on the window curtains. Sarah left Tina's room. In the kitchen Lomax cowered in a corner; the back door was open, and Mrs. Moon swept it shut.

The door bolted, Mrs. Moon turned, her eyes smoking coals in the lamplight; she ignored Lomax and brushed past Sarah on to the front room. The front door slammed shut.

Lomax sat, knees to chest in the corner, the idiot boy's muc-muc going wild. He twisted his neck from side to side, gibbering and blubbering; the drool ran from his cloven lips in long streams, caught, and curled, clung to his wrists, his hands, then broke and flowed anew.

He knocked his head, back and back again, against the counter and the wall, hubba-dubba, hubba-dubba, not hard enough to crack his skull, but plenty loud. His hands slapped his cheeks, nearly gouged his eyes; he wrapped and unwrapped his knees, forearm muscles popping. His fingers twined; his knuckles cracked. He shook his hands, wringing the wrists, eyeballs rolling white-black, white-black. Drool cascaded in foamy bubbling strands from his split pink gum; the stringy gush spilt along his thighs—clear blood from an open wound.

"What do I do about Lomax?"

From the front room: "Nothing."

Lomax kept the fever pitching. Sarah was not sure if she heard right. Mrs. Moon was back in the kitchen. "You have a gun?"

Sarah shook her head. Drake kept only one gun.

"Knives?"

Plenty. Sarah tore open the drawer under the counter, and the carving tools clattered to the floor. She found two big ones and held them by the blades, offering the handles. Mrs. Moon declined. "For you."

"But you'll want a—"

Mrs. Moon was in the front room again. Sarah followed. A large shoulder was coming in the broken window, but Mrs. Moon had a chair and swung the legs, grazing the shoulder and hitting the wall. Jagged glass still poked sharp spikes which caught, snagging the curtains, shredding them. The chair legs broke the crystal slivers and the dry glass fell. The window was empty.

Now at the back door more pounding; the clapboard jolted, knocked and the door frame groaned. The big man had slipped around the house. Dashing to the kitchen, Sarah passed Lomax, sunk in the corner. He kept blubbering in a blind endless fit. Mrs. Moon still had the chair. "Put the knives away."

Another rock exploded the kitchen window, showering the counter with bright powder and razor chips; the glass tinkled around Lomax, falling like a dry hazard snow on his arms and head. He barely noticed. Sarah scraped under the kitchen table, clawing for the knives and forks that tumbled helter skelter from the yawning drawer. Inside, Lomax boiled like water in the pan—outside, the man was running wild. Sarah held two knives in one fist. Damn him. Damn him. Suck an egg and crack the shell between your teeth. Bones to the butcher, fear to the thief. Sarah scrabbled in the knives. Damn him, chop-chop.

No relief.

He bruised the door and his vile pounding shivered timbers through the wood, like smoke through windy leaves. Drunk with his fists' heavy stones, Simple never gave up. Want some more, ladies, do you?

Do you?

Lepke closed the door to Eve's room behind him. Tate was waiting, hoping for another shot once Lowell was through. Lepke's hair was tousled; his throat was splotched red, pinked instead of sweating. Lepke kept his advice short and sweet.

"Well Mister Barber, comb out the tangles and shave it off."

"I see." Lowell didn't.

For once he stopped pacing; he wrung his hands, like a squirrel fondling a beechnut. He hopped from foot to foot, a little lover's jig. Tate lost patience with the fox trot.

"Come on, Lowell, I'm ready for seconds."

"Cool off, big boy." Lepke the sophisticate.

Lowell swallowed hard. He almost never did it without his barber's smock. This was no time to run down now and get the garment. These fellas would never understand. But could he straighten out in regular attire? Would he droop, a supple worm missing his chance? A frightful situation. Some whoremaster. If the others even suspected they would noways let him live it down.

No, down would be where he stayed . . . forever and ever. The barber with the limp razor. Shudder at the notion. No dilly dally. No wishy washy. Batten down the hatches, unfurl the mainsail, Watch Out, Watch Out, keep lively there, Hup-Two, Hup-Two, Hup—

Bart Lowell grabbed the door handle and went searching for El Dorado

---

Josie Baskum stared at her drunken husband and contemplated a good ear-boxing. Well, after all, J. J. was her lawfully wedded washout. She tried a new tack.

"Maybe you didn't hear me, Mister Baskum . . . I said someone busted my bedroom window . . . they may still be outside. I need protection."

J. J. wasn't easily persuaded. "I heard you the first time, you fat whore. I can't possibly understand why any man in his right mind would even want to beat you, much less touch you. If you're so worked up about it, why don't you step outside and give the bastards a piece of your mind? You've terrorized braver men than me."

That did it. Josie hauled off and belted Baskum on the ear; he fell sideways out of the chair, knocked over like a tenpin. Head ringing, he was on his feet, eyes glazed and bulging; the whole side of his face was red. Josie lost her nerve. Baskum swung his fists above his head and charged, knocking the table. Josie scampered out of his way.

He threw a hammy fist. She ducked and Baskum spun like a top. He chased her out of the kitchen—up the stairs, into the bedroom, thrice round and then down the stairs again. He finally caught her by the couch and threw her on it. A couch leg broke; the divan teetered under her weight. Her housedress and nightgown balled up around her middle—she trembled there, all thighs and crotch—somehow not believing.

"J. J. Don't. I'm sorry. J. J.!"

Baskum undid his belt and opened his fly.

"J. J. please."

He dropped his trousers and dived for glory. She squealed, blubber quaking. But wait!

She felt it now—her husband was missing one crucial item. He was soft as a day lily—no angry Jack. The dumb dong couldn't cut the mustard. As though the sky cracked open with the everlasting, Baskum was finished before he started. He was leaning on Josie's body, trousers wrapped at the ankles; Baskum lifted himself off his wife. Josie yawned.

"What's the matter, honey?"

He pulled up his pants. He walked a tight circle in the room, as if to reassure himself that all the parts were in working order. But of course, they were not. "Nothing's wrong. Nothing. Don't feel like it, that's all."

Josie ran her hands down her naked thighs, not bothering to pull down her nightgown. "Well, I can see that."

"Now don't get smart."

"Why, J. J.!"

"Don't make an issue of it."

"Now, now . . . " She stroked her laden thighs again. "J. J.?"

"Yes."

Josie leaned back on the teetering couch. "Come here . . . I want your face."

Baskum obeyed, on his knees before his naked wife.

Claire Lowell took Preacher Simon on the floor, a foot from the crib. She had no trouble; Preacher gave no resistance. Easy as pie. A man so seldom questions his desires. Shocked, maybe . . . reluctant, maybe . . . but question? Never. She took him, in little bits and pieces. Not all at once. She showed him where to lay his hands.

Here.

And here.

She pulled him out and drew him on. With no grandfather

clock or church-tower face to mark the minutes and the hours, Preacher was abandoned to his loins, beaten. Claire's rhythm struck the only time. Variation on the act is repetition nonetheless—Claire had him once and once again. No inkling that his wife had disappeared, no care for her whereabouts, no honor but the second, third and fourth . . . her thighs over his shoulders, round his neck, vulva parted, outer labia swollen, inner slick—smearing fingers, tongue, chin, lips, nose never the same for blowing, blowing, ever, ever again. This he must have practiced there and then five times at least. Tongue tired, she guided his finger above the bone, and he could rest, staring as Claire trembled oblivious to his concentration. He mapped each simple fold and curve: how the inner met slice to pink slice a scalloped rose flesh shell; valleys dip on either side—to no avail the ground through which a soldier never passes, but may slide as though trenched, face first. He folded his own ripe oiled flower ever larger, ever open . . .

She murmured a lifesong low and long; she held on by the short hairs at the back of his neck, forcing his face to work again. She used the tips of her fingers to spread her balm for him, more swollen than before—each lip and ridge parted in relief—she let him take his time, she let him listen, convulsion to convulsion to convulsion, dart and flick, a jump, slash by grazing, renting gasp, fingertips straining, pelvis rocked—little brother tongue kissed big brother, meeting at the bottom of the hour. She pressed the bone against his face and made him hold it there till she was done, brass heart pounding. A shudder passing, gained and broken, ankles twisting, easing off . . . easing . . . off.

She dragged him unwilling over her thighs; his turn had come. She wanted him to the hilt . . . always to the hilt. The cradle rocked on unnoticed. The child slept to the words below . . . a prayer to sunken heavy flesh, eaten both soft and hard, plum squeezed, juice running. Love spread on a painter's canvas—the oil never dries. She spoke his name in the horn of his waiting ear, a dusky voice in the wettest hollow. Only this room existed, only this night . . . only this floor. A dark house, eyes turned in, watching Syrian women, big African women squatting, jeweled Arab women, gashed cut from birth—nipples hard like fruit pits, the syrup shining . . . the syrup.

"Had enough?" Eve was getting edgy; she had set up her ducks and now the time had arrived to shoot them down. Yohanna Johns' house was trussed up with twine, a big bird ready for roasting. A broom was planted, bristles up in the dirt front of the house. The cow flop was laid out, a welcome mat. Ladder in place. Hatchet ready.

Sykes took the heavy blade in hand. Had he, in fact, *had enough?* Not of Eve, not of her getting him to do the things she liked, of getting him to do the things against his better judgment, to do the things whether he liked them or not—of Eve, it appeared, he could not get enough.

Eve loosened her grasp on the wooden handle and watched Sykes walk toward the house. She found a tight grove of bushes and pressed her body into the leaves. The branches quieted their rustle as Sykes stepped up on Johns' porch, avoiding the cow patties and the string. He cut quite a figure, standing there in the darkness, a tall blond man with a hatchet hanging from his hand, relaxed; he flowed with the night, practiced . . . professional. Eve repeated her lines; she murmured them over and over, getting a feel for the words. She could not thank Marybelle enough. Helping Sykes with his revenge seemed a fitting bold thing to do: friends in fraud and hope.

Sykes swung the hatchet at the door-frame molding; he chipped a piece off, wood tore, slivers fell to the porch. He slashed again, driving the hatchet deep into the molding. Johns could not help but notice. Sykes dashed off the porch, careful about the string and the flop. He ran right by Eve in the bushes.

"Pssst. Here . . ."

He stopped short, saw her and crouched down. A light came on in Johns' upstairs window. The curtain rose; Eve went into her act.

"*Eeeeeieieieie.*" Shadows flashed behind the upstairs window. Again. "*Yohanna . . . Yooo-haaa-naaa.*"

"*Yooo-haaa-naaa . . . I'm wayy—ting.*"

The light vanished from the window. Yohanna Johns was coming down.

"*Yooo-haaa-naaa . . . I hurt . . . the mustard stings . . . Oh, Yooo-haaa-naaa, I hurt.*"

The lamplight flashed on the ground floor. Johns was close.

"*Yooo-haaa-naaa . . . My duppy's walking . . . Yooo-haaa-naaa.*"

The front door burst open. Yohanna stood in his nightshirt, a storm lantern in his hand. The glow lit his face and little else. The wick was trimmed very low. He saw the broom-handle jammed in the ground, and the ladder leaning against the house. He clutched his chest.

"Roxie."

The hatchet was jammed in the door frame, head high. Johns saw it and nearly passed out; the lantern trembled, the flame dancing within the glass. Elroy and his two brothers were up and gathered at the door, staring out.

"In the house!" The dumbbells were too dim to understand. "Get in the house!"

They fluttered backward, too fearful to disobey.

"Yooo-haaa-naaa." Cruel, yes. But just.

"Roxie . . . Roxie . . . where are you?" Johns set the lantern on the porch; the lamplight caught the twine, but he did not notice.

"Yooo-haaa-naaa . . . puuut owwwt the liiight. It hurts my eyes."

"Yes, yes, anything." He snuffed the light and the twine vanished.

"Yooo-haaa-naaa . . . doo you love me?" A woman's words if there ever were any.

"Yes, Roxie, yes—where are you? Come and let me see."

"I cannot. They keep me . . . hot . . . a very hot place . . . mustard and fire . . . they make me do such things . . . "

Johns tore his hair. "Oh no, not there. Not there."

"Yesss." Eve paused to catch her breath. Sykes stroked the back of her head; she turned her face and kissed his hand. Eve wanted more. For herself.

"Yooo-haaa-naaa . . . you must tell me . . . you must tell me something . . . "

"Anything Roxie . . . anything." Yohanna Johns was all wrought and ragged; he twisted the edge of his nightshirt in one hand, wringing the fabric, almost tearing it.

"Did you Yooo-haaa-naaa . . . did you?"

"Did I what?"

"With another woman . . . did you with another woman?" The truth to tell.

"Oh Roxie, please forgive me . . . I didn't mean it . . . it was just that you were so spooked when you were alive . . . I could barely live with you . . . I went just to look . . . I never did a thing . . . I looked, but I never touched . . . to look . . . I swear."

"*Should I believe you?*" Eve took a deep breath and went for the full cigarette pack. "*Why should I believe you?*"

"Roxie, *please* . . ."

Eve nailed his shoes to the floor. "*I know damn well all about you. You went with that Eve woman . . . you went with her once a week . . .*"

"That's true. I admit it. But I never touched her. I just went to look."

"*Did you pay her?*"

"No, Roxie—I never paid her."

"*Yooo-haaa-naaa, you skinflint . . . I think it's time you paid her. Yes. Yes. It's high time you paid your debts.*" A dog in the manger.

"I'll do it, Roxie . . . I promise."

Now all men must pay the price. "*Come out here where I can see you better . . . they're calling me . . . I must leave.*"

"Wait!"

And the price is always high, a full purse. Yohanna moved, stepping off the porch. His ankle caught on the twine, he tripped and went sprawling, over the edge of the porch. Hands outstretched, he tumbled neck and chest in the cow manure, sliding a distance on its wet surface. "Roxie!"

"*Promise Yooo-haaa-naaa.*"

Flecks of cow flop speckled his face and arms; he strained his buzzard's neck. "I promise."

"*Good-bye, Yooo-haaa-naaa.*"

"ROXIE!"

Eve and Sykes crept back to the car. Johns never saw them go. Out on the road, Eve touched Sykes' thigh. "Satisfied?"

"Yes."

"Is there anything else I can do?"

Sykes held the wheel with one hand; with the other he touched the back of her neck. "Maybe. They got other switchboards other places. I'll be through here soon. Tired of the bones in Blue Vista? Feel like plugging calls somewhere else?"

Eve almost smiled. Most farmers were familiar with cow flop. They know its look, its shape, its smell. But you would have to go a long way to find one that was proud of falling in the stuff. Now

Government men were much like that. Most of them were familiar with females. They knew their look, their shape, their smell. But you would go a long way to find one that was proud of bringing a dame along. Maybe with good reason. Maybe Sykes was getting what he wanted. Eve was getting close. "You offering me a ride outta here? Or what?"

Sykes traced a line with his finger from the back of her neck to the lobe of her ear. "Or what."

Bart Lowell closed Eve's door behind him and went looking for heaven. Marybelle saw the hall light slash across the room and die; the door closed, but again, why bother to look? One more was not going to make a difference: two down, one to go.

She lay on her side, back to the padding of the gent's feet. He tiptoed around the end of the bed, keeping his distance from the woman breathing low and smooth. Somehow one silk stocking had slipped down her thigh, toe and heel limp, dangling unsatisfied. Bart took the stocking toe between thumb and forefinger; with ginger guts he pulled the silk till it slid off her leg.

Most women were dissatisfied with their looks—thighs too fat, too thin, breasts too big, too small, not the right shape, nose too long, eyes too flat, lips too full, not full enough, ass too round, too large, too small . . . the list goes on and on. Bart never took these notions seriously. In all the time he had lived with Claire, one trick and one trick alone she demanded to while away the time. One trick among thousands, but one trick done well beats a million mediocre alternatives: he had heard all about the Latins, the Cubans, the giant Negroes and the French; he had suspected the Italians for some time, but he could never prove it. Not to mention the Swedish and the Dutch; of the Japanese, he had never heard a bad thing, but knowledge alone never saves men's sabers from rattling hollow in their scabbards. Instinct.

Instinct, that most barbaric primordial hunch: when to go and when to stop; when yes, when no. Even though Bart was under the gun without his smock, he tiptoed round the end of the bed and calculated his chances. The woman had been taken twice already, but Lepke and Tate had failed to raise her with them. He would lay money on it. She was a sweet receptacle at best, a warm wet slit for a bully's thrust. Pity, they had tried so hard and gained so little.

Take a barber without his white barber's smock and what have you got? Charm? Probably not. Class? Who knows? Instinct? If you're lucky. Bart took off his trousers and lay down beside the woman's half-stockinged scissored legs. He reached around one smooth thigh, gently walking his fingers. Better one trick done well: breach the iron maiden.

And Marybelle was no easy touch.

What did this clown think he was up to? Another expert. One kiss between two shoulder blades, one hand groping, one useless. She waited dripping moments and then the finger reached its mark, flicking gently. Oh no . . . not a tickle, no, something much warmer —surprising—a pleasant electric heat. She could not stop her buttocks from shaking; they trembled on their own, far away from her control. Another animal, not part of her—the gamekeeper's private stock, the hunter's prey—the Devil's serpent, finding the mistress all alone. How many fingers did he use? One? Two? Was it the pinky, or the thumb? Did he move fast or slow? She could not tell; pinky and thumb blurred across her flesh, brushing bone and nerve, fingertip to swollen lump, an opiate with pumping blood—the knob behind, just the head, more please.

Damn you.

More fingers strumming—shaking ass, a knob.

Damn you.

Strumming blurred to the bone—nervous swollen lump—the pinky and the thumb. The knob.

Damn you. Gimme that stuff.

Flashy fingers flicking sticking, marking gently buttocks shaking.

Damn you. Gimme that real stuff.

Fast or slow?

stuff!

Stuff!

STUFF!

A drop of sweat broke from her neck and ran between her shoulder blades, down her back, and to the crease. He blew air on the trickle, chilling it, she shook again and somehow bit the pillow.

stuff . . .

Her face, fire-engine steaming, she turned and felt for his warm armpit. Everyone gets everything they want . . . sometimes they even get what they deserve. She kissed him in his soft hollow flesh. She kissed the hair and sucked the odor of a man.

Ollie Cottle had watched Hanson come into the garage, flash on the swinging naked bulb and poke around in the broken-down Model A. From his cot in the back, Cottle had kept a hand over his face, keeping out the glare—then the light went out and Hanson along with it. Woken, and now wide awake, Cottle lay in the dark. He saw a face of cinnamon . . . a girl . . . thirty years ago. A swell girl. Birmingham? No, New Orleans.

A good family girl, white dress on Sunday—Papa dark as a thundercloud. And young Cottle fawning around the door where Papa would not hear him. Don't play with that trash in the street. The moon waned fast; the girl was lost to a steamboat stoker. And then the Great War . . . the days slipped by so fast, the time for love a wrinkled fruit; he never got that girl, and now he wished he had. A young man's world is planted season to season; but the old man withers, a broken vine that dies in winter. Not forgotten, oh, no, influenza and the white-dress girl crinkled like a paper flower. No gravestone, but a wooden cross. No steamboat stoker, left town and playing with another woman. Papa still dark as a thundercloud, he wept away his child's peace. And young Cottle had stood by the swampland's edge, thirty paces from the grave, watching her box lowered away.

Cottle got off his army cot—no sleeping now; he knew Hanson kept extra bulbs for the fixtures someplace. Damn the memory. Cottle could not sleep. And the Model A waited for his dark brown hands.

June Tate stood under Eve's rooming house window and saw the curtains flutter out, hanging over the sill. A low moan drifted down from the second story, a dazzling wail, not forlorn, but panting frail from a woman's hot breath. A sucking tart could get that riled up by Tate? June liked him well enough; when he was nice, he even made her grunt, in his slow heavy way. But this?

This hifalutin' Kisses-Two-Dollars window show was something of a bargain. Did the brew slosh over the rim of a three-handled devil's cup; was it worth the wait? The back door of the rooming house slammed shut, a rackety bang stranded in the square. The lovers' hisses and coos oozed out the windows. At first, June did not notice Lepke sneaking across the square from behind the rooming house. But his footsteps echoed hollow and she turned to look.

"You there. Hold it. Lepke, come here."

Lepke froze, except for his walrus belly, wobbling out of control.

"I said, come here. I meant *here!*"

Lepke came toward her, sheepish, a chickenliver quivering in the pan. "Yes, June?"

"Have you seen Tate?"

"No, June."

"Are you sure you haven't seen Tate?"

"No—I mean, *yes,* June."

June looked up at the open window and Lepke followed her eyes to the curtains hanging like a ladies' hem over the sill. Again the shackled breathing, the bedsprings rocking, wearing down the sheets' fine weave.

"I think you're lying, Lepke."

Drake saw the muzzle flashes against the leaves, and splinters showered from the door frame—bullet's ricochet. No point in squatting by the door all night.

"Out the back, circle round . . . and quiet." Drake sent another rocksalt shell screaming into the night. The leaves shivered together. Ryder would circle from one side and Henry would come from the other. Feet scraped in the bunkhouse; Drake loaded up another shell. With all the bunkhouse windows broken, Ryder slipped out fast, bare feet silent in the night. Eddy stayed behind with Drake; his sickle would not be any use out there. They waited. In the lull even the crickets returned. Drake counted to one hundred. Then three hundred, then five. A birdcall in the woods, *cockatoo, cockatoo.* His man was close, but not close enough. Drake pulled the trigger and the charge shrieked in the moonlight. One shot back, then another muzzle flash.

Heavy thrashing, two shouts, the clatter of weapons falling to the dirt: the leaves in the woods were dancing, branches snapping, bodies crashing. "Get him! Get him!"

The skinny blond Bull dashed from the trees, angling toward the water tower. Ryder broke from the leaves, stumbling. Henry and his brother, too, came charging out. Henry held his shotgun at port-arms; his brother's wormy straw boater snagged on a twig and dangled swinging head free.

By the doorway Drake watched Daryl split like a jackrabbit toward the trestle. Eddy, eyes creased to slits, jumped from Drake's side and sprang from his squat running. Ryder flew past the door, legs outstretched and paced Daryl, gaining. Drake got up and stood outside the bunkhouse. His two men caught the skinny blond Bull at the water tower. They backed him up against the metal spars. "Easy, boy."

Drake saw Ryder scratch the back of his head where the eye-patch cord creased his hair; the man was through fooling around. Daryl nursed his thigh; the hoe handle had left its mark. A last surge; Drake saw the panic lunge in the blond Bull's eyes. He broke through the two men for a final sprint, but Ryder took a step back and slung the hoe at his ankles—it caught and Daryl went sprawling. Eddy had the sickle around the boy's throat.

"We said easy, boy . . . don't you listen?"

Daryl let the sickle lead him back to the bunkhouse; he was limping bad—every time he dipped, the sickle point scratched his throat. "Sit."

Drake paced slowly around the sorry hero. "Now, why don't we talk about my little girl?"

Daryl was trembling. "Simple didn't tell us nothing."

Drake glanced at the ground, as if he had not heard correctly. He spun, kicking Daryl in the knee. The Bull shrieked, spit dribbling from his lips. Drake squatted, his face close, his voice low.

"I said, let's talk about my little girl."

A darkened shade hung over the square, the deep blue night; the moon stared down at the oak like a bright tin target in the carnival at two cents a shot. Eve and Sykes pulled the Studebaker into the square and parked at the diner. They saw Lepke and June

Tate standing under the rooming house window, right in front of the jailhouse door. June was poking Lepke in the chest with one stiff finger, and each time she did, Lepke's hands fluttered by his sides. June's voice was soft and they could not hear her words across the square. But each time she came to the end of a sentence, she made her point and jabbed Lepke again, and harder.

As they walked across the square, June's voice got a little clearer.

"Liar . . . *you know* . . . thick as thieves . . ."

June heard the footsteps coming closer and left off jabbing Lepke. She shook her head when she saw Eve standing in the darkness.

"Why, I thought—"

"You thought what, June?" Eve hung on Sykes' arm. Sykes seemed rather pleased with himself, having a woman draped on his arm and all. He winked at Lepke, but the chef was not interested. His face was pulled and drawn; he stared at Eve and then back up at the window. Then he stared at Eve again. Then back at the window. The curtains trembled and softly a woman's voice: *"Oh . . . oh . . . oh . . ."*

Eve was close enough to see all the color leave Lepke's face.

Hanson and Parker Watts sat in the wreck of the Blue Vista Flats First (and only) National Bank. Hanson, now convinced that Parker Watts was not holding out on him, had joined the search and promptly helped Watts overturn what was previously intact. Piles of banking files were scattered, stacked, and scattered again. Chairs were broken in half, a desk rent to splinters, the whole teller's cage pulled apart, bar by brass bar; the total contents of the safe deposit boxes lay in heaps on the vault floor. Hanson had even gotten up on a stool and searched the spinning rim of the ceiling fan, nearly cutting his fingers off. Parker Watts still possessed enough wits to turn the damn machine off before Hanson began clawing into it. They combed the wall moldings, they ran their palms along the floor, they even tapped the walls, listening for hollow spaces. Now they sat on their bottoms and contemplated the mess. Parker was on the verge of tears.

"I was working in the bank all day . . . didn't even go to the diner for food, been sitting in the teller's cage—never budged an inch... put them in the drawer... didn't take them out... never had to check, because I knew where they were... didn't hide them someplace..."

Hanson was dumbfounded, like the schoolchild stumped by an arithmetic problem: Two Plus Two equals... equals... teacher may I go to the bathroom? But no exit from the classroom could relieve this child's bladder problem. Hanson was hooked, he wanted those coins. Was Parker Watts better off alive... or dead? If he was dead, it would serve the son-of-a-spinster right, but perhaps the banker was better off alive—that way, he could at least keep searching. The damn things were probably right under their noses somewhere... typical. You search and search, you pull and prod, you turn everything upside down and all the while the damn things have been winking like a whore on a street corner, only closer. Hanson slapped his forehead—how stupid could you get?

"The floorboards, the coins slipped through the floorboards."

"*The floorboards!*" Parker Watts jumped to his feet and went dashing around for a crowbar. "Of course, why didn't I think of it —*the floorboards!*"

Yohanna Johns cleaned himself as best he could; now he noticed the string tied from porch post to porch post but he thought nothing of it. He put his ladder away in the barn. He plucked the broom from the dirt and with the ax he chopped the broom-handle and the straw bristles to bits. He gathered the broom bits in a pile and planned to sow them in the field. Roxie would like that. The ax he treasured as a gift from the Beyond.

Never much of a believer in institutions of any nature, Johns never kept his money in the bank. He had a strongbox wrapped in oilcloth and buried in the ground. He fetched a shovel and took his paces from the front door: three forward, one to the left, one forward, another to the left. He marked the spot, lit the lantern and began to dig. Two feet down, the dirt pile had grown and then he struck the oilcloth, black in the black earth. Johns struggled with the heavy box, tugging it up to the surface. Sweat dripped down his skinny arms, but he did not bother to wipe it away.

Unwrapped, the strongbox was metal and bound with studded

metal bands. Johns used no padlock. If a person finds such a treasure, they can usually cart it off and crack the chest with no time pressure. Saws, sledgehammers, chisels, dynamite—strongboxes ain't safes, and safes ain't safe. Johns figured keeping the box hid was his best bet. If no one can find it, no one's going to crack it. So who needs a lock?

By the lamplight, he opened the box and looked inside. His life's profits were laid inside, stacked bill by bill by bill, wrapped with rubber bands—a quarter century's cash-crop profit—the thrift of wisdom and old age. Cash. Cold cash. He counted out three hundred dollars. A mighty sum. Then he put twenty-five dollars back. Thinking even better of the notion, he put another twenty-five back. Two hundred and fifty dollars. Not to be chintzy—during the whole time he had never touched Eve, he only looked. Fair is fair.

Baskum got up off his knees, his face smeared with his woman's juice. In the process Josie had quaked and shaked and broken the other three legs on the divan, but Baskum did not care. He was rampant now. And she was a fat cat gone to the dogs. He dived for his wife's pie but, nimble-kneed, she slipped off the couch and pranced to her feet. Baskum hit the couch and almost broke his pipestem. He struggled around and heard his wife leave the room.

"I'll be back . . . sit tight."

He sat, indeed, praying for salvation . . . aching for the touch . . . he heard the front door open. Searching for stranger.

"J. J.!"

He was off the couch grabbing for his pants. Josie was at the front door, looking down. Something caught her eye.

"J. J.! What's that?"

Baskum poked his head around his broad wife and looked down at the doorstep. Light from the open door fell on the stairs. A strange sight indeed: feces collecting flies in the night. Baskum put his hand on his wife's swell hip.

"Looks like baked Alaska. Don't you think?"

"It's shit."

"Well said." He pulled Josie away from the door and locked it. "Forget the baked Alaska, gimme a slice of the cake."

"Fresh."

Baskum led Josie to the kitchen. "Nonsense, we *are* married you know."

"You're still fresh."

"Never mind that. Get on the kitchen table."

"The table?"

Baskum let go of his waistband and dropped his trousers once more. "Yeah, the table . . . on your stomach."

Josie stretched out on the table, its legs creaking. She rather liked him when he talked dirty. He was not such a chickenliver after all. Worse husbands could be found. And better lost.

"Fresh."

Preacher Simon kissed the hot swollen mole over Claire's upper lip. He sucked on the flesh drop and felt her mouth part. Her teeth, white ivory, were clean and perfect—not what Preacher expected. No tobacco stains, no hot weed breath. Claire pushed him away, fingers pressing his chest at arm's length; she leaned back against the door. She fished a cigarette from her skirt pocket. Lit, the dead match was dropped to the carpet. She ground the matchstick with her foot. Tobacco smoke filled the hallway, the only drug for a night's long serenade. Once again Claire brought her hand between Preacher's thighs and cupped him.

"See you . . . "

Gone. The door slammed and Claire's footsteps receded in the night. Yes, she would see him. This would not be the last. No momentary interlude, no fleeting grunts and groans, no one-time grasp in the endless heat. Other nights were promised. Delivered by Western Union, by hand . . . in person. Thank you very much.

Preacher found the dead matchstick crushed in the padded carpet; he pulled it from the curly threads and blew on it, dusting the sulfur chips, cleaning the tiny firestick off. He kept the dead match like a souvenir, one stick of two rubbed boy-scout style. He went back to the parlor where the empty night held him in her arms, and once more he rocked the cradle, wishing he was rocked, and not the child. The little girl was still asleep and he was drawn to her swaddled nakedness, drawn to peel the sleeprags from her small round body. She had not wet herself. The nipples on her future breasts were pale as butter; such gentle things could not be teased erect. As nipples, their promise lay ahead, in running days and the long dark dawn . . .

Knees dimpled, thighs chubby, not yet stretched to fine long ladies' legs, a pink slice clean and heavy with fatted flesh—would the child listen to its urgent call? He wet his finger with his own saliva and touched the fat-lipped promise, afraid of nothing, not of consequence, not of morals, not of witness, nor of sin. He touched the child between her chubby thighs and watched her wriggle from this adroit first coaxing in a desperate land.

Sloppy Seconds! Fat Chance! Not the way Bart Lowell was taking his time. Hell, he must have taken the woman as water, and then she drowned him. Brought him back to life and drowned him again. Sheriff Tate was tired of waiting; if he plugged the dame again, no doubt the feat would be long and laborious. Not a quick pop like the first. He stopped pacing in the rooming house hallway, left Bart Lowell to his diversions, and clumped down the stairs, the back way out.

A small group of voices chattered away out front of the rooming house, the sounds creeping around the side of the building. Instead of going home to bed, where he surely ought to have gone, Tate rounded the building on the empty barbershop side and peeked around the corner.

"Tate! Get your dumb butt over here."

Too late. June saw him. He withdrew back around the corner.

"And I mean *now!*"

No use hiding. She would get him now or she would get him later. Better get it over with. Tate puffed up his chest and turned the corner with dignity; taking long strides, his boot heels smacked smart and official on the pavement.

Sarah crouched next to the bruised wooden door, her knife ready. The handle was cool in her palm, moist as the sweat between her fingers. Lomax was a dribbling wreck—still crouched in the corner of the kitchen, still drool-dripping, yapping incoherently.

For the moment, Simple's battle lulled to distant thunder. No pounding on the walls, no shattered glass, no broken window frames or howl in the gloom. Three bodies breathing, gentle gasps for air; the lamplight flickered and three shadows loomed preposterous against the walls.

The lull crumbled like an avalanche, crashing at their feet. The kitchen door squealed on its hinges and burst open. Sarah was knocked back on her elbows; the knife skittered. Simple loomed into the kitchen, hands outstretched. Mrs. Moon turned to face him. She rushed him, the hair flying back from her head, fingernails going for his eyes.

His large hands wrapped around her throat, squeezing windpipe, bruising bone. He took his time with her, her arms flailing, useless. Simple lifted her body by the neck, her heels left the ground. She stood on the balls of her feet. Lomax moved on all fours, quick as a cockroach, scuttling along the floor. He parted his cloven lips and gnashed Simple's ankle, ripping a lump of flesh in his teeth. Simple hollered, kicked, but he still held Mrs. Moon by the neck.

The knife was up. And, slowly, Sarah came behind and placed the razor point under Simple's double chin.

"Enough." The blade creased red in his flesh, pressing. "Let her go." Simple breathed through his nose in short whiffs; the skin of his chin was growing more irritated around the blade point. Slowly, the muscles in his arms relaxed, and he lowered Mrs. Moon. The woman fell to her knees, coughing. Lomax scuttled back to the corner.

The knife blade turned in the hollow of Simple's underjaw; Sarah almost jabbed it home. He rose on the balls of his feet.

"Relax. Let's go outside."

The knifepoint kept Simple on his toes, his sagging chin reddening over the blade. When the metal point creased his skin, his breath came fast, in shallow gulps. Sarah brought Simple to the door on tiptoes; the big man went through the door first, the blade still at his throat.

Mrs. Moon breathed deep and long and then she stood up slowly, hands at her tender neck. She took a broom from the kitchen corner and followed Sarah out on the porch. Sarah made Simple step down off the porch before she did; the knife never moved from his fatty chin. The two women led the man into the field fifty yards or so away from the house. Simple was quiet; his piebald scalp sweated like an overripe melon, dew dripping and close to rotten. The moon was waning fast, but Sarah was looking elsewhere.

"Down, Mister... on all fours." Simple got down on all fours. Sarah handed the blade to Mrs. Moon. "Keep his head to the ground. Now Mister, drop your pants."

"What?"

"Do it. Or kiss metal."

Simple struggled with his pants, face grinding the dirt. The trousers fell over his behind and to his knees in baggy loops. His cheeks were spread wide to heaven and he shivered. Sarah had the broom-handle. The wooden rod touched the inside of Simple's buttocks.

"Don't, lady." The broom-handle slid in the crack; his thighs wobbled, but he kept his ass rock still. The rolls of skin around his neck moved together like eels. Simple barely breathed. The knife was not necessary now. Mrs. Moon stepped back several paces. She held the blade in her fist; the metal did not tremble and did not move. Sarah pressed him, the broom-handle on the pucker.

"Where's my baby?"

Simple squirmed away from the wooden rod, but Sarah kept it close. "Don't, lady . . . I don't know. I don't know. Don't—"

She jammed him and he took it, face and lips in the dirt.

"*Lady!*"

He did not know, but she rammed him all the same. "LADY!"

She wrecked him there and then, cheeks spread to heaven. At the end she beat him on the neck and he lay quiet like a dead man, unconscious, barely breathing.

A small breeze tickled the back of Sarah's neck. She looked around for Mrs. Moon. She was gone and the knife lay on the ground. Sarah looked back to the house. Mrs. Moon was walking slowly toward the porch, and through the open door Sarah saw Lomax struggle to stand upright. The idiot boy tottered on his wobbly knees and grasped the door frame for support. He stood on the porch and Mrs. Moon went to him, her hands reaching out to touch his pasty skin, to knead the flesh and know its life. Lomax reached out and touched the windchimes; they tinkled a merciful chant upon their scales. Mrs. Moon turned her dark eyes to Sarah and she felt the windchimes' trembling through her bones, their crystal tune played from a hangman's knot strung from the porch roof molding, the mother-of-pearl dead-eyes swinging through an endless night. Sarah dropped the broom and it fell next to Simple's breathing body. Sweat flowed down from under her arms, and her anger with it, evaporating on her skin.

Drew led him and he followed, his tongue dry and pressed flat against the roof of his mouth. They crept up to the charred ruins of Moss Greene's farmhouse and crouched among the timbers; she gently placed the sawed-off tree branch on the dirt as though setting it aside for future use, out of harm's way. They could see two figures: Tina sitting alone, tied like a packing crate that breathed, and Meriwether angling off in the darkness, hand on Tina's thigh. He had not heard them slither close. Buck felt a tight pounding in the flesh of his palms. Inside, from his heart on out, a rolling wave gathered in his body, like the current of the wind as it bent wheat stalks in the field. Drew took the unknown drifter's bloody hand from the sack and laid it palm up, fingers curling on the ground. The mucus grew thick in Buck's throat, a warm glue that made it hard to swallow but easier to keep staring at the hand. The grown men's words were a faint echo, "Stay here boy . . . we'll be back."

Well, what you gonna do now, boy? Run for it? Go looking for the big folks? What you gonna do now?

Drew struck a match; the sulfur head flared, hissing. Buck flinched from the glare. No guesswork here. His father's rules were crossed—broken. And how he was gonna live with it. Right, boy?

Meriwether pulled the gun and looked from side to side. The Bull breathed deep, nostrils wide for any present scent. Drew held the match flame under the candle. The wax dribbled on the dead man's palm. She pressed the waxy soft candle bottom to the dead man's flesh, the wax cooling, and the candle stayed upright, centered in the drifter's palm. Meriwether caught the faint glow through the charred timbers.

"Who there?"

The charcoal from the burnt timbers smudged across Buck's hands. With two fingers he touched the soft waxy bottom of the candle and the flesh of the dead man's palm. He'd seen this before, that first night—Drew had done it then when the little green garter snake lay dead on the riverbank shale where Tina killed it: *A dead man's hand works better every time . . . the Devil don't know all the tricks . . . a dead man's hand works better . . .*

The rolling wave inside Buck's body curled like a serpent under his skin. The wax was still warm and the dead hand cool; the great wind's wave blew outward from his heart, the wind that broke the wheat stalks' backs and scattered road dust before the storm. A hard fist grew in Buck's chest and his ribs wrapped tight around it.

Suddenly a low growl rolled close along the ground. The dog exploded from the fallow field, padded feet scratching dirt, tongue lashing teeth. Meriwether turned his head, gun aimed. The dog leapt, its black fur shooting through the moonlight. The gun muzzle flashed, cracking the air. The slug blew the dog's skull back over its haunches and it crumpled to the ground, a low growl still caught in its throat. Meriwether took a step back, gun held high. Drew touched the match flame to the candle's wick. The waxy thread sputtered, flamed, glowing on their faces. Meriwether's eyes jumped to the candle's flickering light.

Drew had said this all before . . . a dead man's hand works better . . . no hot-and-bothered thinking blood to fuddle up my good intentions . . . before at the riverbank *he'd* held the candle and a dead man's hand works better . . . before, a little green garter snake lay dead—and now . . .

Again, a low growl, a growl deeper than a mad pit-dog's final warning. The Bull's head whipped back to the dog's carcass, gun in his fist. Buck raised himself and looked through the burnt timbers. On the ground, the dog moved its blasted head. Its rounded skull and matted fur were fleshy mush. Then the dog's tongue darted over its wet nose and teeth. It sniffed the air, filling its nostrils with Meriwether's dirty smell. Hackles raised on the dog's fur . . . slowly its legs curled under the straining gunshot body, muscles and tendons shifting with the weight. Blood ran down its haunches and the dog took one step, muzzle on the Bull's scent.

Buck heard Drew breathing sweet and calm near his neck . . . *a dead man's hand works better, better on a dog than on a tiny snake . . . better without a living hand to hold the candle, to fuddle up her good intentions . . . she never liked to see a wild thing die.*

Meriwether pulled the trigger; a dirt spray shot from the dog's feet. It moved on the Bull, teeth bared. He shot again, dancing backward—falling in the candle's light. The gun muzzle flashed four more times, fast, the bullets splattering the dirt at the dog's moving paws.

Buck let go of the burnt timber and stood up. Meriwether was sprawled on the ground and in the candle's glow, the bodies cut shafts of shadow breaking up the light. Drew stood behind Buck; her olive skin was melted wax, supple smooth. The candlelight fell on the Bull's white face and the dog standing like a stone nearby. Meriwether's tick-tack eyes darted to the dog and then to Buck. His red hair bristled.

Drew's hand was on Buck's arm and he let her rest it there, her fingers cool and lovely on his skin. A gypsy moth fluttered near the candle's flame, grazing the heat; its paper wing scorched and shriveled. The moth fell to the dead palm, righted on thread legs, and walked along a finger. Drew's voice washed across Buck's cheek, spoke through bedsheets and a woman's lacy handkerchief. "You're never ready, when they set you free."

Buck felt the tangle of alfalfa leaves and the rustle of her skirt, pulled way up above her knees. A breeze blew across the field and a dark devil spun to life from the charcoal rubble of the farmhouse. The candle fluttered and the wind whipped the wick, snuffing out the flame. The glow died. Good and evil mixed together in the void. Drew's cool lover's fingers fell from his arm, and Buck saw his own body stretched out in white linen, a dozen mournful faces peering down into his grave.

In the night's darkness, the dog's glistening jaws went slack, and Buck heard the broken animal fall, slumping to its side. No candle burned to hold it steady on its paws. The Bull leapt to his feet and the moon broke coldly through a cloud; the gun was in Meriwether's fist. Drew was gone.

She was slipping through the farmhouse rubble, making for Tina and the ropes that bound his sister. Buck saw it clear now. The time had come. Him and the Bull.

No melted honey dripping safe around his skin. No gentle words. No mad dog brought back to life from a dead man's palm and a silly candle stub. No woman's courage and no maiden's question of, "Who? Who do you love better than you love me?" He did not bother calling Drew's name. She was grappling with Tina's ropes, her hands prying around the little girl's wrists.

And then Meriwether came for him, like he promised all along. The fields' wind gathered in Buck's body and curled strong in his two hands. Meriwether's gun was blue in the moonlight; his finger creased around the knuckle, tightening on the trigger, and the chamber turned. Buck saw the dark barrel point like a snout and he dipped to the ground, sloping among the timber. The farmhouse's broken beams and charred wood rose around him like a dead jungle; partial walls and empty skeleton doorways covered him from Meriwether's line of fire. He saw the Bull through the meshed wood and the gun's hammer fell with a dry click. And then another dry click. Meriwether threw the gun away, and the glittering sodcutter blade coursed with his body. He saw Buck moving through the beams and stepped onto the charred porch, entering the wreckage through the open front door which was missing a jamb and part of the clapboard wall.

"You can't hide, Walker boy."

Meriwether's head turned and he saw over Buck's shoulder that Drew was still struggling with Tina's wrists; the girl's hands were bound too tight, angry and unyielding. The Bull moved lightly on his feet, holding his weight in the pit of his stomach. His knees were bent in a knifer's crouch, hard to knock over. He saw the easy way to go about it all—he made for Tina and Drew, the burnt charcoal hissing softly under his feet, each step dry against the wood.

"Come on out now, Walker boy."

Buck squatted low and slipped under two crossed beams; he moved to cut Meriwether off. Buck felt around him and a piece of brick came to his hand. Meriwether loomed dark against the moonlight, coming within a yard of the fallen beams. The red hair bristled over his head; Meriwether's lips parted, a tooth missing in the blackest gap. The seconds slipped slowly through Buck's fingers. And then Meriwether took a step closer.

Buck rose and hefted the brick, feeling the weight of it in his fist. He threw it and caught Meriwether on the shoulder with a dull slap that rocked him. The Bull went down to one knee. Drew was moving again, pulling Tina up from where she sat and around the side of the farmhouse—keeping the wreck between her and the Bull. The moon vanished behind a cloud and Meriwether was rising off his knee. Buck jumped the crossbeams; he landed a kick on Meriwether's side as he rushed past, through the yawning door and around the burnt porch. Buck crouched next to the dead man's hand.

Meriwether was up again and walking quiet; the clouds parted.

The moon slipped through their shredding vapor. The Bull's jackal eyes were white blown glass. Buck scrabbled on the ground and found the smooth tree branch. He held the branch up and out; Meriwether eased around the burnt porch, this time toward Drew and Tina. Buck moved again to cut him off, past Drew still tearing at Tina's bonds; he met Meriwether halfway. The sodcutter blade reached out like a splash of water, cooling the air. It touched his forearm and Buck's skin peeled back in four layers. Buck swung the tree branch for Meriwether's waist. It snapped against his hip, shattered pieces falling on the ground.

The Bull staggered to the side, his chest heaving, and the wind screamed out his nose. Then the knife was up and he crossed the air in front of him, slashing out. Buck slipped back again into the fallen timber and he heard Drew dragging Tina behind him, keeping his body between them and the Bull. Buck kept lower than the waist-high clapboard and the charred windows burnt open at the top. His ankle brushed cool metal. He reached down: a brass doorknob, big as his fist. He held it in his palm. His hand was wet where the blood flowed down his forearm; no pain, but the air was cold in the open slash where the skin rubbed together. Buck took the black charcoal dust from his hands and spread it on his face, darkening his skin against the Bull's night eyes.

Meriwether rose once more, not even holding his waist; he breathed silent, the wind full in his lungs. He scanned the wreck of the farmhouse, looking for Buck in the fallen rubble.

"You pray, kid?" So soft . . .

In the moonlight the Bull's corded muscles seemed tight like rope. "Start praying now, kid."

Buck reached out into the rubble again and found a chair leg, hard as a club. Meriwether, outside the clapboard, passed the burnt-out window. The moon vanished behind another cloud and the shallow light faded, flattening the world. Buck leapt through the window, his body lunging forward, club swinging . . .

Nothing.

The air moved and hot water seared the back of his leg . . . the calf . . . his pants were cut and the sliced skin rasped on the fabric. The clouds dissolved and the silver light came down like rain. A low chuckle from where Meriwether squatted like a dwarf, with his back to the clapboard and his knife below the window frame. "You done praying?"

The Bull stood up, taking all the time in the world. Outside the wreck they circled low and even, pace by pace. Meriwether's eyes drooped with an opium smoker's smug satisfaction and in Buck's hand the doorknob was slick, slippery with his own blood. The sodcutter blade slashed with no warning. The metal touched his chest, stung, and Buck's shirt was torn. His nipple gone. The air grew rancid in his lungs. The sweat and blood mixed together. He could beat the man forever, it was the knife that made the difference.

The moon was there ... hanging in a black sky ... "Who do you love better? ... " Meriwether reared on two hind legs; Buck drew back, letting the Bull press in. Eyes on the knife ... anything for that knife. Okay, come on ...

Steady like a gravedigger, the Bull came, edging in close, his red lips working, jaw awry. Meriwether hooked the blade, the reaching glint, a splash of hot water wetted Buck's cheek. He swung the doorknob and flattened the Bull's nose across his drawn face. The brass knob slipped from his fingers, gone and rolling on the ground. He whipped the chair leg and clubbed the Bull's elbow. The knife slashed out, crossing the fingers of Buck's club hand, and the chair leg fell away from his fist. Meriwether limped back, clutching his arm; he gulped air, his nose spread nearly to his lips. He tucked his elbow in close to his body, but in the Bull's free hand the sodcutter waved back and forth like the head of a cobra.

The knife ... anything for the knife ...

Meriwether came again. Buck turned his back to the broken window frame and held both hands out, fingers open, waiting for the knife hand. It came, waist high, the splash of hot water and Buck jerked back against the clapboard.

The blade found his hand as it passed across his waist. Buck opened his palm, and the blade slid through the soft skin, deep and out the other side, like through the flesh of a melon. Buck's palm was against the knife handle, and his free hand came across, gripping Meriwether's wrist. His own palm slid off the blade and he pulled the Bull closer to him. Both hands circled Meriwether's knife fist; no pain from the gash in his palm—but the wet flow. Buck rammed Meriwether's knife wrist against the clapboard; the Bull's free hand thudded across his shoulder.

In close, Meriwether's chest and body rubbed along Buck's side, and the lean hard-bitten meat was tough as though hung for smoking. The smell of his lizard's body was like soft putrid eggs, shells cracked and open to the air. A sickly smell of heated sugar, the thousand ants that gather at a drop of blood, the sulfur of his sweat. Meriwether's face was close and each pore opened like a black well of dirt. His devil's breath washed across Buck's face, a warm mildewed rag plastered firm and held in place.

Buck rammed the knife fist again, and the clapboard creaked. The Bull's grip was loose. Buck's hands tightened around Meriwether's fingers and cracked the Bull's knuckles on the farmhouse wall. Meriwether's fingers loosened, their grip broken, and Buck's thumb tore the knife handle from Meriwether's fist. His own palm was wet around the sodcutter; the other hand held Meriwether by the hair, chin up, back against the creaking clapboard.

The hair wrenched in Buck's fist; Meriwether's arms and hands beat on his neck and waist. The sodcutter flashed high in the moonlight and down across Meriwether's neck, splitting the pulse over the Bull's dead white throat.

A fountain spilled from his neck, down his shoulder, and Buck let the red hair go. Meriwether broke away, hands under his own chin; he danced toward the river, across Moss Greene's fallow field. His hands slipped twice from his neck and the fountain splashed off his shoulder. He staggered, his knees bending, turning in a circle, his head to the sky.

He was many yards away and stumbling fast; his dark body slapped against the riverbank bramble and the hands flew from his neck once more. The fountain only dribbled now, and the Bull fell over the river's steep bank.

Who do you love better? . . .

Buck looked at the sodcutter, wet in his fist; he tossed it in the farmhouse rubble and pressed his palm's gash hard to his thigh. "Me . . . " Buck whispered. "Better than them all . . . "

Drew had untied Tina's hands; the limp rope lay strewn on the ground. They came to him, treading softly on the charred farmhouse porch. And the three of them found the dog left in the tangle of burnt timbers where Meriwether had wanted to shoot it dead. The dog was still panting. Tina sagged against the clapboard wall and Drew took Buck's hand. The dog was lying on its side, its shattered head down, tongue rolled to white. The heavy panting stopped, the haunches stiffened. The animal stretched and jittered as if pulled by the neck and tail. Then its hackles raised, smoking, shriveling, and the dog smoldered, long overdue, burned with a low blue flame and the flesh peeled away in strips, the bones' end, the tired bones' relief, the guts untangled, charcoal dust sinking deep into the earth.

Drew stood on her woman's hips, her head held high; her fingers touched the gash on Buck's hand and felt his sweaty skin. The gash was deep and raw. She wrapped his trembling hand in her handkerchief; she seemed more lovely than ever before, more lovely than when she shrugged the blankets off her shoulders in the back seat of the car, more lovely than when her knees bent in the alfalfa field and when she grabbed his thighs in her strong hands.

Tina's jitters had fallen from his sister like the Bull's defeated rope; her eyes were calm and the panic gone. The scaredy-cat in Tina had been spooked right off and now Buck could see the grown-up woman grown within her . . .

"Let's go . . . it's late."

Thin End of the Wedge

FOR EVERY EVIL UNDER THE SUN,
THERE IS A REMEDY, OR THERE IS NONE.
IF THERE BE ONE, TRY AND FIND IT;
IF THERE BE NONE, NEVER MIND IT.

Up the stubby steeple in Preacher Simon's church, the grinding gears deep in a brass heart loosened in mercy. Springs uncoiled, cables ran, weights dropped, little brother broke off a kiss with big brother and the clock's hands moved.

A weak breeze dipped into the empty square; beyond the screen door of Lepke's Diner, the Emerson radio hummed to life and a frail tune drifted faintly across the moving air. In the Sheriff's jail, the switchboard buzzed for a short second and then went silent like an old man clearing his throat once and for all.

In Preacher's hallway the grandfather clock shuddered; the clock chimed five times and the pendulum began to swing in a slow, steady arc.

The sun climbed up in the sky and soon it was truly the bright morning's daytime hour. Ollie Cottle, in the garage, laid down a monkey wrench and lowered the engine hood over the Model A's metal guts. He climbed in the driver's seat; the car started sweet as cream, and he drove it out onto the concrete ramp by the gas pumps.

Before Cottle even had a chance to climb out of the car, Drake Walker's pickup truck swung into the square, the boy driving; the truck rolled up onto the garage ramp. Then the Moon woman and her folk were climbing down out of the back, pulling things from the Walker truck they had taken from their Model A not three days ago. But Cottle saw that three days had changed the boy. Buck stood taller, his head thrust back and ready to smile. He was not the skulking kid Cottle had seen coming into the garage for that Moon gal, all hungry and scared and not knowing which way to go. Cottle shook his head; he thought he had the kid figured. Now, maybe not.

"Well, dem friends of yours got deh money, or what?"

Buck came around the side of the Model A and faced Cottle. "Well, you fixed it, or what?"

Buck was smiling. Cottle chuckled, touching his mouth with the back of his hand. "Don' get wise wit' me, boy. Ah fixed it good 'nuff get dem outta de county. But after that, it's de will a' God."

"That's good enough." Mrs. Moon came up beside the large Negro and laid a hand on his hard arm. "I've got faith in your talents of mechanical persuasion."

Buck helped Lomax into the Model A's front seat; the idiot boy let him do it, like he had let him hold the water can back in the cotton rows. He plopped his soft bottom on the seat cushion and looked up at Buck, his eyes in focus and his muc-muc spread in a sly wet grin. Buck leaned toward Lomax's pink fleshy ear and whispered, "You watch it now . . . Cottle may be wise to me, but now I'm wise to you." Lomax turned away, the focus falling from his eyes. Buck closed the car door.

Cottle was still waiting for his money. Drew paid him, holding the coin sack in one hand, those same gold coins, as though the sack had no bottom, and Cottle took them without so much as a second glance. The coins flowed from Drew's hands to his brown wrinkled palms like mercury spilling from a broken thermometer. And before Buck could stop them, Mrs. Moon was in the Model A's driver seat, her hands at the wheel. And Drew was sitting in the back, her legs curled on the blankets' fold.

She was looking at him through the car's open window and Buck felt his ankles grow heavy, as though weighed down with chains, and his hands grow weak as though palsied and old—there was nothing he could do.

Not a damn thing. He was standing on the concrete garage ramp and she was sitting in the car. No way to say: please, please let's start over again, start to finish, the terror too, stretch the seconds and count them over again. But Drew's eyes were half closed and stared at him and Buck knew it was this time once, and only once like this. Only one time. Deep in the alfalfa and step by step in the ruined farmhouse. He did it once, never a child again.

Drew leaned toward the open car window, her voice soft, the honey flowing. "Come kiss me . . . "

And he did, leaning over so his back hurt, lips parted for him so he smelled her woman's scent and the wetness that she let him taste. And then she kissed his hand where the bandage covered the punctured skin. "No more fearful mornings . . . "

The car engine growled to life; Mrs. Moon leaned out her window, one hand dangling down the door. "You take care now, Buck Walker. Live healthy and sober, and don't stay up late nights."

Buck said nothing; he watched the car roll down off the concrete ramp and this time Drew was looking out behind. She waved once through the back window, her eyes deep on him, on what he was and what he had become.

The car headed west up the U.S. Route; its engine whine was high in the air, fading as the seconds passed. A dust devil spun from its back tires, spun once like a lazy dancer, and whirled itself to nothing. Ollie Cottle had gone back into the garage and Buck stood out on the concrete ramp alone. He touched his forearm, his nipple, his cheek, where Meriwether's sodcutter had splashed like hot water. In the morning light the cuts were not as bad as in the darkness. Only his palm, where the blade had run through him like butter. They had not stitched it up, but taped the cut closed from both sides and let nature do the rest. He looked under the bandage where Drew had kissed him; there the blood had dried and was flaking off, the new skin pink and fresh, sealed with a scar and her lover's kiss.

Across the square Sheriff Tate was peeking through the curtains in his jailhouse window. Buck caught him staring and the curtain dropped; Tate's face vanished. Buck knew the Sheriff had come to some conclusions all by his lonesome, watching the Model A drive off, knowing the Walker kin were still alive, knowing he would have heard about it by now if Drake's people had come to any trouble. But Tate would still be wondering how the other side turned out. And yet the Sheriff did not know the half of it. The drifter's body that floated like a log face down—now it lay pulled up on the riverbank, drying in the sun, one hand missing. Buck touched his own bandaged hand; sooner or later they'd find Meriwether with his throat cut, blood drained in the river.

But Buck had those things figured out.

Sheriff Tate could have them both, two angry fighters of the night, and Cottle could break new ground, digging two holes behind the church's white picket fence. No great loss to God or man, or even the Sheriff's precious law. The rest, the town—even Simple at his lonely bunkhouse—they could take care of themselves, smart enough to shut their loose traps and count their blessings like the passing days.

Up the U.S. Route he heard the dumb clip-clop of horses' hoofs. Around the corner of the garage Moss Greene's two dappled mares walked side by side. They were dirty and unbrushed, mud dried and cracking down their sides. Loose tack and metal bits were wrapped around their necks, dangling halfway to the ground. They looked a sorry mess, but breathed easy . . . now free—their wagon and their angry rider fallen from his crazy rage. The mares ambled over to where Buck stood and started nuzzling his hands—hoping for a feedbag or anything at all. Buck tied them to his truck's fender, and patted each once on her broad horse's cheek.

"Take a load off. I'll be back, take you home and feed you something. Don't worry."

Buck stepped off the concrete ramp and headed toward the Sheriff's jail. The dead men waited, like all dead men wait. He'd save Tate some trouble, take him by the hand and show him where to look.